W9-CFK-912

THE FOOTLOOSE GUIDE
GREECE

THE *footloose* GUIDE

GREECE

MAINLAND AND ISLANDS

ROBIN GAULDIE

Series Editor: Andrew Sanger

SIMON & SCHUSTER

LONDON·SYDNEY·NEW YORK·TOKYO·SINGAPORE·TORONTO

First published in Great Britain by
Simon & Schuster Ltd in 1992
A Paramount Communications Company

Simon & Schuster Ltd
West Garden Place
Kendal Street
London W2 2AQ

Simon & Schuster of Australia Pty Ltd
Sydney

A CIP catalogue record for this book is
available from the British Library
ISBN 0−671−71040−0

Typeset in Sabon & Futura by
Falcon Typographic Art Ltd, Edinburgh
Printed and bound in Great Britain by
HarperCollinsManufacturing, Glasgow

Illustrations by Julian Abela-Hyzler

CONTENTS

INTRODUCTION

Greece is as much a state of mind as it is a country. Four thousand years of civilization and wave after wave after wave of invaders and occupiers have turned it into a patchwork of history and geography, from the northern snows of Epirus to the blinding sun of southern Crete. Its coasts and mountains have been settled by pre-Hellenes, Greeks, Romans, Slavs, Franks and Turks, not to mention a dozen other forgotten peoples.

For many visitors, the towering legacy of Classical Greece, the age of the city states, casts a shadow which obscures much of the country's more recent past. But beside and between the toppled columns of ancient Athens, Delphi and Olympia, there are Frankish castles, Venetian fortresses, and Turkish mosques.

This chessboard of history is not unique in Europe. What is unique is the way in which Greek culture has to some degree survived all these waves of invaders – rather as if the British, despite the arrival of Romans, Saxons, Danes, Vikings, Scots and Normans, still spoke a version of the language used at the building of Stonehenge.

It sometimes seems that Greeks are far more interested in their future than in their cluttered past. Certainly they spend far less time than most Europeans – certainly less than the heritage-obsessed British – in bemoaning lost glories. And they are extremely quick to latch onto the new. Tiny villages which less than a generation ago had no electricty now have not only TV and electric light but satellite dishes and microwaves, little island hotels make their bookings by fax, and restaurant owners who only a couple of years ago were laboriously figuring out your bill on the back of a cigarette packet now add it up on their PC.

This love of the new has a downside: all over Greece, a complex and vigorous popular culture of music and dance is waning under the impact of world pop culture, just as Greece's superb vernacular architecture – like the archetypal white houses and blue domes which have become a kind of visual shorthand for the whole country – has in many places been supplanted by modern and often hideous concrete buildings.

Tourism has been a huge part of this process, promising easy money in places where ownership of two goats, half a dozen hens and an olive grove was prosperity. It has also slowed down the population drift which throughout the past century has decanted people from remoter islands and regions into Athens and a handful of other cities. Deserted ghost villages and empty farmhouses are very much part of the Greek landscape, but the promise of employment and amusement at least during the summer season has brought many younger Greeks, Athenians and expatriates back to the islands their families came from.

And tourism has also played a part in eroding the once-instinctive Greek spirit of hospitality. This philoxenia survives in force, however, off the main tourist beat, and even a few words of Greek will miraculously win friends, open doors and influence the availability of food, drink and beds. Impatience, rudeness, drunkenness and a reluctance to adjust your attitude to Greek ways of doing things, on the other hand, are guaranteed to produce the opposite result – just as they would anywhere.

Geography and history are inseparable. This is especially obvious in the islands, where one little inhabited rock may have a history, landscape and architecture quite different from its nearest neighbour. And local politics can change even more sharply.

On the mainland, where rugged mountain ranges cut off one valley from another, there is the same rich variety – a variety which is sadly not reflected in most of Greece's smaller rural towns. Strikingly, almost every settled part of Greece is next door to landscapes that look like, and sometimes are, pure uninhabited badlands – from the main square of any provincial town you can look up and out into harsh, spectacular and unforgiving hill country. Often, the harshest landscape resolves on closer examination into patches of cultivation – the silvery-green ripple of olive groves clinging to a hillside or handkerchief-sized vineyards and barley fields. But there are also pockets of real wilderness where only half-wild herds of goats find enough to graze.

Arriving in the empty, sun-hammered main street of some rural metropolis on a summer day, you wonder where all the people went. To see a Greek town or village at its busiest, you need to get up at dawn. By eight in the morning the street cafés will be busy with people taking their first coffee of the day. Around midday, business slows or stops as most people retire for an afternoon nap through the hottest part of the day. Life starts again in the early evening, many offices working a second stretch from late afternoon to early evening. After that comes the *volta* or *peripato*, a stroll through the town's main square or esplanade. Dinner is eaten late, and the day ends well after midnight for many. In fact, in summer at least, Greeks tend to divide the 24 hours into two short wake/sleep cycles instead of one long night and day.

Erratic geography makes Greece a country of micro-climates. Spring comes earliest and dies quickest in Crete, far to the south, while you can swim virtually year round in Rhodes; and there are ski runs on Mount Parnassos and in Pilion. Even in June, when the southern tip of the Peloponnese is already parched, you can see from the beach the snow-capped tips of the Taigettos range. This, of course, is one of Greece's greatest charms. Tired of the blazing summer heat of the southern islands, you can head for the cooler northern mountains. Party time on Paros or Mykonos is a healthy corrective to the culture shock induced by yomping round too many ancient cities, and party fatigue in turn can be remedied by days or weeks flatlined on some quieter island.

Since winning its independence in a century-long struggle which ended only in the early 20th century, Greece has looked firmly westward, systematically rejecting the oriental influences of four centuries of Turkish rule. But there are still many reminders that this is a country on the eastern brink of Europe: the unfamiliar rhythms and nasal semitones of traditional music, the universal blue beads which ward off the Evil Eye, and the tiny cups of poisonously strong coffee. These, as much as the braying of donkeys, the insistent buzz of cicadas, the clatter of goat bells on a barren hillside or the miraculous sight of a school of dolphins racing an island ferry, are part of the complex cobweb of Greek life, a web from which it is hard to break free once you have been caught up in it. The hardest part of any visit to Greece is going home.

THE PRACTICAL SECTION

GETTING TO GREECE

FROM THE UK

By Air

Cheapest flights are "flight only" charters offered by leading tour operators such as Thomson and Falcon Flights, with several services weekly from most major UK airports during the holiday season, from late April until the beginning of October. Athens, Corfu, Kos, Crete and Rhodes are the most popular gateways and the best-served by charters.

Scheduled flights by British Airways and Olympic Airways go from London and Manchester to Athens several times a day. Olympic Airways also flies to Thessaloniki several times weekly. Some of the cheapest scheduled fares are by Kenya Airways, which stops at Athens once a week en route to Nairobi.

By Land/Sea

Overland travellers can connect with international ferry lines at Venice (for Patras), Ancona (Patras or Igoumenitsa), Brindisi and Bari (Patras, Igoumenitsa and Corfu). Journey times are between ten and 30 hours and fares start at about £40 (Ancona to Patras) to about £50 (Brindisi to Corfu or Patras).

The main overland route to Greece, using the main international highway or rail route through Yugoslavia, is at present (early 1992) off limits because of fighting between the Yugoslavian republics. Those determined to go overland all the way could detour through Hungary and Bulgaria, entering Greece via Bulgaria.

FROM THE USA

There are scheduled flights by TWA from San Francisco and Los Angeles and by TWA and Olympic from New York.

GREEK FERRIES

The Greek islands and mainland are linked by a vast fleet of ferries. Some – such as the big international vessels on the Adriatic routes – are modern and comfortable; others, especially on routes to smaller islands, are elderly and spartan. Generally, the smaller your destination and the further it is from the trunk routes, the smaller the boat. Many of the larger and newer boats are Scandinavian-built. Some are superannuated ex-Channel ferries. Until quite recently a vessel called the Achilles operated a meandering circuit from Piraeus through the Cyclades to Crete, across to Rhodes, then up through the Dodecanese and North East Aegean islands to Thessaloniki, then back to Piraeus via the Sproades and Evia. The circuit sometimes took up to a fortnight and it was not unusual for the Achilles to be a day or more off-schedule – not surprisingly since it had started life in Dumbarton in 1918 as the Channel Queen. Most services are now remarkably reliable and service is usually interrupted only by very bad weather or (more frequently) by wildcat strikes.

SCHEDULES AND ROUTES

Most major island groups are served at least seven times a week from Piraeus. Infuriatingly, competing services are not usually staggered and often go not only on the same day but within half an hour of each other. The main "trunk routes" are between Piraeus and Crete via the eastern Cyclades, between Piraeus and Rhodes (non-stop and via Kos and Kalymnos) and east to Samos via Mykonos. Chios and Lesbos have their own non-stop ferries sailing seven times a week in high season.

The whole network is geared to transporting people and cargo between Piraeus and the islands. Getting from one island group to another is more problematic, especially if you want to go from, say, one of the smaller Dodecanese islands to one of the lesser Cyclades. This usually means changing boats at one of the "hub" islands where different services connect. The main ones are:

Mykonos: Virtually all Cyclades services plus connections to the North East Aegean and Dodecanese.

Heraklion: Change between Piraeus/Cyclades routes and eastward services to Karpathos and Rhodes.

Rhodes: Services from Crete connect with Dodecanese routes.

Samos: Services from Piraeus via Mykonos connect with the Dodecanese and the North East Aegean routes.

Sometimes it can be easiest to give in and go back to square one at Piraeus.

Finding out far in advance what goes where and when it is sailing is almost impossible. The National Tourist Office in the National Bank on Syntagma Square in Athens will give a copy of the weekly Piraeus sailings, published each Thursday. On the islands, ask at the harbour ticket agencies or at the Harbour Police office; the harbour cop, in his immaculate white flares and standard issue Ray-Ban aviator shades and droopy moustache, ranks with the priest as one of the prominent figures of any Greek port village.

BUYING A TICKET

Almost all boats have three classes – Alpha, or luxury, Beta, or tourist, and Gamma, or "deck" class. You will usually be given a deck class ticket unless you ask for one of the other classes. On all but the smallest boats, "deck" gives you the right to a pullman-style seat indoors – first come, first served, but it is almost always more pleasant on deck than in the crowded third class saloons.

Tickets are sold by the shipping line's own offices or by ticket agents. These lads are often economical with the truth. An agent may tell you his tickets are cheaper (in fact fares are fixed by the government) or that buying one on board will cost 20 per cent more (untrue). Since no island agent represents every ferry serving the island, the information they will give you about sailings is usually incomplete – agents are reluctant to tell you about competing services.

The only answer to this is to shop around as much as you can. Usually, all the ticket offices are clustered together on the harbour and a quick walk down the row will give you a better idea of what is running than taking any one agent's word for it.

Fares: Deck class fares are cheap. The longest haul, between Piraeus and Rhodes, costs about £15, and an average island-to-island hop is about £5 to £6. Mile for mile, the longer journeys are cheaper. Hang on to your ticket throughout the journey – tickets are usually checked after each stop.

FOOD AND DRINK ON BOARD

Whenever you can, take your own. There is always a snack bar selling coffee, alcohol and soft drinks but the food—usually soggy microwaved pizza, toasted sandwiches or cheese pastries – is dire and the prices are loaded.

HYDROFOILS

The Flying Dolphins fleet of Soviet-built hydrofoils offers fast service from Piraeus to the Argo-Saronic islands and in summer down the Peloponnese coast to Monemvasia and onward to Kithira. In high summer, hydrofoils also operate around the Cyclades from Mykonos and up and down the Dodecanese from Rhodes. Another hydrofoil network links Volos in northern Greece with the Sporades. For those in a hurry, the hydrofoils are an ideal – if more expensive – alternative to the conventional ferry. They cost about twice as much and get you there in half the time. Generally, only one-way tickets are sold and if you must be back in Athens by a certain date it is usually worth booking your return journey as soon as you arrive. Like the ferries, hydrofoils have a snack and drinks bar on board.

CAR AND MOTORBIKE HIRE

You can hire cars (usually Japanese four-wheel drive soft-tops), mopeds and motorcycles on almost all islands and in larger towns on the mainland. Having your own transport makes it possible to see and do far more, but there are hazards – as can be seen from the large numbers of visitors wearing slings, bandages and plaster casts at many popular resorts.

Driving in Greece has its own hazards. Roads – though mostly tarred – are always serpentine and often potholed. Blind corners are the norm and overtaking on them is a national pastime. Greece has one of the worst accident records in Europe. Drive with care and make sure that you have maximum insurance to cover you not only against injury but for personal liability. Small owner-operated car rental agencies have been known to demand vast compensation for accident damage and it is not unheard of for the local police to threaten to hold unlucky renters until they cough up.

Renting a car is expensive. You will almost certainly find it cheaper to book in advance with one of the major international rental companies before leaving (see page 53). As for renting mopeds and motorcycles, the best advice is not to – at least not unless you have considerable experience riding one. Few renters offer helmets and many bikes appear to be inadequately maintained, while local lorry and bus drivers have no mercy on anything on two wheels. Motorbike and moped offer a great way of getting around the Greek islands, but think hard before hopping on – and check the brakes.

INTERNAL FLIGHTS

Olympic Airways, the Greek national carrier, has a large internal route network on the mainland and in the islands. Prices have risen sharply with the reduction of government subsidies on unprofitable routes. Most flights are hugely over-booked all year round though it can be worth putting your name on the waitlist – there are almost always a great many no-shows by booked passengers. You have a better chance of getting a confirmed ticket if you book through Olympic Airways abroad, especially if you are booked on a connecting international Olympic flight. Aircraft vary from Boeing 737 jets on services to larger islands and regional airports to twin-engined Dornier puddle-jumpers to smaller airstrips. Olympic has one of the world's best safety records, which does not stop the lady sitting next to you from crossing herself repeatedly on takeoff and landing, nor deter the passengers from enthusiastically applauding each safe arrival.

BUSES AND TRAINS

Long-haul buses are usually the fastest and most comfortable public transport in mainland Greece. They are frequent, efficient and cheap, and the network operated by the KTEL consortium of regional bus companies extends almost everywhere – though smaller towns and villages have less frequent services. Off the beaten track on the mainland, and on smaller islands, the school bus is often the only public transport and its timings can be idiosyncratic. Larger towns often have two or more terminals for services in various directions, so check that you have the right one.

Confusingly, the Greek State Railway Organization, OSE, also operates buses to complement its not very extensive network. These leave from the railway station.

Trains are often elderly, usually painfully slow and always very cheap – about two-thirds of the cost of a bus ticket. First class is rarely any more comfortable than second.

Most routes are roundabout, and some are spectacular and worth taking just for the dizzying scenery. The best of these is the Diakofto to Kalavrita rack-and-pinion railway near Egio in the Peloponnese – definitely worth doing in its own right. The only rail service which can compete with the bus for speed and convenience is the Athens/Thessaloniki express.

WHERE TO STAY

HOTELS

In theory, hotels and guesthouses in Greece are graded from A- to E-class and prices are fixed by the government. In practice, there is rather less rhyme and reason – a recently modernized E-Class hotel may have better facilities than an older hotel of a higher category, and a great many family-run pension-style properties have escaped the grading system entirely and charge whatever the traffic will bear.

Generally, A-Class hotels are too expensive for most travellers and in any case there are few outside Athens. B- and C-Class hotels are usually large, comfortable, modern, and boring, expensive in season but offering good value if you are touring off-peak. Most of these are in major beach resorts or near the biggest archaeological sites.

D- and E-Class hotels are usually small and old-fashioned, often spartan, and occasionally tacky. There are plenty of them in small provincial towns and island harbours, where they are often a good bet; in bigger cities like Athens and Thessaloniki they can be sleaze-pits, especially near the railway stations. You are unlikely to find D- and E-Class hotels near the beach.

PENSIONS AND ROOMS TO RENT

All over Greece, families and individual owners run small guesthouses or rent rooms in their homes. Standards are very uneven; the better of them, with new rooms, en-suite shower and WC, solar-heated water and beach-view balconies, are far and away the best value for money on most islands. Others can be cheap but nasty and some – especially when the islands are crowded – are a simple rip-off.

STUDIOS AND APARTMENTS

A relatively recent development, many of these have been built for package-tour clients and are very good value outside peak season. They are usually on the beach and while they cost a bit more than a simple room they can save you money because you can cook your own meals instead of spending in restaurants. Ideal if you are planning a longish stay in one place.

CAMPING

On the mainland – especially on the Ionian coast, the western Peloponnese and in Halkidiki – campsites sometimes offer pleasanter accommodation and better value than hotel or guesthouse. At the better campsites, services usually include a mini-market, laundry, hot showers, café-bar and often a swimming pool. In the Cyclades and on other islands campsites are for those on a minimum budget and facilities are usually rudimentary and none too clean. **Freelance camping** is officially frowned on but plenty of people do it. It's very much a matter of play it by ear – if asked to move on do so, or you may be accommodated in the local nick. Generally, most Greeks do not appreciate minimum-budget travellers camping on their land or sleeping on their beaches.

PRICES

Places to stay listed in this guide as **expensive** cost around £30 per night for a double room (£15 each for two). For this, you should get the works – a terrace, en-suite hot shower/loo, and usually a built-in sink, fridge and a cooking ring for making coffee.

Moderate/Medium: £10 to £15 per double/twin room for which you can expect similar facilities, probably not so new or so smart.

Cheap: £5 to £10 a room. Take pot luck – what you get varies very much according to season and demand.

Very cheap: Under a fiver. Only campsites and the most basic rented rooms come into this category. Expect a bed and little more.

In Athens expect to pay up to 50 per cent more than elsewhere for the same type of accommodation.

Most places give you ten per cent off if you stay two nights or more. Between Easter and mid-June and from the end of August to late October official prices go down by about 30 per cent and you can usually negotiate a discount for privately-rented rooms. Easter can be a major headache as millions of Greeks living in Athens and abroad return to their islands and villages for a big family reunion. Every hotel and guesthouse is bursting at the seams and if you have not booked finding a room is difficult to impossible in many places outside Athens.

FOOD AND DRINK

The row of languidly dangling octopuses decorating the terrace-canopy of a harbourside restaurant should brace you for some surprises. Greek food can be mediocre in some of the smartest places, but wonderful in a simple waterfront ouzeri with rickety ill-assorted tables and a two-ring gas cooker in the back.

The line between the traditional restaurant (**estiatorion**) and the **taverna** is blurred. Old-style establishments usually have high, tobacco-stained panelled ceilings, oilcloth-covered tables and – in most cases – a charcoal-fired spit or grill. Restaurants specializing in roasted or grilled meat – usually lamb or chicken, sometimes pork – are called **psistaria** and are usually good value. A **psarotaverna** is a fish restaurant. These are often more expensive than the rest, but offer the best food in Greece. An **ouzeri** is a snack-tavern which is permitted only to serve the range of cold snacks called meze – slices of vegetables, nuts, chips, sausage or bits of octopus – which traditionally accompany a round of ouzo. A **kafeneion** is a traditional café and a **zacharoplasteion** a pastry-shop selling coffee, soft drinks, and an array of tooth-achingly sweet sticky stuff. As well as these home-grown institutions, most Greek towns now boast a sprinkling of pizzerias, toasted-sandwich bars, and hamburger joints. At harbours, bus terminals and rail stations you will always find a stand selling souvlaki or giros, the Greek answer to doner kebab.

Greek fish. Swordfish steak is often frozen and less than irresistible. **Galeo** or hake is usually served with a reeking garlic dip. Shrimps (**garides**) and **astakoi** – langoustine, but usually called lobster – are expensive but well worth it as a treat.

The old Greek habit of letting food cool off to tepid before serving (hot food being believed to be bad for the stomach) is dying hard, but most restaurants now recognize that foreigners like their food served piping hot. Greek diners usually order each course separately, so a full meal is like an extended picnic lasting all evening, a succession of snacks rather than a formal starter/main course/dessert. If you order everything at once, it usually comes all at once – or in some unexpected order, the chips turning up as an afterthought.

Often, you will be invited to visit the kitchen to view what is on offer. In fish restaurants, you choose your fish, which is then weighed before your eyes and the price calculated –

fish are priced by the kilo and prices fixed by the government. A visit to the kitchen will also reveal whether they have a microwave. If they do, take yourself off forthwith, as the microwave has done Greek cooking no favours.

Prices in restaurants often seem to vary unpredictably. This is because the government, in its passion for categorization, classifies them like hotels from A to E Class and fixes the prices they can charge accordingly. The price depends less on what you are eating than on where – for example, a smart place with a romantic harbour-side terrace will usually charge a good deal more than a smaller taverna a few streets inland.

WHAT TO EAT

Lamb (**arni'**) and chicken (**koto'poulo**) are the commonest meat dishes, either spit-roasted or baked in the oven. **Klef'tiko** is lamb sealed in foil or greaseproof paper and slowly oven-roasted. **Giouvet'si** is veal baked in noodles. **Moussaka'** needs no introduction. **Pasti'tsio** is a macaroni pie with cheese and minced meat and **souvla'ki** is chunks of lamb skewered and grilled. **Koukoure'tsi**, pieces of liver and kidney bound together by intestines and spit-roasted, tastes much better than it sounds.

Horia'tiki is the traditional Greek salad, usually comprising tomatoes, olives, onions, cucumber and green peppers topped with a slice of sharp, salty feta cheese. **Phasola'kia** is an oily stew of green beans in tomato sauce. **Giga'ntes** are butter beans stewed in oil and tomatoes. **Meletza'nes**, aubergines, turn up in vegetable stews with cheese, tomato and onions. **Gemista** is tomato stuffed with rice and herbs. Dips such as **tzatziki**, a pungent garlic, yoghurt and cucumber mix, and **taramasalata**, made from fish roe, are common appetisers. Contrary to what you're often told, houmos and pitta bread are not Greek but Middle Eastern, and rarely found in Greece.

Fish come in all shapes and sizes. Squid (**kalamares**) are sliced into chunks and deep fried in butter; octopus (**oktapodi**) is stewed in its own ink and served hot or cold. **Barbounia** – red mullet – are, I think, over-priced and overrated and seem to get smaller every year. Presumably all the big ones have been devoured long since. **Melanurgia** or blacktail is one of the tastiest.

COFFEE

Traditionally, Greek coffee (kafe Elliniko') comes in a tiny cup accompanied by a tall glass of chilled water and is drunk without milk. The last half-inch is a thick brown sludge which you leave. You drink the water first. For coffee without sugar, ask for **skito'**; half-sweet is **me'triou** and very sweet indeed is **glikou**. Greek office-workers do not have coffee machines; they order it in from a neighbouring café, and at mid-morning you will often meet café-waiters hurrying down the street with a precariously-swinging aluminium tray loaded with cups and glasses.

Greeks are also addicted to iced instant coffee, called frappé and served in a tall glass with chunks of ice, with or without sugar and condensed milk.

MONEY MATTERS

You can change cash, travellers' cheques and Eurocheques at banks, post offices and most travel and tour agencies, which usually charge a small commission. Banks are usually open 08.00 to 14.00 weekdays but hours vary – in smaller places they are often open only 08.00 to 12.00 and only on selected days of the week. Post offices usually open 08.00 to 17.00 but often keep shorter hours in smaller villages. Travel and tour agencies usually close in mid-afternoon but reopen in the evening. Eurocheques are the most convenient way of carrying money with you – keep your cheque card and cheques separate.

Credit cards are widely accepted in souvenir, clothing and jewellery shops in Athens and major resorts but not in most smaller hotels, guesthouses and less expensive restaurants. Greece is still very much a cash economy and almost every-where a big wad of drachmas speaks more persuasively than credit cards ever can.

CURRENCY

Greece suffers from severe inflation, which hurts locals much more than visitors. In practice, the drachma tends to slide downhill against the pound, the dollar and other currencies just enough to compensate for the annual increase in prices. Coins come in 10, 20, and 50 drachma denominations, notes in 50, 100, 500, 1,000, 5,000 and 10,000. Ten drachmas is now worth so little that most people will round bills off to the nearest 20 – sometimes in your favour, sometimes in theirs.

YOUR BUDGET

You can travel in fairly lavish style on £200 a week without having to economize on food, drink, transport or accommodation. Watching the pennies you can even be fairly comfortable on as little as £100 a week, especially if you eat picnic lunches (no hardship) and are staying put rather than island-hopping. £150 a week is a realistic no-worries budget allowing £15 a day for bed and board and the balance for fares and extras.

KEEPING IN TOUCH

THE PERIPTERO

This is such a gobsmackingly useful institution that you wonder why other countries don't have them. At one of these streetside kiosks you can make a phone call, buy cigarettes, sweets, chewing gum, combs, hairspray, ballpoint pens, film, condoms, toothpaste, aspirin, newspapers and magazines, soft drinks and a whole bunch of other stuff. In a pinch, if you can't find anywhere else to change money, you may be able to sweet-talk a periptero man into changing some foreign cash into drachmes. Dollars are most acceptable as the dollar exchange rate is always known. There is a periptero on every other street corner in Athens and most towns and it is a small place indeed which does not support at least one.

PHONING HOME

International and local phone calls are easiest from the offices of OTE, the Greek telecommunications organization. Calls are metered – you dial from a booth and pay after you hang up. When OTE is closed, you can make local and sometimes international calls from a periptero kiosk. These also use meters. In resorts, many travel and tour agencies also have metered phones and fax facilities.

Getting your call through is another matter and can raise the blood pressure of even the most laid-back. Calling from (or even within) Athens is particularly frustrating and it can take half an hour or more to reach your number. One tip is to try early in the morning (between 7.30 and 8.30) or in mid-afternoon when the city takes its collective nap and phones are less busy. Calling the UK costs approximately £1 per minute.

NEWSPAPERS, BOOKS, MAGAZINES AND TV

British and other foreign newspapers and magazines reach Athens and the main resort islands one to two days after publication. The English-language daily, *Athens News*, is an eccentric and amateurish institution but its coverage of national news and translations can be amusing and revealing of local attitudes. The English-language *Greek Weekly News* is more professional and informative. *The Athenian*, a monthly magazine for Anglophone expats, is a good source of up-to-date information on restaurants, nightlife and special events in and around Athens.

BOOKS in English are generally much more expensive than in Britain but there are many second-hand bookshops in Athens and on the more popular islands which will give you a good trade-in deal. In Athens, the following stock new and second-hand books in English:

Compendium (Nikis 28, Syntagma). Fiction, nonfiction, guidebooks, maps and used book exchange.
Reymondos (Voukourestiou 18, Syntagma). Books, newspapers, magazines.

TV junkies will be glad to know that Greek TV stations broadcast films and shows – especially sitcoms and soaps – from the UK, US, Canada and Australia in English with Greek subtitles. Olympic Action Radio on 102.1 FM broadcasts

BBC and Voice of America programmes on alternate days, 24 hours a day.

READING TIPS

Among my favourite fiction, non-fiction, specialist guides and personal reminiscences of Greece are:

Mani and *Roumeli* (both Penguin), by Patrick Leigh Fermor, recount splendidly idiosyncratic journeys of exploration through ancient, medieval and modern Greece. His diatribe against tourists and guidebook writers in *Roumeli* makes uncomfortable reading!

Eleni, by Nicholas Gage, and *The Flight of Ikaros*, by Kevin Andrews (Penguin), give two different views of the tragic and horrific Civil War of the 1940s.

The Mountains of Greece: A Walker's Guide, by Tim Salmon (Cicerone), is for serious walkers prepared to tackle tough but tremendous tracks, mainly in Epirus and the Peloponnese. *Landscapes of Western Crete* (Sunflower Books), by Jonni Godfrey and Elizabeth Karslake, is essential for anyone planning to visit this mountainous region and is a detailed guide to easier walks, car tours and picnic spots as well as marathon explorations. In the same series, Sunflower publishes *Landscapes of Corfu, Landscapes of Samos* and *Landscapes of Eastern Crete*. Also useful is *Exploring Rural Greece* by Pamela Westland (Christopher Helm) – particularly good for touring itineraries off the beaten track.

A Traveller's History of Greece, by Timothy Boatswain and Colin Nicholson (Windrush Press), is a concise if rather dry run-down of Greece's past from Neolithic times to the present day. Good for an overall view, not so good at putting places in context.

The Greek Myths (two volumes, Pelican) by Robert Graves. The great poet's interpretation of the whole of ancient mythology is still the definitive one. Scholarly and fascinating – but definitely not light reading.

The Mediterranean Ferry Guide: 1. Eastern Mediterranean by Frewin Poffley (Thomas Cook) is a useful rule-of-thumb guide to what goes where. Also lists ferries to Italy, Turkey and Yugoslavia.

Athens and Attica (Phaidon Press) is a handy illustrated, detailed guide to the ancient and medieval sites of the capital and its hinterland.

WHAT TO PACK

CLOTHES

Your travelling wardrobe depends on when you plan to go. Between June and September you won't need warm or waterproof clothes unless you intend to head for the highest parts of northern Greece.

INDEPENDENT TRAVELLERS' SURVIVAL KIT

I usually carry a very lightweight sleeping bag and mat for long overnight boat trips or the occasional emergency night under the stars when every bed in town is spoken for. A sleeping bag which unzips all the way round is preferable to the "coffin" type in summer – you can unzip it when it gets too hot. Also:

Swiss Army Knife with corkscrew, can and bottle opener and other useful tools. Get the one with the tiny tweezers – good for removing thorns and sea urchin spines.

Metal spoon for yoghurt.

Metal/plastic mug.

Water bottle.

SPONGE BAG/MEDICAL KIT

As well as the usual essentials you will need:

Insect repellent containing **Deet** – try Jungle Gel or Autan, both available in sticks.

Insect bite soother like Anthisan is also a good idea.

Painkillers – aspirin or paracetamol – for headaches, tooth-aches and hangovers. Avoid painkillers containing codeine, which is a controlled substance in Greece.

Sticking plasters for the almost inevitable blisters.

Antiseptic ointment and **Antiseptic wipes** for cuts and grazes. **Water sterilizing tablets** – Greek tap water is perfectly safe to drink but if you plan any long walks these tablets mean you can purify water from a well or spring. Alternatively, take a bottle of **iodine tincture** – doubles as antiseptic and water purifier.

Sunblock/sunscreen: Never underestimate the power of the Greek sun. It can burn you badly as early as April and as late as October. All main brands of sunscreen, sunblock, oils and lotions are sold at beach resorts, though they cost about 50 per cent more than in the UK. If you are passing through Athens, there is a branch of **The Body Shop** just off Kolonaki Square with the usual good range of organic and cruelty-free sun products.

PHARMACIES

In Greek towns and villages the pharmacy (**Farmaki'a**) is marked by a red Maltese cross and sells most medicines over the counter without a prescription – including a number of remedies only available in the UK on prescription. Most pharmacists speak good English and are very helpful in recommending cures for the more common ailments. Condoms (**capotes**) are sold in pharmacies and in periptero kiosks.

SEEING THE SIGHTS

ANCIENT GREEK SITES

Starting in Athens, you could take in half a dozen or more of the finest and best-known ancient sites – the Acropolis, Corinth, Mycenae, Epidavros, Olympia and Delphi – in a fairly hectic week or a more relaxed ten-day to two-week itinerary, getting around by hire car or by bus. More remote sites, such as the Macedonian ruins at Vergina and Pella, the sanctuary of Zeus at Dodona, or the Necromanteion at Ephyra, are in some ways more impressive because they are less visited, and are well worth the extra effort it takes to reach them. An alternative western circuit from Athens could take in Delphi, Dodona, the Necromanteion and Olympia, as well as Nestoria in the south-west Peloponnese, in a week of touring.

In the islands, the sites not to be missed are Minoan Knossos and Roman Gortys on Crete, Lindos on Rhodes, Delos, and the Sanctuary of the Great Gods on Samothraki.

WHEN TO GO: Off-season – late March to early April and mid-September to the end of October – is the best time to tour the great centres of ancient Greece. The weather is milder, though still usually sunny, and the sites far less crowded than in summer. Even at Delphi, the best known, you can sometimes have the place almost to yourself.

MEDIEVAL GREECE

Byzantine, Frankish, Venetian, Genoese and Turkish castles are scattered all over Greece like broken toys, often little-admired and hardly publicized. The Peloponnese is the richest hunting ground, with crumbling fortifications crowning every hilltop.

Not to be missed are Acrocorinth, above the ancient Hellenistic site; Mistra, near Sparta; Monemvasia, in the south-east Peloponnese; Methoni and Koroni, the massive sea-forts called "the eyes of Venice"; the fortress of the Palamidi at Nafplion. In the islands you should see the Genoese castles on Limnos, Chios and Lesbos, the Venetian fortifications at Chania, Rethimnon and Heraklion, and the Tolkienesque walled town of the Knights of St John on Rhodes.

WHEN TO GO: Any time of the year, the pleasantest being spring and autumn. All the island castles are within a few minutes' walk of good beaches.

TRADITIONAL GREECE

Fast-vanishing traditional costumes can still be seen worn by older men and women in south-west Crete, Skiros, Olympia on Karpathos, Rhodes, and on special occasions in Epirus and Macedonia. Greece's splendid variety of vernacular architecture is preserved in government–supported "traditional settlements" on the mainland and islands (see p 115). Go to the Cyclades for white geometric villages as seen on cards and posters – Paros, Naxos, Mykonos and Santorini have especially lovely villages. On the mainland, the mini-fortresses of Mani and the timbered mansions of Pilion deserve a detour or a special trip.

WHEN TO GO: Year round. Folk music, dancing and traditional costumes are most in evidence at Easter, at the mid-August feast of Panagiria (Assumption, August 15) and at name-day festivals celebrating the patron saints of islands and villages.

WALKING IN GREECE

For day hikes: Samos, western Crete, northern Corfu, Pilion, some of the smaller Dodecanese islands, Thassos. For serious walkers: the White Mountains on Crete, the Epirus ranges around Mt Timfi and the Zagorochoria, the Taigettos in the Peloponnese, Mt Parnassus and Mt Olympus. The NTOG leaflet on the E4 European hiking route from Macedonia to the southern Peloponnese lists some of the more challenging walks. Watch out for fierce shepherd dogs in the northern mainland.

WHEN TO GO: Spring or early summer in Crete and the Peloponnese. All through the summer in Samos, Pilion and Epiros.

BEACHES

Greece has thousands of beaches, some idyllic, many fine, some downright squalid. Long beaches of fine sand are rare, and inevitably attract mass-tourism development. But there are plenty of little coves of fine clean white pebbles and glass-clear water and many beaches are a mixture of coarse sand and small pebbles. These smaller beaches usually have more shade than the long sandy stretches which look so inviting in holiday brochures. They are also more sheltered from the Meltemi, the infuriatingly strong wind which in summer can blow up from any direction and is like the hot blast from an oven, turning exposed beaches into a hell of driving sand.

The best **island beaches** are on Corfu, Crete, Kos, Rhodes, Paros, Samos and Mykonos. Long, sandy **mainland beaches** can be found down the west coast of the Peloponnese and on the Kassandra and Sidhonia peninsulas of Halkidiki in the north.

Tourism must carry the can for a great deal of the rubbish cast up or left behind on many beaches. HELMEPA, the Hellenic Marine Environment Protection Association, estimates 40 per cent of the garbage it collects in its beach clean-up campaigns is plastic, an awful lot of it in the shape of suntan oil bottles, old sandals, carrier bags and soft drink containers. Each summer, the Greek islands experience a population explosion and garbage disposal facilities simply can't keep up. Tourists, after all, do not pay local taxes, nor do they take their garbage home with them.

But local people are to blame too. Islanders and mainland villagers have been accustomed over millennia to having the sea obligingly devour their relatively tiny amounts of rapidly biodegradable organic trash. Kitchen scraps, old leather shoes, wood and paper vanish quickly. Even old tin cans and glass bottles, though unsightly, are eventually ground down to sand. This cavalier attitude persists, but plastic neither rots nor rusts, and the affronted Aegean just spews it back.

In general, Greek municipalities in tourism areas make a big effort to keep beaches clean. Make a point of finding a bin for your trash.

WHEN TO GO: The wind is at its worst from late July to the end of August and is fiercest in the Cyclades. Only the most dedicated self-baster sunbathes for much of the day in August. Early summer (June to mid-July in most of the Aegean, late April and May in southern Crete) offers hot sun but chillier sea. Wimps or those pampered by heated swimming pools may prefer September, when most of the crowds have gone and the sea is at its warmest after months of summer sun.

KEY DATES

BC

6500:   Stone Age settlements in Greece

3000:   Bronze in use on mainland. Seafaring Bronze Age trading culture develops in Cyclades.

2200–1700:   Early Minoan civilization in Crete develops into Minoan palace culture.

1600:   Appearance of Mycenaean city-culture on mainland, spreading to islands.

1500:   Explosion of Thira volcano.

1200:   Waning of Mycenaean culture, destruction of Mycenaean palaces.

1100:   First Dorian Greeks; movement to the Aegean islands and Asia Minor coasts.

776:   First Olympic Games.

800–600:   City-states take shape. Athens and Sparta expand and become more powerful.

545:   Persians conquer Greek colonies in Asia Minor.

490:   First Persian incursions into Greece. Battle of Marathon.

480–79:   Persian invasion of Greece.

478:   Delian League marks zenith of Athenian expansionism.

431–404:   Peloponnesian War between Sparta and Athens ending in Athenian defeat.

371:   Battle of Leuktra. Theban victory ends Spartan hegemony.

359–336:   Reign of Philip II and rise of Macedonia as greatest power in Greek world.

338:   Battle of Chaironia destroys all remaining opposition to Macedonia.

336:   Alexander becomes King on assassination of Philip II.

336–23:   Reign of Alexander.

323–196:   Macedonian kingdom and client states.

196–86:   Piecemeal conquest by Romans culminating in sack of Athens by Roman general Sulla.

AD

0–300: Roman rule in Greece.

324: Constantine moves capital of the Empire to Byzantium, renaming it Constantinople. For the next three centuries, Christian Emperors gradually impose Christianity and wipe out older religions and traditions.

395: Olympic Games ended.

529: Non-Christian schools of philosophy in Athens suppressed.

600–700: Eclipse of Byzantine power. Invasions by Slavs. Corsairs and Saracens conquer Crete and raid the Aegean coast.

800–900: Byzantium regains control of Greece.

1204: Latin/Venetian Fourth Crusade sacks Constantinople. Venice and the Frankish Crusaders divide Greece among them.

1261/1262: Byzantine Emperors recover Constantinople and mainland Greece. Venetians retain control of islands and coastal fortresses.

1354: Ottoman Turks reach Europe.

1429: Turks take Thessaloniki (Salonika).

1453: Fall of Constantinople.

1460: Turks take Mistra.

1480: Turks besiege Rhodes unsuccessfully.

1499–1501: Turks take Nafpaktos, Zakinthos, Koroni and Methoni from Venice.

1522: Turks conquer Rhodes.

1537–40: Turks besiege Corfu and take Monemvasia and Nafplion.

1566: Turks capture Chios and Naxos.

1571: Turks checked at Battle of Lepanto.

1577: Samos falls to Turks.

1669: Fall of Heraklion completes Turkish conquest of Crete.

1684–1715: Venetians reoccupy Peloponnese.

1799–1814: Ionian islands occupied successively by France, Russia and Britain.

1821–30: War of Independence, ending with Battle of Navarino and destruction of Turkish fleet by Britain, France and Russia. Peloponnese, Cyclades, Attica and the Sterea Elladha become the new Greece.

1831: President Capodistrias assassinated.

1833: Otto imposed as King by Britain, Russia, France and Bavaria.

1864: Britain returns Corfu and Ionian islands to Greece.

1866: Rising against Turks in Crete fails when Britain, France and Russia block Greek intervention to preserve status quo.

1881: Turks cede Thessaly to Greece.

1912: First Balkan War. Greece gains Thessaloniki, Ioanina and Chios.

1913: Second Balkan War. Bulgaria attacks Greece. Greece formally annexes Chios, Lesbos, Samos, Ikaria and Crete.

1914: Outbreak of World War I. Greece divided between pro-Allied faction led by Prime Minister Venizelos and neutralist, German-leaning Royalists. After pro-Venizelist army coup and series of Allied ultimatums, Greece joins war in 1917.

1919: Encouraged by Britain and France, Greece lands troops at Smyrna (Izmir) in Turkey.

1919–23: War between Greece and Turkey in Asia Minor ends in defeat for Greece and exchange of populations. Hundreds of thousands of Greeks driven out of Turkey to Athens and other Greek cities.

1924–36: Series of coups, counter-coups, and rigged elections as Venizelists, Royalists and generals vie for power. In 1936 King George suspends constitution; General Metaxas becomes dictator.

1939: Italy invades Albania.

1940: Italy demands access to Greek ports. Metaxas refuses on October 28 ("Ochi Day").

1941: German invasion and conquest.

1942–44: Anti-German resistance by Royalist and leftist groups. British support only Royalists. Frequent fighting between resistance groups.

1944: British troops land in Greece, entering Athens in October. In December, police massacre demonstrators in Athens. Fighting between leftist forces and government and British troops in Athens.

1945–49: Civil War between Royalist right, supported by Britain and US, and Communists, ending after Stalin withdraws support.

1967: Colonels' coup led by Col. Papadopoulos imposes right-wing regime. King Constantine leaves Greece.

1973: Plebiscite ends monarchy. Secret police chief Ioannides deposes Papadopoulos. Student protest sit-in at Athens Polytechnic crushed, many students killed.

1974: Junta's backing for right-wing Greek coup in Cyprus backfires when Turkey invades Cyprus. Crisis ends with collapse of the junta. Constantine Karamanlis becomes caretaker president.

1975–1981: Nea Demokratia, right-wing government, takes Greece into EEC in 1981.

1981: PASOK, the left-wing Pan Hellenic Socialist Alliance, wins election under Andreas Papandreou.

1984: PASOK re-elected.

1989: PASOK defeated in election but no clear winner.

1989–1990: Series of elections fails to produce governing majority.

1990 (April): ND forms government under Constantine Mitsotakis with one-seat majority.

THE POLITICAL SCENE

Politics has always been the prime topic of conversation in the Greek kafeneion, an institution which rivals the British pub as the centre round which social life revolves. Political discussion is always guaranteed to raise voices and tempers, and the most intense clashes of opinion are often between members of the same side rather than partisans of right and left. But since the welter of recriminations which ended eight years of rule by Andreas Papandreou's Pan Hellenic Socialist Alliance (PASOK) in 1989, politics have been in the doldrums. Even the nightly TV spectacle of the former president and his associates on trial, charged with massive fraud, has lost its savour. The Bank of Crete scandal which erupted in 1989 spelt the end of PASOK's reign.

Whether the 73-year-old Papandreou's divorce and remarriage to a 35-year-old former air hostess cost him votes is debatable: given the rather cavalier attitude of many male Greeks to their womenfolk it may well have been seen as a token that Andreas, as he was familiarly known, was still a fit and potent leader. PASOK loyalists still insist that the Bank of Crete scandal has the grubby fingerprints of the CIA all over it. Certainly Papandreou, with his stagey wooing of Libya and other Arab states and his continual threats to evict US military bases from Greece, was not well liked in Washington.

What finally tipped the balance against PASOK – far more than the opportunist mouthings of its political rivals would suggest – was the electorate's feeling that the flamboyant Papandreou had failed to deliver on many of the pledges on which he was elected in 1982. PASOK was the first genuinely left-wing party ever elected in Greece. Papandreou made a sweeping promise of "alaghi" – change – but many Greeks felt that the government had both failed to carry through many of the changes it promised and been unable to control the far-reaching changes being wrought by outside forces, particularly after membership of the European Community.

Joining the EC has not been an unalloyed success. True, new markets have been opened for Greek products, and EC funds have helped bring better roads and other services to the remote communities. Greece's many small farmers have benefited from subsidies. But the Community's common agricultural policy has increased prices of many commodities and fuelled inflation.

One side effect has been a minor "orange mountain" which has led some Greek farmers to dump their crops – hitherto unthinkable. In Crete, sultana farmers complain that they have become dependent on Community subsidies which may be withdrawn. And the Greeks, perhaps Europe's most fiercely nationalistic people, look askance at the signing away of the slightest shred of a sovereignty won in a bloody century of rebellion and insurgency.

No other non-communist European country has experienced such rapid social, economic and political change in the past decade as Greece. And in the last four years practical concerns, primarily inflation, unemployment and frequent strikes, have alienated many voters. PASOK failed to to do anything to improve Greece's lumbering, antiquarian and disproportionately large bureaucracy. Instead, Papandreou – in time-honoured fashion – found slots in the system for PASOK placemen and grafted on still further layers of pen-pushers to staff new commissions, ministries – including a short-lived ministry of tourism – and bureaux.

PASOK's share of the vote in the three elections it lost in 1989 and 1990 was around 40 per cent – roughly the same proportion which under the British electoral system has won the Conservative Party landslide victories and more than ten uninterrupted years of power. The loyalty of the PASOK vote made three successive elections necessary before Constantine Mitsotakis and Nea Dimokratia – with the help of the sole deputy elected for the tiny right-wing splinter party DIANA – emerged with a clear ruling majority.

Nea Dimokratia is usually translated as "New Democracy"

though "New Republican" is an equally valid translation and perhaps better conveys the party's free-market, pro-NATO and anti-leftist stance. Founded by the elder statesman Constantine Karamanlis in the aftermath of the 1967–74 military junta, Nea Dimokratia was hammered into a disciplined and modern right-wing party by Mitsotakis during its eight years in the wilderness. "Mitsi" – it may be some time before the kafeneon pundits accord him the honour of dubbing him "Kosta" – is a veteran political infighter from way back, but whether his party has anything going for it apart from popular disillusionment with PASOK rule remains to be seen, even after two years in power.

PASOK's opponents may have overplayed their hand by bringing Papandreou and other PASOK figures to trial for offences connected with the Bank of Crete scandal, in which Papandreou is charged with siphoning off state funds into PASOK and private coffers. As the trial got under way, Papandreou – flamboyant as ever – challenged the court's competence to try him, while PASOK militants took to the streets.

The state prosecution fumbled and fudged its case as the trial got under way, and events came to a dramatic halt with the collapse in court, and subsequent death, of a key witness, George Koutsougiorgas. At the time of writing the case drags on, televized daily, and the prosecution case looks weaker day by day. Greeks – united by their general contempt and distrust of politicians of any stripe – are increasingly of the view that the real truth behind the missing millions will never emerge.

The third player on the Greek political stage is KKE (pronounced "kappa kappa eh"). Though it commands a staunch following and between 15 and 20 per cent of the vote, and is said to be the country's second biggest owner of real estate, the Communist Party in Greece is suffering from a lack of direction. Many of its policy-makers spent much of their careers exiled in Moscow or Bulgaria, but ironically KKE clung to die-hard Communist doctrines long after other Eastern European Communist parties – and even the Kremlin itself – disavowed them. At the time of writing a terminal split between old guard and reformists in the Party seemed imminent.

Such a split opens up an opportunity for PASOK to woo disenchanted reformist Communist Party members and voters, but whether this can happen in a political environment plagued by personalities is doubtful. Both Papandreou and Mitsotakis are ageing relics of Cold War, pre-EC politics, and until both leave the stage there seems little likelihood of an end to political stagnation.

A small nation afloat in a stormy geopolitical ocean over which it exerts little control, Greece clings to its Western alliances while denouncing a host of real and imagined slights to its independence and interests. Foreign policy is coloured by a strong streak of not entirely unjustified paranoia on the touchy subject of Turkey. For almost 40 years the two have been NATO's least likely allies, with Greece's military planners in no doubt that Turkey is as big a threat as the defunct Warsaw Pact, crumbling Yugoslavia or maverick Albania. The United States is seen as favouring Turkish claims on its affections over Greek interests. Since Turkey's staunch support for the US during the Gulf War, this has become an even bigger worry. In 1974, the two countries almost went to war over Cyprus and since then there have been frequent sabre-rattlings over the oil and mineral rights to the Eastern Aegean seabed. Politicians like the maverick and compulsive turncoat Mikis Theodorakis who extend the hand of friendship eastwards make themselves targets for abuse from all directions.

The realignment of Europe, crisis in the Balkans, and the advent of the single European market are even greater causes for anxiety. On its way into the 21st century, Greece has a flock of political albatrosses round its neck, and they certainly won't be shaken off easily. Trapped in the mire of Cold War positions, none of the country's politicians have shown much sign of adapting to a new Europe or a new world order.

Meanwhile, Greeks continue to muddle along as always, fatalistically shrugging off the idiocies and idiosyncracies of government. With inflation still high, many people hold down two or three jobs to make ends meet. Governments are frequently accused of failing to deliver and a great many Greeks regard taxation as a one-way street. As a result, ducking and diving is a national pastime, encouraged by a largely cash economy in which more than half of the workforce is self-employed. No love is lost between working Greeks and a burdensome bureaucracy which insists everything must be done in person and in triplicate, creating a climate in which, as a café philosopher once told me, "everything is forbidden and everything is permitted".

ATHENS
Love at Second Sight

Nobody falls in love with Athens at first sight, but sooner or later any committed lover of Greece must visit its sprawling, noisy yet relaxed capital. This is the home of almost half of Greece's people – four million out of nine million – and Athens street life has a better claim than the increasingly touristified fishing harbours of the islands to represent the "real Greece" so many visitors claim to seek. Given the chance, Athens will grow on you, but the best – and for many people the only – reason to visit it is to see its ancient crowning glory, the Acropolis, and the other archaeological sites and museums.

If you're not set on seeing these, your best bet is to bypass the city by taking a charter flight directly to the islands or one of the mainland regional airports.

If you have to use Athens International Airport but do not plan to spend time in the city, consider taking an Olympic Airways domestic flight onward to one of many island airports or going straight to Piraeus or Rafina for ferries onward to the islands.

Greece's capital is an odd and sometimes uneasy blend of ancient, medieval and modern, and it can come as a jarring surprise to the visitor to find that the old has been obliterated by the new to a greater extent than in almost any other European capital.

Athens can seem a gritty desert of identical apartment and office blocks, stamped out and plumped down along the geometrical plan of the 19th-century city with no regard for aesthetics or indeed for comfort. In high summer, when the city swelters at 40°C or more, the multi-storey blocks trap the heat and turn streets into baking, smog-filled canyons. The city's traffic problems and air pollution are legendary, creating

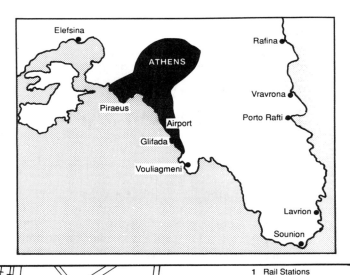

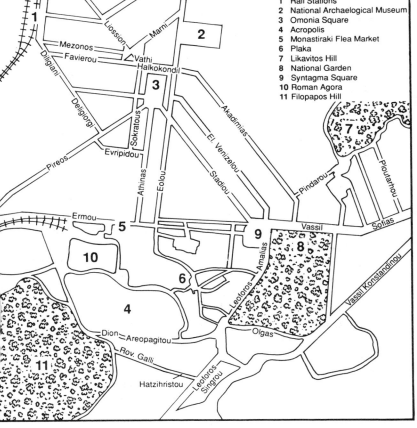

1 Rail Stations
2 National Archaelogical Museum
3 Omonia Square
4 Acropolis
5 Monastiraki Flea Market
6 Plaka
7 Likavitos Hill
8 National Garden
9 Syntagma Square
10 Roman Agora
11 Filopapos Hill

a choking cloud which ruins ancient marble and human lungs with horrid impartiality. The city is gradually coming to grips with the problem, but the campaign to curb pollution has a long way to go.

But an older, calmer city lives side by side with the traffic and cement of late-20th-century Athens. Corner stalls sell traditional snacks like roasted corn, sesame-seed rolls and pokes of salted nuts, sunflower and melon seeds. Lottery ticket peddlers work the streets with their bundles of tickets on tall poles. And around noon, when the city grinds to a halt for its afternoon siesta, Athenians – most of whom have been up since dawn – retire to the cool depths of high-ceilinged, open-fronted cafés to drink coffee and play backgammon. Only tourists are foolish enough to brave the heat and traffic fumes at a pavement table on a summer day; for Athenians, sitting outside is for the evening.

In side streets and on hillsides only a few steps from the city centre, there are pockets of traditional houses and tree-lined squares full of rickety café tables, and marooned on roundabouts and traffic islands in the middle of busy main streets you come across little medieval churches with pan-tiled roofs and massive timber doors. Hints of an even older city crop up everywhere – tumbled columns in a little park or lining a stretch of metro track at Monastiraki station, or a marble pillar pressed into service to hold up the sagging ceiling of a basement taverna in the Plaka.

Though people have lived here for 7,000 years (on and off), modern Athens, little more than 150 years old, is one of Europe's youngest cities. It grew up with the fledgling Greek nation, thanks to Otto I, the Bavarian princeling whom the great powers of Europe made Greece's first king in 1832 and who moved his court here from Nafplion on the Peloponnese, the newly-independent country's first capital.

It is hard to believe that when Otto and his carpetbaggers arrived Athens was a huddle of shepherds' huts below the long-deserted, tumbled ruins of the Acropolis. Otto's Bavarian architects, used to the whims of princes, set out to build Greece a modern European capital with wide boulevards and streets on a grid plan which you can still see. Athens in the last century was a gracious little capital of villas and mansions in the style called neo-classical, with stuccoed façades and mock-Ionic porticoes and pilasters.

Only a few are left. Much of the city was flattened by fighting and bombing by Allied and Axis forces during the Second World War and in its immediate aftermath, when Allied forces turned on their erstwhile allies in the left-wing Greek resistance. Many more have been torn down by developers over the past 30 years, and the grand avenues of Syngrou and Alexandras have been turned into ugly dual carriageways lined with dull buildings and crammed with speeding vehicles.

The end result is a city singularly lacking in architectural charm, a lack highlighted rather than relieved by the elegant ruins of the Parthenon rising above a sea of drab, angular concrete boxes as a poignant reminder of ancient Greece's architectural brilliance. But there are, happily, signs that Athens is becoming more aware of the need to preserve what remains of its old heart. Most of the work going on in the pretty streets of the old Plaka district is now restoration not demolition, and the surviving blocks of older Plaka shops and houses buffer the timeless beauty of the Acropolis from the raw modernity of the city centre.

GETTING YOUR BEARINGS

Syntagma, a long rectangle shaded by trees and full of café tables, is the hub of the visitor's Athens, with the Acropolis not far away to the south-west and Mount Lycabettos, the city's other big landmark, north-east. On its west side, the neo-classical façade of the Parliament building gives some idea of the grandest aspirations of 19th-century Athens. Outside, sentries in the white kilts and pom-pommed shoes of the Evzones, Greece's elite guards regiment, pace up and down like clockwork toys in a rigid, mechanical slow march.

Two of Syntagma's remaining three sides are lined with big hotels – including the city's grandest, the Grande Bretagne – and international airline offices. The west side is full of practical addresses – the main Athens Post Office, American Express and Commercial Bank of Greece. The main national tourist office (EOT) is inside the bank at Ermou 1, on the corner of Ermou and Syntagma.

Exploring Plaka

Built on the north and west slopes of the Acropolis, Plaka is the oldest part of the city, bounded roughly in the north by Mitropoleos and in the west by Fillelinon and Kidathinion.

Apart from the ancient Greek and Roman sites of the Acropolis itself, the Plaka has two small museums — the Goulandris Museum and the Kanellopoulos Museum, both in traditional mansion houses — which are worth checking out. It is, however, far more a place to wander, and eating, drinking and shopping are the order of the day, and for that matter the night.

The Flea Market proper starts on Odos Ifestou, beside the Monastiraki metro station (on the right as you face the station). In recent years it has spread into neighbouring streets and now extends all the way up Pandrossou to Plateia Mitropoleos (Cathedral Square), where a sign boasts the Pandrossou Flea Market.

There is a world of difference from the posh end of the market to the scruffy bottom end. Start at Pandrossou for leather bags, fleecy flokati rugs, ceramics (mostly imitations of ancient styles from the National Archaeological Museum) and jewellery for the tourist trade. Things get funkier when you cross Monastiraki into the older flea market street of Ifestou, by which time you will be well acquainted with the characteristic smell of all Greek tourist flea markets. The pervasive perfume of perfunctorily-cured leather flavours the air of souvenir shopping streets all over Greece.

Hephaestos (Ifestos) was the armourer and general ironmonger of the gods, and appropriately this street is full of shops and stalls selling all manner of army surplus kit (from a century or more of local, regional and world conflicts) fashion denims and T-shirts. Ifestou and other nearby streets are good places to look if you have to replace luggage or camping gear.

Some stalls resemble miniature war museums, with stock which includes rusty German, Italian, and British World War 2 helmets and bayonets, miscellaneous used shellcases and occasionally the threadbare remnants of elaborate pre-war Greek Army uniforms and traditional costume.

The real junk is sold at the corner of Ag. Filippou and Adrianou, where in the early morning you will find people selling the kind of stuff which ends up among the unsold leftovers of charity jumble sales: old ballpoint pens, tap fittings, last year's calendar, broken coat hangers, rancid old clothes and shoes.

East of Syntagma, across the busy artery of Amalias, the National Gardens are the main lungs of a city which has less urban greenery than any other European capital.

Omonia, Athens' other main central square, is at the centre of a busy commercial district and is a crowded traffic and public transport hub with little to offer the visitor except a glimpse of everyday Athens life.

Walk west of Syntagma along Ermou or Mitropoleos and you are heading for the most entertaining part of the city. **Plaka**, and the flea-market streets around Monastiraki, still have a whiff of the old Athens despite their dedicated pursuit of the tourist drachma. Entertaining places to wander through, they are untouched by the hurtling streams of traffic which carve up much of the rest of the city and they are richly endowed with pavement cafés and restaurants.

Kolonaki, the fashionable suburb a few minutes' walk north-west of Syntagma on the lower slopes of Mt Lykabettos, gets you away from the undiluted tourism of Plaka and its surrounds and from the busy commerce of the city centre.

Chic Greeks frequent the cafés and restaurants on Plateia Filiki Etaieria, the central square of this district dominated by the wooded pinnacle of Lycabettos behind it, one of the major Athens landmarks. These, and the expensive shops and piano bars on Tsakalof, are a good deal costlier than more modest tourist traps in the Plaka, though they offer little better quality or service – you are paying for the chic company, the smart location and the pink tablecloths. Kolonaki can seem like a poor imitation of smarter European capitals, but climb Lykabettos – or take the lazy way up by cable car – for a wonderful sunset panorama of the city.

DON'T MISS . . .

The Acropolis

It makes sense to visit the Acropolis before all else. It is the most prominent landmark of ancient Athens, and the city's other main archaeological sites can all be seen from it.

Above the banal sprawl of modern Athens the pure white columns of the Acropolis – literally, the high city – beckon irresistibly to all but the most hardened philistine. Semi-hardened philistines being dragged towards it against their better judgement by determined travelling companions will be pleased to learn that the climb to the site through the Plaka streets is dotted with attractive cafés and bars.

Marble white against a clear sky, the Parthenon, the main building of the Acropolis, is the central symbol of Greece, a country which is identified with its ancient past far more than most. A 20th-century Athenian still speaks a version of the language of Plato and Pericles and has at least some central ideas – democracy, for one – in common with them. We know who commissioned these buildings, who designed them, and we know what they were for, which is more than you can say for Stonehenge. Sadly, you will never be alone on the Acropolis, but even when crawling with visitors its buildings convey a powerful sense of the vitality and genius of classical Athens, two and a half millennia ago.

Entering the Acropolis you pass through a gate built in

Rebels Without a Cause

The bouzouki-loving mangas of Athens have long vanished from the scene but remain an inspiration to some of the city's younger bohemians. Mangas spoke their own impenetrable slang and were stylists to a man, wearing sashes, trilbies cocked at an angle, peg-top trousers and jackets slung over their shoulders at "full Zorro". They were a product of the great exchange of peoples which followed the tragic and pointless Greek-Turkish war of 1919 to 1922. Huge numbers of Greek refugees from Smyrna and Constantinople flocked to Athens, bringing with them their own music and dance and a whiff of the east – hashish.

Life was hard at first and its hardships were reflected and celebrated in songs called rembetika whose subject matter closely echoes the blues of Black America. Drinking, jail, dope and the fickleness of womankind are among the common themes.

Rembetika songs and music, which flourished in the 1930s, were almost submerged in the 1960s and 1970s by vulgarized, over-amplified versions but have made a comeback in the last decade, popular with younger Greeks because of their elements of protest and defiance of convention. Many of the pony-tailed self-styled "anarchists" who hang out in Exarchia, the slightly sleazy district around the Athens Polytechnic, see themselves as modern-day mangas.

Roman times (AD 267) on what was originally a bastion of the **Propylaia,** or main entrance to the site.

A wide first-century AD staircase leads to the Propylaia, built by the architect Mnesikles in 437 and regarded as one of the peaks of ancient Greek architecture. Five gateways, originally with massive wooden doors, led through its marble façade. High steps led to the inner temple, with shallower steps to the large central doorway through which sacrificial animals were taken to the altar. On either side of the stair are massive vestibules, each with six Doric columns. These originally held statues, shrines and resting places for pilgrims.

On the left of the staircase as you climb to the Propylaia, a square-sided column is the marble base of a monument to Agrippa (second century BC). On the right stands the Temple

The Site of the Acropolis

The crag on which the ancient temples stand is roughly 16m high and 16m by 260m wide. This natural defensive site was occupied from around 3000 BC and fortified with a massive Cyclopean wall around 1300 BC. On the advice of the oracle of Delphi these walls were pulled down in 510 BC, a move the Athenians had cause to regret only 30 years later when the victorious Persians sacked and burned the buildings on the Acropolis with the rest of the city.

Successive Athenian governments began rebuilding work but the site's most famous temples were built in the latter half of the fifth century BC, during the rule of Pericles, Athens's Golden Age.

It remained the wonder of ancient Greece until its fortunes began to wane as worship of the old gods faded. Buildings were damaged by fire and rebuilt during the Hellenic period and the site was treated with less reverence under Roman rule. In AD 437 the proselytizing Christian Emperor Theodosius II had the site "purified" and the Parthenon became the church of Agia Sofia – the Holy Wisdom.

The Acropolis became a fortress again in the unstable years after the fall of Byzantium, when it was held first by a Frankish bishop, then by the Frankish Dukes of Athens. Under the Turks, who pulled down many of the ancient temples and modified others, it became a fortified mosque. An exploding powder magazine destroyed the Propylaia in 1645 and the Parthenon, also used by the Turks as a powder store, suffered the same fate in 1687 when a lucky shot by the besieging Venetians set off another blast.

Restoration began in the 1830s and continues today.

of Athena Nike, Athena as the goddess of victory, with Ionic columns. Many of its frieze panels are copies. Most of the originals are in the British Museum. The temple, begun by Kallikrates in 447 BC, was completed 20 years later. It contained a wooden statue of Athena Nike, holding a pomegranate in one hand (the pomegranate was regarded as sacred fruit and appears in several myths) and a helmet in the other.

Statues of Nike were usually winged, but this one was

wingless, apparently so that the victory-bringing goddess could never desert her city. The temple was pulled down by the Turks and restored in 1835 and in the 1930s.

Passing through the Propylaia, the main attraction is ahead of you and a little to the right. Between the **Parthenon** and the Propylaia, foundation stones and boundary walls are all that remain of the shrines of Artemis Brausonia and Athena Ergane (Athena of the craftsmen) and of the Chalkotek storehouse (450 BC), the statue of Athene Promachos (454 BC) and the bronze chariot erected in 506 BC.

The Parthenon is built on a site where Athene was worshipped from the seventh century BC and probably much earlier. Destroyed by the Persians in 480 BC, it was eventually rebuilt under Pericles between 447 and 431 BC. Eight columns by 17, it is the epitome of the Doric temple, and despite its great size – the columns tower to a height of ten metres – and massiveness it seems light and graceful.

The Parthenon's builders used sophisticated structural and optical tricks for the greatest visual impact and design strength. The columns slope invisibly inward for stability, and the corner columns – which should appear larger than the others – are in fact slightly smaller, tricking the eye into "seeing" a larger space. Such geometrical subtlety is not seen again in European architecture until the age of the great cathedral-builders of the Christian West more than 1,500 years later.

The marble austerity of the Parthenon is deceptive. Inside, the temple was elaborately and colourfully decorated with murals and friezes, many of which are now in the British Museum. In the fifth century BC the Parthenon and the surrounding buildings were as gaudily painted as a Hindu temple. Red, blue and gold were the preferred colours.

The temple and its grounds were cluttered with equally brilliantly painted statues and pagan icons. The greatest, the gold and ivory statue of Athene Parthenos made by the great sculptor Phidias, was 12 metres high and contained almost 1,000 kilos of gold. In 426 it was removed to Constantinople, where it was destroyed; there is a Roman copy in the National Archaeological Museum (see page 47).

The **Erechtheion**, built between 421 and 406 by the architect Philokles, ranked in importance with the Parthenon and is in its own way equally impressive. An olive-wood statue of Athene was worshipped here from 480 BC.

Irregular in plan, the Erechtheion is on a smaller and more intimately human scale than the elegant geometries of the Parthenon, partly because it was built not from scratch but to incorporate a number of older shrines. Its eastern portico has six Ionic columns. Its best-known feature is the **Porch of the Caryatids**, where six larger-than-life female statues support the roof. The originals are in the Acropolis Museum to preserve them from the ravages of Athens's corrosive and polluted atmosphere.

Remaining features of the Acropolis site include the remains of the Ergasterion (workshop) of the sculptor Phidias; the foundations of the shrine of Zeus Polieus; and the sites of the Altar of Athena, the Old Temple of Athena, the Royal Palace (where foundations and inscriptions dating from the 15th century BC have been found) and the fifth century BC foundations of the House of the Arrephoroi, the girl-acolytes of Athene.

At the north-east tip of the site – the highest point of the Acropolis – the 19th-century belvedere offers a panoramic view of the city, with Lycabettos to the north-east and Philopappos Hill, known to the ancients as the Hill of the Muses, to the south-west.

The Agoras

The other sites of ancient Athens are laid out around the base of the Acropolis, within the limit of the ancient city walls of which little trace remains.

After the Acropolis, the most important classical site is the **Greek Agora**, sometimes called the Ancient Agora to distinguish it from the more recent Roman Forum next to it, behind Monastiraki. North of the Acropolis, the Greek Agora was the heart of ancient Athens, a noisy mixture of marketplace and debating floor – rather like Speaker's Corner, Portobello Road and the House of Commons rolled into one. Its most striking surviving building – better preserved, though less dramatic, than the Parthenon – is the Temple of Hephaistos, also called the Thesion. Built in the fourth century BC, it was dedicated to the god of smiths and to Athene. Around the temple are columns and remains of temples to Aphrodite, Zeus, Athene, and Apollo and of public buildings including the Bouleuterion, the fifth century BC meeting house of the Athenian senate.

The **Roman Agora**, once connected to the older Greek site, is half-lost among the narrow alleys and souvenir stalls of the streets behind Monastiraki metro station. Its most prominent landmark is the eight-sided Tower of the Winds, built in the first century BC. It was a combination of waterclock-tower, planetarium, sundial and weathervane. Also notable is the four-columned Doric west gate to the Roman Agora, likewise built in the first century BC, and the remains of the Library of Hadrian (AD 132) whose columned courtyard can be seen from outside the agora but is not open to visitors.

The Temple and Theatre of Dionysos, and the Odeon of Herod Atticus

On the south side of the Acropolis, these two main sites stand out among a number of more or less featureless foundations.

Built in the sixth century BC, the **Temple and Theatre of Dionysos** is the oldest venue for the performing arts in Europe. Plays by Sophocles, Aeschylus and Euripides were first performed here. Dionysos, god of drunkenness, was also god of transformation and disguise and so of masks, which were central to Greek drama. By 330 BC the theatre had expanded to seat 17,000 for the Dionysia, the annual festival of theatre. Behind it, against the rock of the Acropolis, are columns on which stood monuments to choregoi, the chorus-leaders who were the impresarios of Greek theatre. The remains of the temple of Dionysos Eleutheros, built in the fourth century BC, can be seen in front of the theatre.

West of the Theatre of Dionysos and connected to it by what remains of a 170-metre two-storey colonnade, is the rebuilt **Odeon of Herod Atticus**. Built in the second century AD, it was rebuilt this century and since 1955 has been the venue of the Athens Festival of music, theatre and dance as well as the summer sound and light shows. Its acoustics carry the slightest noise to all points of the huge theatre.

Politics in the Agora

In legend, Athens was ruled by kings of the line of Theseus, but an unusually enterprising populace did not allow them to become absolute rulers. By the seventh century BC the city was ruled by nine archons who were appointed each year. After a year in office, an archon became a life member of the council called the Areopagus.

Athens was not yet a democracy. Only a small aristocracy called the Eupatridai (literally "the sons of good fathers" or more colloquially "the well-born") could become archons or Areopagites. Those excluded from the system came to resent it, not least because they were called on to fight for the city even though they had no say in its policies.

In 620 BC the archon Drakon introduced Athens's first legal code. Harsh and inflexible, it made death the penalty for many crimes. It may have been intended to suppress a swell of anti-aristocratic feeling. Like most such attempts to stave off revolt, the more liberal reforms of the archon Solon (594 BC) probably encouraged it. Solon broke the aristocratic monopoly, created four social classes and founded the 400-member citizens' council called the Boule. He is seen as the founder of the Athenian state, and the lower chamber of the Greek parliament is still known as the Voule.

The failure of Solon's reforms led to chaos and internal strife and the general Peisistratos made himself tyrant or dictator. In ancient Greece such rulers were often aristocratic demagogues who came to power by promising to defend the common people against the rich. Peisistratos ruled from 546–510 BC but his son Hippias proved less adept and was kicked out of Athens with Spartan help in 510.

Reactionary Sparta intervened again and again in Athens and other Greek cities to bolster conservative oligarchies against more democratic rivals. The Athenian leader Kleisthenes laid the foundations of a grassroots democracy based on village units and made the assembly the heart of the system. From this evolved the Athenian democracy which flowered in the fifth century BC and more than 2,200 years later inspired the principles of modern democracy.

In Athens, the belief in the small democratic unit persisted. Aristotle belived the ideal city-state should be so small that all its citizens could hear the voice of a single herald. But Athenian democracy was strictly limited. Women had no voice, nor did those not born of Athenian parents, and slaves had no rights at all. It could also be random – in an attempt to prevent public office-holders mutating into an aristocracy, citizens were required to serve in the assembly as well as simply to vote, and government posts were awarded by lottery. Military commanders (strategoi) were elected and the ten elected generals held the most powerful posts in Athenian government, a situation open to abuse.

ALSO WORTH SEEING . . .

More Roman relics are to be found some distance from the Agora and the Acropolis, close to the National Gardens on a site north of Leoforas Amalias. The striking **Arch of Hadrian** is next to the busy traffic of Amalias. Nearby, within the National Gardens, is the **Olympion.** This temple to Zeus took seven centuries to build and was completed during Hadrian's reign.

Close to these ancient sites, a couple of more modern buildings survive as mementoes of Athens's 19th-century flowering. The **Zappeion,** in the middle of the National Gardens, is a neoclassical exhibition hall now used as a meeting place by the Council of Europe.

The **Stadion,** built in 1869–70 with funds given by the millionaire Averoff – who also bought the Greek Navy its first battlecruiser – was the venue for the first modern Olympics in 1896. It was modelled on the stadium built in the second century AD by Herod Atticus, King of Attica.

THE MAJOR MUSEUMS

The National Archaeological Museum
(Tositsa 1 – take the 2, 4, 5, 11, or 15 bus from Syntagma or Omonia. Entrance fee. Open 08.00 to 18.00.)

Most of the great sites of Athens have been denuded of their statues and decorations by centuries of pillage or in the interests of preservation. To imagine what they looked like when thronged with pilgrims and cluttered with statuary, a visit to the National Archaeological Museum is essential. The museum also contains treasures from Greece's other great ancient sites. There are 56 rooms, so a full day is needed if you plan to try to see something of each collection.

If you just want to hit the high points, head first for the Mycenaean collection, where Schliemann's phenomenal finds from the site are displayed. The most exciting of all is the beaten-gold "Mask of Agamemnon". Its heavy-lidded, bearded features are no longer thought to be those of Homer's hero-king, but as with so many Greek relics you feel a strong sense of personal connection with this long-vanished ancient ruler. Other key collections include the Cycladic finds. From a culture completely different from that of the Mycenaean mainland, these carved figurines and minimalist long-nosed faces look oddly modern.

The Acropolis Museum
(Within the Acropolis site; included in site entrance fee. Same opening hours.)

The museum is dedicated to finds from the site. Its most striking exhibits are the Caryatids, female figures which supported the porch of the Erechtheion.

The Agora Museum
(Adrianou 24. Inside the Agora site; included in site entrance fee. Open 08.00 to 18.00.)

Inside the Agora site, this museum contains statues, bronzes and pottery work discovered during digs here.

MINOR MUSEUMS . . .

Kanellopoulos Museum
(Corner of Theorias and Panou)

Eclectic collection from the Cycladic era to the Byzantine, willed to the nation by the Kanellopoulos family in 1972 and housed in a gracious Plaka mansion.

Museum of Cycladic and Ancient Greek Art
(Neofitou Dhouka 4)

Excellent private collection casts light on the enigmatic civilization of the Cyclades (3000 BC), Bronze Age Greece, and the Dark Age which followed the fall of Mycenaean civilization.

Factfile

Embassies and Consulates
Great Britain: Plutarchou 1, Tel: 723 6211/19
USA: Vas. Sophias 91, Tel: 721 2951
Canada: Genadiou 4, Tel: 723 9511/19
Ireland: Vas. Constaninou 7, Tel: 723 2771
Australia: Dem. Soutsou 37, Tel: 641 1712
New Zealand: Tsoha 15–17, Ambelokipi, Tel: 641 0311

Airlines
Olympic Airways, Syngrou 96, Tel: 929 2111
British Airways, Othonos 10, Tel: 322 2521

The "Elgin" Marbles

Many of the best preserved friezes and temple ornaments of the Parthenon and other buildings on the Acropolis are kept not in Athens but in the British Museum, where they have been for more than a century.

The "Elgin" marbles — as the British know them — are a continuing cause of friction between Britain and Greece. The fiercely patriotic Greeks see Britain's continued refusal to return the marbles to Athens as infuriatingly arrogant and utterly indefensible.

There is much to be said for the Greek argument that the proper place for such important relics is with contemporary finds in a major Greek museum. And the plan for a new museum designed specifically to house such relics in the best conditions strengthens the Greek case.

The British soldier and amateur archaeologist, Lord Elgin, bought the friezes from the Turkish bey of Athens early in the 19th century, when much of the Acropolis lay in ruins and there was no prospect of its being restored. In Elgin's defence, it must be said that he felt he was saving the marbles for posterity and maybe he did. Like so many other remains of ancient Greece, they could have ended up in the walls of a Turkish fortress or in a pasha's palace.

Nevertheless it is hard to make a convincing case for keeping them in London. Reading between the lines, the British Museum is reluctant to give way because to do so would open the sluices for a flood of similar requests from nations all over the world for the return of dozens of other exhibits.

British Airways airport desk, Tel: 961 0402
Air Canada, Othonos 10, Tel: 323 5143

Changing Money

National Bank of Greece, Karayorgi Servias 2, Syntagma, Tel: 321 0411
American Express Bank, Venizelou 15–17, Tel: 323 4781
Credit Bank Exchange Offices:
Stadiou 40, Tel: 326 0000
Venizelou 9, Tel: 323 4351

Pericleous 1, Tel: 672 5583
Stadiou 2 (Syntagma), Tel: 322 0141

National Tourism Organization of Greece (EOT)
Information Office: Karageorgi Servias 2, Syntagma (inside
the National Bank), Tel: 322 2545

Central Post Offices
Aiolou 100, Omonia Square
Syntagma Square (west side).

TRAVELLING

By Air   Athens Airport has two terminals. The West Terminal is for all
Olympic Airways international and domestic flights. The East Terminal
handles all other flights.

Athens city buses connect both terminals with the city centre and
Piraeus. Olympic Airways runs hourly shuttle buses from the West
Terminal to the corner of **Amalias** and **Syntagma,** departing hourly on
the half-hour in each direction (reduced frequency between midnight and
05.00). Olympic buses also run on the same schedule to the Olympic
office at **Syngrou,** a more convenient stop if you are staying in the
Vikou part of town. Taxi fare between the airport and central Athens
should be between £2 and £3 ($3.50 to $5), taxi fare to Piraeus around
£4 to £5.

By Sea   Most ferries for the islands dock at the main **Piraeus**
harbour, easily reached by public transport from the city centre.
Hydrofoils for the Saronic Gulf islands, the Peloponnese coast and
Kithira leave from **Zea Marina,** 1$^{1}/_{2}$ km north, say 15 to 20
minutes' walk from the main harbour, or most easily reached by
taxi. Ferries also leave from **Rafina,** a smaller port on the east
coast of the Attica peninsula, for Evia and the North-east Aegean
islands. This is a good back-door route in and out of Athens
bypassing Piraeus which is at its busiest and least salubrious in high
summer.

You can buy ferry tickets at the many agencies in central Athens
but it is easier to buy a ticket in **Piraeus.** There are ticket offices
in the Piraeus metro station and on the main ferry pier for all
routes and services. Ticket offices are affiliated with certain ferry
lines and will not sell tickets or give information on competing
services, so don't give up immediately if the first one you visit
tells you no services are available to your chosen destination that
day.

There is (usually) a list of all departures each day at the harbour
police office at the end of the main ferry pier.

Ferries for the Cyclades, Crete, Dodecanese and North-East Aegean islands leave from the main harbour about five minutes' walk from the metro station. Turn left along the waterfront and follow the signs.

By Bus Buses for the north and north-east (Halkida, Ķimi, Delphi, Larissa, Thiva, Trikala, Livadia, Lamia, Volos and Thessaloniki) leave from Liossion 260. To get there take the metro to Ags' Nikolaos, about ten minute walk from the bus station (see map).

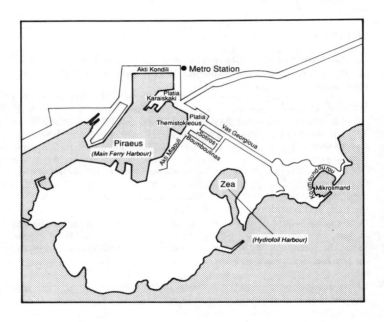

Buses for the Peloponnese, the west and north-west (Patras, Pirgos, Olympia, Nafplion, Kalamata, Sparta, Githion, Tripolis, Messolonghi, Igoumenitsa, Preveza, Ioanina and Kastoria) go from Kifissou 100, well out of town. Take city bus 52 from Omonia (about half an hour).

By Car   Car rental is available in Athens but rates are high. If you plan renting a car for a week or more it is much cheaper to book through one of the international companies such as Hertz, Budget or Holiday Autos before arriving in Greece.

Fast dual-carriageway toll roads connect Athens with Thessaloniki in the north and Corinth and Patras in the Peloponnese.

Car hire agencies in Athens: Avis, Amalias 48, Tel: 322 4951; Budget, Sygrou 8, Tel: 921 4771; Hertz: Vouliagmeni 567A, Tel: 994 2850; Thrifty: Syngrou 24, Tel: 922 1211. Apart from the major international chains, there are many national rental agencies with offices along Syngrou and Amalias.

By Rail   The two Athens train stations stand back to back. The passenger entrance is opposite the corner of Diligiani and Filadelfias. Trains for the north leave from Larissa Station (Stadhmos Larissis). Trains for the Peloponnese leave from the Peloponnese Station (Stadhmos Peloponnissou).

WHERE TO STAY

Finding decent affordable accommodation in Athens can be a problem. A series of purges by tourist police and tax inspectors has closed down many of the city's cheapest guesthouses, hotels and dormitories.

Avoid like the plague the overcrowded and insanitary "dormitories" like the so-called youth hostels close to the rail stations. In summer, these doss-houses are crammed with people sleeping on the floor, in the halls and corridors in generally squalid conditions. A fire in one of these dumps would be a horror story. If you really are on a shoestring budget, consider arriving in Athens early in the morning, taking a day to see the Acropolis and the main museums and heading out that night on any convenient bus or boat.

Cheap accommodation in the outskirts of the Plaka

Student Inn, 16 Kidathinion, Tel: 324 4808.
John's Place, 5 Patroou, Tel: 322 9719.
Joseph's House, 13 Markou Moussourou, Tel: 923 1204.
All three are favoured by a multinational budget-traveller clientele, and are good places to pick up word-of-mouth updates on your next stop.
Pella Inn, 104 Ermou, Tel: 325 0598. Just off Monastiraki, close to Plaka, Syntagma and the Acropolis. Fairly modern, helpful staff, and you can book excursions and ferry tickets here.
Royal Hotel and Imperial Hotel on Mitropoleos, next door to each other opposite the Cathedral, are cheap and clean but drab.

Other cheap and cheerful pensions
To Spiti tis Afroditis, Einardou/12 Selefkou, Tel: 881 0589.
Tony's Pension, 26 Zaharitsa, Tel: 923 6370 Pleasant pension in the quiet Zoukaki area on the slopes above Syngrou, bordering Plaka.

More expensive hotels

If you want good rooms, not just acceptable ones, be prepared to pay £20-£30 ($35-$45) for a double room.
Acropolis View (C-Class), 10 Galli/Webster, Tel: 921 7303, is clean and bright and its balconies really do have a view of the Acropolis. On a quiet side street, overlooking Koukaki and within easy walking distance of the Acropolis and the restaurants and cafés of Kidathinion.
Hotel Austria (C-Class), 7 Mousson, Tel: 923 5151, is nearby and similar.
Hotel Sofos, 18–20 Hormovitou, Tel: 822 6402. Not picturesque, but comfortable and next to the railway stations for late arrivals/early departures.
Blue House, 19 Voukourestiou, Tel: 362 0341. Comfortable central pension. Not cheap, but good value.
Athens House, 4 Aristotelious, Tel: 524 0539. Mid-priced pension.
Hotel Vienna, 20 Pireos, Tel: 524 9143. Mid-priced hotel close to Omonia.

FOOD AND DRINK
The streets around the flea-market are great for grazing on the hoof. Stationary and mobile hawkers sell roast nuts, chickpeas and sunflower seeds or sesame-seed-flavoured bread rings called koulouria, or the charcoal-roasted, chewy corn cobs which Athenians favour, flavoured with a shake of coarse rock-salt.

Adrianou, one of the lower streets girdling the Plaka, is a good place to look for breakfast. The square at the corner of Aiolou and Adrianou has a bunch of pleasant open-air cafés and restaurants. On the corner of Aiolou and Mitropoleou, Kafeneion Athena is good for coffee, yoghurt and freshly-squeezed orange juice, ham and eggs. Dioskouri, Adrianou 39, has coffee, fruit juices and cheese and ham omelettes at affordable prices.

South-west of the Plaka, Kidathinion and Thespidos streets are a strip of shops, cafés and restaurants, many of them mainly for visitors but some catering to a local clientele. The biggest concentration is around Plateia Philomousou Etaireas (not to be confused with the similarly-named square in Kolonaki) where you can eat or drink fairly generously for about £3.50 a head with wine. Philomousou is one of the smarter of Athens's newly-fashionable tea-houses, serving cocktails, juices, pancakes, icecream and salads. Taverna Damigos, at the corner of Kidathinion and Adrianou, is one of the last of the old restaurants. It has been run by the same family for more than a century and the walls of the restaurant are lined with ancient family photos.

The ceiling is held up by an ancient marble column liberated from some ruined temple.

At the foot of Mitropoleos, **opposite Monastiraki metro**, there is a cluster of souvlaki restaurants and modern burger-bar places. Best, biggest and most traditional of the bunch is **O Thanasis** which sells souvlaki from about 40p (70 cents) to take away or to eat there. Just around the corner in Monastiraki itself you'll find the venerable **Biraktaris**, an old-fashioned taverna which has only recently yielded to tourism by putting tables on the pavement outside. It is still favoured more by Athenians than by visitors and its cooking is as authentically Greek as you will find in the centre of Athens. Sample their wines from the barrel.

Turn left at the foot of Mitropoleos for the **Flea Market Café**, a bright new contender on the Monastiraki scene, selling sticky cakes, buns and pastries. Closer to Plaka, **Aiolos**, Aiolou 18, is a smart café-restaurant with a more imaginative menu than most and specials which change from day to day. **Eden Vegetarian Restaurant**, Plessa 3, is a boon for vegetarians longing to break the monotony of their usual Greek diet of bean stew and tomato and feta salad. It's in an attractive old Plaka house.

In Kolonaki, **Kolonaki Tops** and **Lykovrisi** are side by side, smart restaurants with outdoor seating under canopies. Expect to pay at least £25 ($42) for dinner for two. You are paying for the location, not for the meal, and the food isn't outstandingly finer than at the better Plaka restaurants. On the same side of Kolonaki square **Le Quartier** is a café and ice-cream parlour popular with cool young Athenians. **Perix**, on the corner of Spefskippou and Loukianou, is a cheaper and less pretentious place to eat in Kolonaki, with a choice of traditional Greek meze snacks such as dolmades, tzatziki, taramasalata and fried saganaki cheese from around £1 ($1.70) a plate.

NIGHTLIFE

For the visitor to Athens, nightlife comes down to eating and drinking. Most restaurants and bars stay open until 02.00. Establishments describing themselves as nightclubs tend to be either sleazy or plain dull, aimed at middle-aged Greek men. Restaurants advertising bouzouki music and dancing charge over the odds for an ersatz floorshow aimed at gullible tourists, while discos catering to young Athenians are not particularly welcoming to visitors.

PIRAEUS

Piraeus is a great place to leave, a sprawling, smelly, dockside district with few redeeming features. Between the First and

---

Beaches near Athens

Only the most hardened Athenians swim at the beaches closest to the city, where the cleanliness of the water is, to say the least, suspect.

The closest beaches fit for swimmers are at the beach resorts of Glyfada and neighbouring Vouliagmeni, 15 to 20 km from south of the city centre past the airport. The beaches of these resort suburbs are lined with blocks of big holiday hotels and with waterside bars and restaurants, mostly quite expensive. There are frequent buses from the city centre.

Second World Wars it was a rough, tough part of town and some of that lingers, as it does in harbour districts everywhere. Piraeus was also a haven for the mangas and bouzouki musicians and singers and general bohemian lowlife who frequented its rowdy tavernas. This squalid and dirty dockside was levelled by bombing during the Second World War, leaving the grime but not the colour. Nevertheless, with its round-the-clock cacophony of sirens and anchor chains as the island ferries load and unload, it has at least the promise of good things in store as you head into the archipelago.

Athenians used to flock to the fish restaurants around the little harbour of Mikrolimano, about one kilometre from the main commercial docks, but the stink of the heavily-polluted harbour has recently put many people off dining here. The only reason to be in Piraeus is to catch a ferry out to the islands, and fortunately the good metro and bus services from the city centre to the port mean that you do not have to eat or sleep here – though at a pinch you can.

An all-night café on the main ferry pier provides Greek coffee, iced instant coffee, beer, ouzo and soft drinks as well as greasy snacks for those waiting for a ferry departure in the small hours.

GETTING TO PIRAEUS

The easiest route is the east–west metro line which crosses Athens – Piraeus is its western end. Board at Omonia or Monastiraki in the city centre. There is a direct bus service between Piraeus and Athens Airport.

Journey time to the centre is about 45 minutes; for the airport allow one hour.

WHERE TO STAY

Piraeus has its share of really sleazy hotels catering to a floating population of merchant seamen and hookers. If you have to stay overnight, it's worth paying a little extra for a C-Class hotel or better. Three streets in particular, Notara, Filonos and Harilao Trikoupi, are lined with hotels.

C-Class Hotels

Anita, 25 Notara, Tel: 412 1024
Argo, 23 Notara, Tel: 412 1795/6
Atlantis, 138 Notara, Tel: 452 6871
Capitol, Harilao Trikoupi and 147 Filonos, Tel: 452 4911
Cavo, 79/81 Filonos, Tel: 411 6134
Santorini, 6 Harilao Trikoupi, Tel: 452 2147

D-Class Hotels

Achillion, 63 Notara, Tel: 412 4029
Adonis, 70 Filonos, Tel: 452 0330
Faros, 140 Notara, Tel: 452 6317
Piraeus, 1 Bouboulinas, Tel: 417 2950
Lux, 115 Filonos, Tel: 452 0354

RAFINA

27 km from Athens, Rafina is a busy little harbour with some decent beaches nearby and plenty of places to stay. This is a much more pleasant place than Piraeus to wait for a ferry; its harbour-front ringed with fish-markets and seafood restaurants is a world away from the urban blight and you could already be in the islands. There is an adequate, if slightly scruffy, town beach five minutes' walk south from the harbour and a better one 20 minutes away in the opposite direction. **Ferries** and **Hydrofoils** go from Rafina to Andros, Tinos, Paros, Mykonos, Siros, Amorgos, Iraklia, Schinoussa, Chios, Lemnos, Lesbos, Kavala, Evia, Naxos, Kos, Rhodes, Kalimnos, Astipalea and Nisiros. For the North-East Aegean and the more remote Cyclades it is more convenient than

Piraeus; for the Dodecanese and the main Cyclades islands it is just as good, so it is surprising that so few travellers use it as their Athens-Aegean gateway.

WHERE TO STAY
Hotel Bravo, Kokino Limanaki, Tel: 31 488, is a small, C-Class resort hotel on the sea. More convenient for the ferry harbour is the clean, old-fashioned and cheap **Hotel Akti** (Bithymias, five minutes' walk from harbour). **Hotel Korali** (Plateia Plastiria) is also cheap and a short walk from the harbour.

FOOD AND DRINK
Rafina has plenty of fast-food places, both modern and traditional, as well as some better restaurants close to the fishermen's end of the harbour. Near the main square above the harbour: **Steki**, cheap chicken and souvlaki grill; **Labito**, comfortable new café-bar; **Psarotaverna Dallas**, overlooking the harbour (medium expensive). On the waterfront: **Taverna I Rafina**, **Taverna Ta Kala Krasia** and **Taverna O Skalas** all have good fresh fish. **Ioakeim** is a real old-fashioned fish-taverna.

OUT OF TOWN . . .

Athens is easy to get out of, and some of Greece's greatest ancient sites, beach resorts and holiday islands are within easy reach either on an organised trip or travelling independently by bus, train, hire car or boat.

There are plenty of tour agencies in the Syntagma/Plaka area offering tours and excursions. Prices do not vary widely. Many hotels also arrange bookings for coach trips.

Dafni, on the outskirts of the city, is worth visiting for the lovely Byzantine monastery. Built in the 11th century, it has some of the finest Byzantine mosaics and has been a Christian site since the sixth century. Set among olives and cypresses, its walled gardens are – despite the flow of visitors – a calm oasis after the hubbub of the city.

Under the Latin Dukes of Athens, Dafni became a Cistercian monastery – the only one in the East. Abandoned after the Turkish conquest, it was taken over by Orthodox monks in the 16th century. Dafni's mid-Byzantine gilt mosaics, though damaged by intruders including Turkish, Bavarian, British and

French troops, are still magnificent, marked by a realism and humanism which is at odds with more stylized Greek religious art from earlier and later periods. They date from the 11th century.

Dafni's other visitor attraction is a great deal more profane. The Dafni Wine Festival, which runs non-stop through the summer, lets you run the full gamut of Greek wine-tasting. The festival park is open each evening. You pay an entrance fee – about £2 ($3.40) – which entitles you to a glass mug and all you can drink. You then proceed to get thoroughly hammered among the pine trees in the company of a very mixed crowd of others doing the same thing. Wine is served by hosepipe straight from the barrel at a number of booths.

Ten kilometres from Dafni and 20 km from Athens, **Elevsina** is an industrial town of shipyards and cement mills on the shores of the Saronic Gulf. Though its surroundings lack charm, the nearby ancient site of **Eleusis** still makes a considerable impact.

By the seventh century BC Eleusis was the heart of a popular cult based on the fertility-goddess Demeter and was the terminus of the Sacred Way which ran from Athens to the temples here. The site was first settled between 2,000 and 3,000 years BC and a Mycenaean palace stood on its acropolis.

The most striking remains on the site are the tiers of steps carved from the rock at the entrance to the Telesterion or shrine of Demeter. Remnants of Mycenaean and later buildings from the post-Mycenaean age show that this was an early sacred site which changed as it grew in importance. The site also held temples to Persephone, Demeter's daughter, (on a site next to the Telesterion) and her husband Hades, King of the Dead. Only vestiges of these are left. More striking are the Doric Great Propylaia whose columns have tumbled but whose pediments have been reassembled. Inscriptions on the threshold are well preserved. The inner and outer gateways each had six Doric columns and were built under Antoninus Pius in the second century AD. The Romans also built the Great Forecourt around the ancient Kallichoron well. Built in the sixth century BC, the well marks the spot where Demeter,

Marathon and the Persian Wars

Ancient Hellas included city states as far afield as southern Italy and Sicily and the Ionian cities on the west coast of Asia Minor. Conquered by an expansionist Persian Empire, these Greek colonies at the end of the sixth century BC called for help in throwing off Persian rule and Athenian support for them led Athens into war with Persia.

In 514 BC King Darius conquered Athenian colonies in northern Greece and sought to expand Persian power into Europe. The expedition overstretched Persia's ability to supply it and failed. In 492, Darius's son in law Mardonius tried again, only to lose his supply fleet in a storm off the peninsula of Mt Athos. In 490, Mardonius launched a full-scale assault on Athens and its ally Eretria, a small city-state on Evia. The Persians besieged and sacked Eretria, then landed at Marathon on the mainland and prepared to march on Athens. They were stopped by an army of 10,000 Athenians — an enormous force by contemporary Greek standards — led by Miltiades. Outnumbered three to one, the Athenian heavy infantry, the hoplites, charged straight at the Persian line and broke it.

Tradition names an Athenian runner called Diomedon as founder of the modern Marathon. Eager to bring news of the victory to Athens, he ran to the city in full armour, gasped out: "We won!" and — not surprisingly — dropped dead. The Greek historian Herodotus claims 6,400 Persian dead for 192 Athenians (not counting Diomedon).

The Persian force defeated at Marathon seemed vast to the Athenians, but was probably little more than a scouting expedition. Its loss did not deter the Great Kings for long. Persia was distracted by conflict with Egypt, a much more important enemy, but ten years later Xerxes' successor Darius turned west again.

In 481 Sparta emerged as the leader of a league of Greek cities against Persia. Understandably, Sparta wished to draw a defensive line across the Isthmus of Corinth and hold the Persians there, but Athens persuaded the League to make a stand further north to defend Attica.

At a mountain pass called Thermopylae ("the hot gates", because of the thermal springs nearby) the Spartan King Leonidas met 200,000 Persians with a scratch force of 7,000. Leonidas chose his ground well: the position favours the defender. The Spartans held out for two days before a traitor led the Persians through a secret path to attack from behind.

The Persians sacked Athens, which had been evacuated, but in the sea-battle of Salamis lost their fleet and many soldiers to the Athenian navy. In the following year (479 BC) Mardonius marched south again to face an allied army of 37,000 Greeks led by the Spartan regent Pausanias. This time it was the Spartans' turn: Mardonius was killed and his army broken. Greek raiders destroyed what remained of the Persian fleet, beached at Mykale in Asia Minor, and the Persian threat ebbed away. Hellas proved too tough a nut to crack.

Sea power, land power and simple geography saved Greece from the Persian threat. Hoplite citizen soldiers fighting for cities in which they had a voice seem to have outperformed the levies of an absolute monarch. The warrior fanaticism of the Spartans provided a superb cadre for the Greek land forces, and the Athenian triremes, the most effective fighting machines of their time, far outmatched the Persians at sea.

The heroism of the Greek cities and of individual soldiers and commanders eclipses the more prosaic reality that the Persians, despite the size of their invasion forces, outstripped their own ability to supply them. Conquering the Hellenes was never at the top of the Persian agenda.

searching for Persephone after her abduction by Hades, was comforted by the daughter of the King of Eleusis – and was the heart of the cult which grew up on the site.

Other Roman relics include the substantial Wall of Kimon, the ruins of a portico and gallery, and the ruins of two triumphal arches whose inscriptions have survived and are in the Archaeological Museum within the site. The museum is well worth visiting for its collection of statues, panels and ceramics which shed light on the Demeter cult and other ancient settlers on the site.

For an overview of the ancient site – and regrettably of the urban sprawl of modern Elevsina – climb the Acropolis hill whose slope begins just west of the excavations. The hilltop is ringed by a medieval fortress-wall and there are traces of a Mycenaean palace.

South of Athens the main attraction is the spectacular temple site of **Cape Sounion** (Sunion), 70 km from Athens. Perched

The Dekemvriana and the Civil War

When Allied troops arrived in Athens in 1944, loyal Greeks hoped for an end to four years of extreme suffering. What they got, thanks largely to Churchill, Stalin and Harry S. Truman, was more of the same.

Not for the first time, Greece became the victim of great-power politics. At Yalta and Potsdam, Churchill and Stalin carved up the Balkans: a free hand in Greece for the West, freedom for Stalin to do what he liked elsewhere. The wishes of the millions of ordinary Greeks who had suffered during the war were ignored: Churchill was set on reimposing an unpopular alien monarchy and clique of politicians who – in the eyes of many – had sat out the war comfortably in exile.

Churchill and the government in exile had purged the Free Greek forces abroad of all but firm Royalists before returning them to Greece. Later, the Allied administration and the new government made no bones about signing up former members of the collaborationist Security Battalions who had fought for the Germans, to help intimidate liberals and leftists.

On December 3 1944, the Athens police shot 28 unarmed demonstrators and the right-wing death squads of the "X" organization killed 100 more in the next few days. Churchill's response to these events is illuminating. "We have to hold and dominate Athens with bloodshed if necessary", he told the commander of the British forces in Greece.

In the street-fighting of the "Dekemvriana", British troops were pitted against the very Greeks who had so recently been hailed as gallant anti-Nazi allies. Thousands of Greeks died in the fighting and parts of the city were still further pounded by aircraft and artillery. With tacit allied approval, right-wingers and former Nazi sympathizers hunted down any opponents of the monarchy and were recruited into the police. Opponents of the regime were deported to the prison islands of Makronisi and Ikaria. This was the curtain-raiser for a further four years of savage civil war in which atrocities were committed on both sides but which – with the aid of an American force of "advisers" who acted much as they later did in Vietnam – the Right won hands down. Stalin kept his half of the bargain and abandoned the Greek Communist Party and the ELAS left-wing army to its fate.

The scars of this brother-against-brother conflict are only now beginning to heal, and one of the real achievements of the PASOK governments in the 1980s was to begin the healing process by amnestying thousands of left-wing exiles who had fled to eastern Europe after the final defeat of the Communists in 1949.

60 metres above the sea, the clifftop Temple of Poseidon is as fine a relic of the great Athenian temple architects as the Parthenon – perhaps even finer, with the Aegean instead of the cement tide of Athens lapping at its feet.

Built in 444 BC – at the same time as the Parthenon – it is one of only a handful of Poseidon temples. A classical Doric temple, it had 13 columns on the longer sides and six on the shorter. Nine of these still stand on the north side and two on the south. The narrow, slim columns rival the Parthenon for elegance and – silhouetted against the sunset – have become as vivid an image of ancient Greece. On one column, you may find the name of Lord Byron, where he carved it in 1807.

Though Sounion is one of the most popular day-trips from Athens, with flocks of coaches arriving daily, these visitors miss seeing the temple at its best at sunset. If you can spare the time, it is worth staying overnight just for this abiding image. Food, drink and accommodation can be found nearby and at the small beach resort of **Legrena** about four km away.

The main route out of Athens to the east runs through the bleak, quarried and hacked landscape of the Penteli range which rings the capital. The Aegean, merging with land and sky in the summer heat haze or vividly blue in spring, offers an escape route from baking Attica to the islands. The jumping-off point on this getaway route is **Rafina** (see page 57). About ten km south of Rafina on the coast road, **Vravrona** is one of the least-visited ancient sites in Attica, but the ruins of its shrine to Artemis deserve more visitors than they get. Your gain, their loss, since this small site with its odd founder is quiet and evocative of the ancients among its calamus reeds and farm terraces.

Ancient Vravrona was said to be one of Attica's twelve oldest cities, founded by the half-serpent, half-human King Kekrops. The earliest finds on the site date from around 1700 BC and the cult of Artemis here goes back to the ninth century BC. The shrine of Artemis was favoured by the Athenians and was at its height during the classical period. Aristophanes describes how girls dressed as bear-cubs danced for the goddess at the spring festival held at Vravrona every five years.

The most striking ruins are those of the dormitory of these bear-girls or arktoi, of which pillars and foundations remain to indicate a large temple precinct of dormitories, halls, courtyards and dining-rooms. A small Archaeological Museum displays minor finds from the site including jewellery, statuettes, sculptures and sacred vessels, but most of the major finds from Vravrona are in the National Archaeological Museum in Athens.

THE ARGO-SARONIC ISLANDS

The Argo-Saronic islands are the perfect escape from the grit and grime of Athens. They have decent swimming, pretty resort villages and good restaurants, and are easy to get to by Flying Dolphin hydrofoil (one hour to 90 minutes each way) from Piraeus. Aegina, Spetsai, Hydra and Poros are popular weekend resorts for Athenians.

See page 166, for more details.

WHERE TO STAY OUT OF TOWN

Dafni   Camping Dafni, Tel: 581 1562, offers a cheap last resort for the truly banjoed, or those who intend to be. Conveniently within staggering distance of the Wine Festival.

Marathon   Hotel Marathon, Platia Marathonas, Timvos, Tel: 55 122. Small C-Class hotel on the beach.

Sounion   Hotel Saron, Leoforos Lavriou, Tel: 39 144. Largish tour hotel which may have rooms available off-peak.

At **Legrena,** 4 km away, the 64-bed **Amphitrite Motel,** Tel: 39 154, is a pricy but comfortable B-Class.

THE
CENTRAL MAINLAND
Between the Sea and
the Mountains

Lapped by the Gulf of Corinth and hemmed in by the Parnassus massif, this region combines bleakly impressive mountain scenery with a calm, sheltered coastline and a rich vein of history which runs back to the mother-lode of the myths. This is the land of Oedipus and the other tragic protagonists of Sophoclean drama, and of a much bigger cast of ancient, modern and medieval characters.

On Greek maps the region is called Sterea Ellas (the Greek

mainland), a name chosen in the early days of independence from Turkey, when it was the new Greek nation's only foothold north of the Gulf.

THE ROAD TO DELPHI

The main road west from Athens passes first through **Thebes** (Thiva), now an undistinguished industrial town with no hint of its ancient power and glory.

Ancient Thebes dominated Boeotia, the country between Attica and Parnassus, and was a fierce rival of Athens, siding with the Persian invaders during the Persian Wars. After Sparta's victory over Athens in the destructive Peloponnesian War, Thebes became an Athenian ally and – after its military genius Epaminondas and its élite force, the Sacred Band, broke Sparta – became for a while the most powerful Hellenic city. In alliance with both Sparta and Athens it was defeated by Philip II of Macedon, father of Alexander, at Chaironia in 338 BC and razed two years later by Alexander. It remained no more than a village for the next two millennia, recovering only after independence.

Livadhia, the region's other major town some 45 km west of Thebes, is more interesting, with steeply-arched Turkish packhorse bridges spanning the river Erkyna and old white houses with precarious wooden balconies along the banks. Under the Turks, it was the region's chief town. Before them, it was the stronghold of a clan of Catalan freelances imported by the Latin Crusaders during the 13th and 14th centuries. Their castle can be seen above the town, perched above the gorge from which the river emerges.

There are two historic battlefields nearby. **Chaironeia** (Heronia) is about ten km north of the town, left of the main road to Lamia. The site is marked by a huge marble lion, part of a monument to the Thebans who fell in the last great battle of the Greek city states against Macedonia. It was smashed apart by the klepht captain Odysseus Androutsos during the War of Independence – he hoped to find ancient treasure – and patched together early this century.

East of the town, and unmarked, is the site of the battle of Kephisos (1311) where the pragmatic Catalan mercenaries defeated the armoured knights of their former employer, the Frankish Duke of Athens, by luring them into a swamp, after which they took over the whole of the Duchy of Athens.

From Livadhia, the main road east to Delphi switchbacks through steep mountain country on the flanks of the Parnassos massif and passes through the small hill-town of **Arahova** which has become a ski resort on a small scale, patronized by Athenian weekenders. The ski season is fairly short, lasting from January until March, but towards the end of the season there is the attraction of being able, on a good day, to ski in the morning and sunbathe on the coast in the afternoon. Several ski shops in Arahova rent skis and boots, and with several good hotels and guesthouses and plenty of restaurants the town is also a good base for those planning to visit Delphi, only 22 km away; its hotels and restaurants are less likely to be crammed with coach parties.

DELPHI

In its still-magical setting in a giant, natural hillside amphitheatre, Delphi is the biggest tourism magnet in these parts and in summer the ancient site resembles an anthill as dozens of escorted coach parties are disgorged to trek briskly through the columns, straining to hear the shrill patter of their guide above the conflicting strains of French, English, German, Greek, Italian, Japanese and Spanish commentaries. If visiting Delphi is high on your list of Greek priorities – and it should be – you should consider a spring or autumn visit. On a warm day in March you can spend much of the day almost alone, and Delphi's serene impact is not lessened by the distractions of your fellow visitors.

Oedipus and Thebes

"There once was a man called Oedipus Rex
(you may have heard about his weird complex)
He got his name into Freud's index
'cause he loved his mother.
Yes, he loved his mother like no other,
his daughter was his sister and his son was his brother...."

The most famous of all the murder-and-incest tragedies of ancient Greek drama is the tale of King Oedipus of Thebes, the son of Jocasta, Queen of Thebes, and her husband King

THE ANCIENT SITES

The main site contains the Temple of Apollo, the treasuries of the Hellenic cities, and the Rock of the Sibyl, site of the original oracle.

The site is about 400 m behind and above the modern town, which is concealed from sight behind a fold of the hill. The plain below, stretching to the coast, is the famous "sea of olives" – mile after mile of dusty-green trees marching off toward the Gulf of Corinth. The view is hardly marred by intrusive modern elements except for the unsightly towers of the bauxite plant at Itea, about ten km south on the coast.

The site of the Oracle of Delphi and its attendant temples and palaces is the greatest triumph of the singular Hellenic gift of location. If it is possible for a landscape to act as a mood amplifier, then that is what Delphi does. If the state of serenity it induces could be synthesized, Valium would go out of fashion overnight. The grounds of the Oracle are cluttered with temples and treasuries donated by the Hellenic cities which competed for the favour of the gods and more practically for control of one of their world's greatest centres of religious power, prestige and propaganda.

Entering the site and climbing the Sacred Way which traverses it, the first of these to catch the eye is the Spartan Monument (to the right of the path). Built around 404 BC, it was a thanksgiving gift to the gods for the city's victory in the

Laius. The Delphic oracle foretold that he would one day kill his father and marry his mother. The parents nailed the baby's ankles together and ordered a shepherd to abandon it in the mountains.

But instead of killing the child the shepherd gave it to another shepherd from Corinth. He in turn brought Oedipus to the childless king and queen of Corinth who raised him as their son, naming him Oedipus — "Swollen-foot". When Oedipus was a young man he heard of the oracle's prediction and — to avoid fulfilling it — left Corinth, swearing never to see his supposed parents again.

But on the road Oedipus met his true father and — not knowing that he was Laius's son — killed him in a quarrel over who should give way. Arriving in Thebes, he found the city terrorized by the part-beast, part-woman monster, the Sphinx. In the interests of fairness (and dramatic necessity) the Sphinx posed all who met it a riddle, lunching on those who failed to answer it. The riddle: what goes on four legs in the morning, two legs at noon and three legs in the evening? Oedipus's answer: man, who crawls in the morning of life, walks upright in his prime and with the aid of a stick in his twilight years. The Sphinx was so infuriated by his cleverness that she hurled herself off a cliff, and the Thebans made him their king, marrying him to Jocasta, who bore him sons and daughters who were, of course, also his brothers and sisters: the prophecy was fulfilled, but Oedipus did not find out until 15 years afterwards, when plague and famine struck Thebes. Tiresias, the blind seer, divined that this was a punishment for harbouring a man guilty of his father's blood. Oedipus pronounced a curse on the perpetrator, whoever he might be: but his investigations revealed the awful truth and in horror and guilt Jocasta hanged herself and Oedipus destroyed his own sight with her golden cloak-pin and was condemned to wander, friendless and homeless, for the rest of his life.

Not a pretty story. Sophocles gives it a happier ending, with Oedipus called by Zeus to a death "without a pang, without grief or agony — a passing more wonderful than any other man", but in the original version Oedipus was finally hounded to death by the vengeful Harpies at Colonus in Attica.

Skiing in Greece

Skiing has become popular in Greece only recently, and the country's small resorts are cheerful and unsophisticated, catering almost entirely to Greeks. Few will want to go to Greece just to ski — snow is unreliable and the runs aren't up to Northern European standards — but since the ski season lasts from January until late April and the slopes are within easy reach of Athens, it's quite possible to combine a couple of days' skiing with a spring beach holiday or a winter sightseeing tour.

The best and most popular slopes are at Mt Parnassus, behind Delphi, about three and a half hours by bus from Athens; there are tows, and skis can be rented at the ski station which is run by the National Tourist Organization of Greece or at the nearby village of Arahova, a pleasant place to stay at any time of year. Parnassus Ski Centre (0234) 22493/ 22689/ 22694.

Another accessible ski centre is at Hania on Mt Pilion, about half an hour by bus from Volos and close to the delightful traditional villages of Makrinitsa and Portaria, which have year-round accommodation. Information on skiing and snow conditions at the NTOG Information Centre; Plateia Riga Fereou, Volos, (0421) 23500/ 24915.

Peloponnesian Wars. Next to it is the Monument of the Kings of Argos, semi-circular and dating from 365 BC.

Like other Greek sacred buildings, these and others on the site were crammed with statues in marble, gold, ivory and painted wood and may have been garishly painted. Contemporary writers say the Spartan Monument held 37 statues and its neighbour 20. Others were certainly equally crowded, as the cities which endowed them competed for status.

On the left as you climb further, one after another, are the Treasuries of Sifnos, the Boeotains, and Thebes. None of these are particularly striking, but immediately above, left of the Sacred Way where it turns sharply to the right, is one of Greece's most meticulously restored ancient buildings, the **Treasury of Athens**. Like the Spartan Monument, it commemorates a great victory, this time over the Persians at Marathon, and was built in 490 BC. The treasury is almost complete (it was rebuilt in 1906) though the metopes crowning its Doric columns are copies. The originals are in the Delphi Archaeological Museum.

The Sacred Way now passes the rectangular foundation of the Bouleuterion, Delphi's administration building, on the left. Above it on the right side of the sacred way a disappointingly nondescript hummock of rock is the site of the original Oracle of Gaea and beyond that, on the, left, is the Stoa of the Athenians. On the right, the Treasury of Corinth was the last major building on the Sacred Way, which culminates in the Crossroads of the Tripods and the pillars of the great Temple of Apollo. Imagine this crossroads gleaming with Delphi's most precious objects. These included huge gold and silver bowls resting on tripods of precious metals. As Hellas declined, they inevitably attracted looters such as the Phocians, who melted some down while they controlled Delphi around 350 BC. Many more were removed to Constaninople in the fourth century AD to decorate the Emperor's new capital.

The **Temple of Apollo** began as a simple hut thatched with laurel leaves but according to Homer had by his time become a building of bronze (probably on a wooden frame). A stone temple, built in the seventh century BC, was destroyed by fire and rebuilt by a consortium of Hellenic rulers and noble families. This in turn was destroyed by earthquake in the fourth century BC and rebuilt with contributions from all over the Greek world. Completed in 330 BC, it is 60m by 24m with 15 Doric columns on its longer sides and six on the shorter ends.

The fourth century BC **Theatre**, above the Temple of Apollo, seated 5,000 people. Its 35 rows of benches are well preserved, as are those of the Stadium, also dating from the fourth century BC. It seated 7,000 spectators. Behind the banks of seats loom the cliffs of Mt Kirfi in a great arc; an athlete or actor might easily feel that his audience included the gods themselves as well as mere mortals, a setting calculated to inspire a virtuoso performance. Almost 650 metres above sea level, the higher banks of seats offer the finest view of Delphi and its surroundings. The ruined fortifications behind the stadium were built by the Phocian occupiers of

Delphi in the mid-fourth century BC to complete its natural defences.

Below the sanctuary site, the Kastalian Spring is little more than a trickle of clear water in a narrow cleft in the cliffs. Questioners of the oracle cleansed themselves in its pools before going to the Temple. It is often unpleasantly littered, as it is not part of the fenced-in site. On the opposite side of the main road to Arahova, two Doric temples to Athena, the remnants of two more treasuries, and an elegant tholos or rotunda make up the secondary site of the Marmaria. The Old Temple of Athena, built in the fifth century BC, was replaced in 373 BC by the New Temple after being damaged by several earthquakes. The fourth century tholos displays Doric at its best, though only three of its 20 columns now stand.

THE MUSEUM

Do not leave Delphi without visiting the Museum, which is between the Sanctuary site and the coach park. Its most famous exhibit is the bronze Charioteer of Delphi, which is given pride of place in its own hall. Its oldest is the Omphalos or "navel of the Earth", the conical stone which stood in Apollo's temple and was the soul of Delphi. It is a slightly spooky feeling contemplating the Omphalos, so unimpressive visually yet once the centre of a complete belief system.

More immediately striking are the ivory and gold head of Artemis and a life-size silver bull, the sacred animal of Zeus, from the sixth century BC. Also well worth seeing are the metopes of the Athenian treasury, the friezes of the Siphnian treasury, and the Sphinx of Naxos which sat on a pedestal close to the Temple of Apollo.

MODERN DELPHI

Modern Delphi is a strip of hotels, restaurants and souvenir shops either side of the main east–west road and exists solely to service the ancient site. From its hillside it has fine views over the olive plantations which stretch down to the Gulf of Corinth. Other than that, it can be recommended only as a place to spend the night.

NEAR DELPHI

If you are looking for somewhere a little more interesting to stay while visiting ancient Delphi, try nearby **Amfisa**, an attractive old-fashioned town about ten km away, which as well as a sprinkling of inexpensive hotels and restaurants has a small medieval castle overlooking the town from a pine-clad hilltop. Below it, there is an unmodernized older quarter of tall houses with shutters and balconies around and above a café-lined central square (about 300m from the modern square by the bus station).

The north shore of the Gulf of Corinth, despite its magnificent mountainous backdrop, is less than gripping. Mostly rocky, it has few good beaches but a scattering of small towns make pleasant enough stopping-off places if you hunger for the sight of the sea.

Open to Interpretation
The Oracle at Delphi

If the ancient dramatists are to be trusted, the Delphic oracle's stubborn refusal to give a straightforward answer to a simple question caused many of its supplicants an inordinate amount of strife. Look at the whole messy Oedipus business, for example.

Gaea, the Earth Mother, was worshipped at Delphi from the 14th century BC through priestesses who were inspired by intoxicating fumes rising from the earth. As the Dorians moved into Greece, bringing their male-oriented pantheon with them, Gaea was dethroned — in legend and in fact — by Apollo and his followers and the site became his greatest sanctuary. The weathered, unadorned conical stone called the Omphalos, now in the Delphi Museum, was the exact centre of the ancient world, located by Zeus who released an eagle from each end of the earth; they met at Delphi.

The oracle was one of the keys to the twisting diplomacies of the Greek cities, whose rulers consulted on all great affairs of state. That its *Pythia*, or high priestess, spoke in riddles was only partly because she was stoned out of her mind on laurel fumes; it was also to the advantage of Delphi and its priesthood to to maintain a monopoly on revealing her meaning. Occasionally, that meaning could be explicit, as when the Oracle called repeatedly for the overthrow of the Athenian tyrant Pisistratos. Among his strongest opponents was the powerful family of Alkmeonidis, who contributed huge sums to rebuild the Temple of Apollo and win the Oracle's favour. Occasionally, the predictions were right on the money: in 336 BC the Pythia foresaw the assassination of Philip II of Macedon. It is tempting to believe that the priests of Delphi occasionally took an active hand in making some prophesies come true.

With the decline of the city-state system under Philip and Alexander, then under the Romans, the Oracle's prestige waned. It was plundered by several Roman emperors, including Nero, and by the second century AD it was more of a tourist attraction than a sacred place. The Christianizing Emperor Theodosius ordered the temple to be demolished at the end of the fourth century AD and in the fifth century AD a Christian church was built on the site.

Itea, the small town on the coast which you can see from Delphi, is an unremarkable modern town and commercial port dominated by a large bauxite works and sited on a wide bay. Eastward, the coastline is barren and bleak and the sea largely inaccessible, and the handful of villages and hamlets on the coast do not offer much reward for the considerable difficulty of getting to them.

Much more attractive is **Galaxidhi,** 14 km from Itea on the west side of the same natural harbour. Another town that time has forgotten, Galaxidhi was a prosperous port in the 19th century. Its commerce seems to have been eroded by the coming of road haulage or siphoned off by Itea. Galaxidhi's tall old shuttered houses, built by sea-captains at a time when all cargoes went by sea and schooner owners were the wealthiest people in Greece, are a reminder of its former prosperity.

It is now sleepy and little-visited despite being the pleasantest place to stop off along the north shore of the Gulf. There are no beaches, but a handful of sandy-pebbly inlets on the rugged coast of the headland which shelters it from the open Gulf offer secluded swimming. Around Galaxidhi and to the west, along the main coast road, the landscape is barren and unforgiving and the coast, plunging steeply into the sea, is featureless until you reach the minimal settlement at Ag. Nikolaos, where a thrice daily ferry service runs to Egio on the south shore, a useful connection if you are planning a return to Athens taking in Corinth and Mycenae. Ag. Nikolaos consists of little more than the ferry pier. There is no accommodation.

The next stop along the north shore is **Nafpaktos.** Like Amfisa, it was a stronghold of the Catalan mercenaries of the Grand Company and after them of the Venetians. A derelict medieval fortress squats on the hill above the cheerful little port, which is a mixture of modern blockhouse-style architecture, older 19th-century townhouses, and crumbling medieval walls enclosing the castle, the tiny old harbour and an adequate town beach. Pink explosions of oleander flowers in gullies and gardens give Nafpaktos a pleasantly tropical air.

Ten kilometres west of Nafpaktos, the Gulf of Corinth

The Battle of Leparto

Off Nafpaktos, then called Lepanto, a Christian fleet in 1571 met a huge Turkish navy in a great sea-battle. Led by Don John of Austria, a bastard of the Holy Roman Emperor Charles V, the 200 Venetian, Papal and Spanish galleys were crewed by a rag-tag of volunteers, mercenaries and pirates from all over Europe. Sir Thomas Stukely — another royal bastard whose father was said to be Henry VII — commanded three English ships, the legendary Genoese privateer Andrea Doria led a large contingent of French and Italian soldiers of fortune, and Miguel de Cervantes — later to write *Don Quixote* — fought aboard a Spanish galley. The great Turkish admiral Ali commanded 300 Turkish vessels crammed with Janissaries, the fanatical converts from Christianity who were the feared shock-troops of Islam. Victory would leave the way open for the Ottomans to sweep through the Adriatic and ravage Italy itself.

Turkish naval tactics in the 16th century would have been instantly recognizable to a Greek admiral of the Persian wars: ram and board. The Christian ace in the hole was the galleas, a huge gun-platform mounting 40 big guns and bristling with musketeers. Don John had six of these floating fortresses. As their first salvoes tore into the crescent line of the Turkish fleet, the wind changed to favour the allies. The outgunned and outmanouevred Ali fell to a musket-ball, and the Turks lost 25,000 men and 180 ships.

---

narrows to a bottleneck between **Rio** on the south shore and **Andirio** on the north. A ferry service runs between the two; Andirio is otherwise uninteresting.

TRAVELLING

By Road   Frequent buses from Athens to Thiva and Livadhia and onward into Thessaly and northern Greece via Lamia. Frequent buses also go direct to Delphi and west to Missolongi. You can connect at Amfisa with bus services to Lamia and points north.

By Sea   Three ferries daily between Ag. Nikolas and Egio. Shuttle ferries four times an hour (half-hourly from 23.00 until dawn) between Rio and Antirio. Buses to Hafpaktos connect with most Antirio ferries. Bus connections at Ag. Nikolaos are poor.

WHERE TO STAY

Amfisa Hotel Apollon, Gidogiannou 12. Cheap.

Andirio Pension Antirrio (B-Class) is friendly, cheap and convenient if you have to wait overnight for a ferry.

Arahova Pension Maria (B-Class) is not cheap but is the best value for money. **Hotel Apollon** and **Hotel Parnassos** (C-Class) are cheap small hotels, both owned by the same family. The slightly bigger **Hotel Astero** is more expensive. All are open year round. Rates are about 30 per cent lower May to October.

Delphi Pension Odysseus, Filelinon 1, has the cheapest rooms in town. Cheapest hotel accommodation in town is in the E-Class **Hotel Dolphin** and the D-Class **Hotel Fivos** and **Hotel Aspassia**. All are modern and functional, as is the **Hotel Athena,** in a similar price bracket. All are on Delphi's main street, Vassileos Pavlou.

Galaxidhi Pension Galaxa, comfortable, mid-priced. **Pension Ta Adelfia,** slightly cheaper. **Pension Ganymede,** comfortable with a tropical garden, quite expensive.

Nafpaktos Cheap but a bit scruffy, **Hotel Diethnes** (D-Class) on Odos Messolongiou. A little more expensive but still cheap, **Hotel Aegli,** 75 Ilarhou Tzavela. Big, comfortable and affordable, the **Hotel Akti** (C-Class) on Gribovo beach.

FOOD AND DRINK

Eating and drinking in this part of Greece is unremarkable at best; restaurants are geared mainly to snacking-up coachloads of day visitors.

Thiva (modern Thebes) and **Livadhia** at least have plenty of gyros and souvlaki places to leaven the growing mass of burger and pizza bars. **Delphi** is a disappointment: several restaurants including **Maniati** and **Vakhos** have wonderful views but indifferent food. In **Nafpaktos** the best food is to be found in the three small restaurants by the medieval harbour; good fish to match a pleasant location.

THE PELOPONNESE
A Patchwork of History

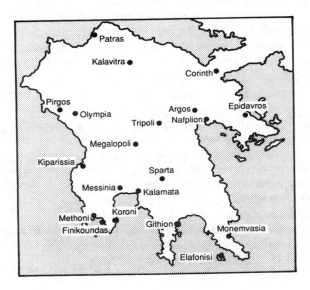

Separated from the northern mainland by the Gulf of Corinth, the Peloponnese is a three-fingered hand pointing south towards Africa. The peninsula is cluttered with history and its hilltops are crowned with fortresses built over more than three millennia, from the massive walls of Mycenae to the airy Byzantine palaces of Mistra, the Frankish castles of Arcadia and the looming Venetian fortresses of Methoni and Coroni.

THE NORTH-WEST

The strip of coast along the south shore of the Gulf of Corinth holds little of interest, and the beaches are at best unexciting.

Patras is Greece's third biggest town, but for the visitor it is simply an entry point and centre for boats, buses and trains onward into the Peloponnese and mainland Greece rather than a destination in itself. It's an uninspiring modern place and only those arriving late in the evening or with onward travel planned for the following day will want to stay overnight.

Egio, a staid clifftop town above the gulf, is notable mainly as a ferry crossing. A pleasant enough little farming and commercial town, its biggest historic landmark is a giant plane tree close to the ferry pier which is claimed to have sheltered the ancient historian and geographer Pausanias.

At **Diakofto**, about an hour by bus or train from Patras, an attractive narrow-gauge railway runs through a steep and spectacular mountain pass to the village of **Kalavrita**. The trip is worth doing for the scenery alone, but Kalavrita also holds a special importance for Greeks on two counts. It was here that Archbishop Germanos raised the flag of revolution in 1821, signalling the start of the final War of Independence which led to the creation of modern Greece; here also, during World War Two, German troops massacred the entire male population of the village: a monument commemorates them.

Between Diakofto and Kalavrita, you can get off the train at **Zachlorou**, from which it's a stiff but beautiful one hour walk to the important monastery of **Mega Spileon**.

TRAVELLING

By Sea   Frequent international ferries to Ancona and Brindisi, frequent ferries to Corfu and the Ionian Islands. Shuttle ferries between Andirio, on the north shore of the Gulf of Corinth, and Rio, 11 km east of Patras. Ferry three times a day in summer between Egio, half an hour's drive from Patras, and Ag. Nikolaos, a tiny port on the north shore. The ferry takes about an hour, but bus connections onward to Delphi are poor, and if you don't have your own transport the Andirio/Rio crossing is the best choice.

By Road   A fast "National Road" dual carriageway and a rail line run along the south shore of the Gulf of Corinth. Frequent buses connect Patras with Corinth and Athens and with the main towns of the Peloponnese.

By Rail   Trains to Corinth and Athens on the line along the south coast of the gulf and to Kalamata and points on the west coast of the Peloponnese.

Mega Spileon

Perched half-hidden in the cliffside midway between Diakofto on the Peloponnesian coast and the mountain village of Kalavrita, the monastery of Mega Spileon — "the big cave" — is one of Greece's more important places of worship. Founded in the eighth century by two Orthodox fathers, the monastery itself, set in these forbidding crags, is rather disappointingly modern on the outside, having been extensively rebuilt this century after a disastrous fire. Inside this drab façade it's a different story. In the monastery's most holy chapel, the icon of the Panagia, miraculously revealed to the fathers Simeon and Theodoros by a shepherd girl, is an oddly amorphous work in dark wax, clearly of a different workmanship from the familiar gilt and crimson icons of most Greek churches. Hung all around its elaborate gold setting are pieces of gold jewellery — watches, chains and rings being the most favoured — left as offerings by the faithful. Under layers of soot left on the domed ceiling by hundreds of years of continuously-burning candles, you can just make out that the dome was once bright with holy frescoes. It's all rather at odds with the sacred cave itself, where a strange diorama of life-sized two-dimensional figures portrays Christ crucified and the two monks putting to flight the dragon which guarded the sacred icon. There's also a museum of grisly relics — the hands, finger-bones and skulls of saints and holy men set in elaborate gold and silver reliquaries.

Also on display are items from all over the Greek world — a cross made in Smyrna (modern Izmir) in 1600 entirely out of gold filigree, a labour of love which cost its maker 11 years and his sight, splendid icons and a wonderful collection of elaborately worked holy vestments from the 18th and 19th centuries.

There is a small entrance fee and — as at all Greek holy places — you won't be admitted in shorts, T-shirts or other "immodest" clothing.

WHERE TO STAY

If you have to stay in **Patras** there are plenty of acceptable hotels right across the price range. Most expensive are the A-Class **Astir** (Tel: 277502) and **Moreas** (425494). Cheaper are the C-Class **Acropole** (279809), **Delfini** (421001/5), **Adonis** (224213), and **El Greco** (272931). There are also a number of cheaper hotels, most of them around the port, catering to people arriving or leaving.

If you're on the way to or from Delphi you may like to stay at **Rio**, where there are a number of hotels and rooms to rent.

At **Egio**, accommodation is in short supply but for the expensive B-Class **Hotel Galini**, whose huge blue neon sign dominates the town centre.

FOOD AND DRINK

There are plenty of places to eat and drink in **Patras**, most of them on or around the main plateia, but none are distinguished. In **Egio** there are a few basic restaurants by the ferry pier.

THE WEST COAST

West and south of Patras, the Peloponnese has some of Greece's finest beaches, hardly known to British tourists and (apart from a string of well-appointed campsites catering mainly to German summer visitors) surprisingly untouched by mass tourism. Anywhere else in the Mediterranean, these sweeping miles of fine sand would be lined with mid-market hotels.

Here there are only a handful at resorts close to Patras and none south of **Killini** which has an excellent sand beach and is a main summer resort for Greek visitors. with A-, B- and C-Class hotels, a campsite run by the NTOG and a choice of village rooms and self-catering apartments. South of Killini, the castle of **Chlemoutsi** is a relic of the 13th-century Frankish kingdom of the Morea.

Pirgos, 97 km from Patras, is a small farming town of no great interest except as a point to change buses en route to **Olympia**, which ranks with Delphi and the Acropolis as one of the great archaeological sites of classical Greece.

OLYMPIA

The sole purpose of the **modern town** of Olympia, which is about 15 minutes' walk west of the ancient site on the main road, is to service visitors to the site. That said, it's a pleasant enough place for a couple of nights' stay, with plenty of places to stay and to eat at a variety of prices, and good road connections with the rest of the Peloponnese.

Ancient Olympia is the only classical site which truly rivals Delphi in its effect on the visitor. Like Delphi, the site of the ancient Olympic Games was a neutral zone amid the twisting politics and power games of the Greek city-states. But the site exudes a different atmosphere from the calm of sacred Delphi. The games were, after all, games: while they had a sacred role too, this site during the four-yearly event must have been a colourful, noisy bustle of hucksters, hookers and gamblers vying for the attention of crowds of spectators from all over the ancient world.

At first sight, the ruins of Olympia don't make as much sense to the eye as those of Delphi. Where Delphi's hillside siting gives the visitor an eagle's view of its layout, Olympia was — for obvious reasons — built on the flat. And while some at least of Delphi's columns and walls have been pieced together, at Olympia the huge marble column-drums lie scattered and it takes an effort of imagination to see the great temples as they must have once been.

It takes very little imagination, though, to people the grassy slopes of the Olympian stadium with cheering crowds: this, you feel, is what Olympia was really all about — the Wembley of ancient Greece. The other main buildings of the site are the fifth-century BC **Temple of Zeus**; the **Heraion** (temple of Hera, wife of Zeus); the twelve **treasuries** built by the city-states to house their sacred offerings; the **Leonidion**, built to house the rulers and VIP delegations of the cities during the games; and the **Prytaneion**, from which the magistrates administered the event. The workshop of Phidias, the most famous sculptor of classical times, can be seen within the much later walls of a small Byzantine church built on the same site.

Fortunately there's an excellent **Museum** at the site, and a visit either before or after touring Olympia is a must if

The Fourth Crusade and the Latin Kingdoms

In 1199 a Venetian fleet was hired to transport an army of Frankish crusaders to aid the Latin kingdoms of the Holy Land. Things went horribly wrong when the cynical Venetians, who had not been paid for their services, egged on the Crusaders to attack "heretical" Constantinople instead. The Franks, who were in it for the loot rather than from any deep religious conviction, were eager. Eastern Christendom's greatest city had been amassing treasures for more than a thousand years. It was a rich prize for the looters, who carried off its wealth after burning much of the city.

For the Venetians, the exercise killed two birds with one stone: they took a percentage of the booty for the hire of their fleet and as a bonus seized the whole of the Aegean for their own. The Venetians got the better part of the bargain by far, and their Duchy of the Archipelago, with its capital in Naxos, was the longest lasting of the microstates the Latins chipped off the rock of Byzantium — it stayed in their hands until 1566, and the Roman Catholic faith of some Cycladic islanders is its last relic.

The Frankish barons, however, being bone-headed soldier types rather than sly Venetian traders with an eye to the main chance, settled for lands on the mainland. Few lasted more than a century. Boniface of Montferrat's kingdom of Salonica (Thessaloniki) was one of the real no-hopers, lasting from 1204–23. Othon de la Roche, a Burgundian, set up the Frankish Duchy of Athens in 1205 but his successors were turfed out by the hard-nosed mercenaries of the Catalan Company around 1300.

The Catalans in turn faded from view and Athens became a Florentine fief until the Turkish conquest. Geoffrey de Villehardouin carved off the Peloponnese, named himself Prince of Achaea (Akhaia) and doled out bits of it to twelve barons whose keeps and castles are still dotted about over hilltops, harbours and mountain passes. The Villehardouins did better than some, but in 1266 the Byzantine Emperor Michael Palaeologos drove the Latin Emperor from Constantinople and in 1271 defeated the Latin princes in battle once and for all.

The Villehardouins lost their key fortresses and their kingdom faded away: apart from their castles, the Latin dukes and prices left little mark on Greek history, but the whole unfortunate episode terribly weakened Byzantium, which was already under pressure from the Turks on its eastern border. Constantinople regained some (not all) of its territory, but never recovered its former glory.

you want to make sense of the cluttered ruins. The scale model of the site in the entrance hall of the museum is particularly helpful in this. The museum's collection includes a statue of Hermes and the infant Dionysos, which is one of the surviving masterpieces of classical Greek art, as well as artworks and artefacts from the whole span of Olympia's history from classical to Roman times, and it helps you to construct an idea of how Olympia must once have looked and how too it changed with the changing fortunes of Greece.

One of the most powerfully moving exhibits is the dented and battered Corinthian helmet worn by the Athenian hero Miltiades at the battle of Marathon and dedicated by him to Zeus. The archaeologists of the German Institute who conducted the dig at Olympia found it buried along with many other pieces of armour and other offerings buried in the seating-banks of the stadium. There's a real sense of connection with ancient Greece in looking at it and knowing who wore it, and when: it makes Miltiades for a moment a real person and ancient Olympia a real place.

Olympia is better looked after than some ancient sites, and an attempt has been made to replant some of its avenues with flowering trees like those believed to have grown there in its heyday. As with Delphi and other major ruins, the best time to visit is in the winter/spring low season or – if you are there in high summer – either first thing in the morning or in late afternoon, missing the tidal waves of coach visitors. The site opens at 08.30 year round.

TRAVELLING

By Train From Athens via Patras, a slow but scenic ride via Pirgos through attractive countryside, climbing slowly from the coastal plain into the hills with the mountain backdrop of Erimanthos always in sight.

By Road Fast and frequent buses to Patras, Athens, nearby Pirgos and Tripoli via Langadia. From Pirgos there are bus connections on south to Kiparissi and the beaches of the western Peloponnese and to Pilos and Kalamata. From Tripoli there are buses onward to all points of the Peloponnese.

WHERE TO STAY
There's no shortage of accommodation in Olympia, from the rather rule-obsessed **youth hostel** on the main street, Odhos Kondhili, (cheap dormitory beds, doors closed at 23.00, showers extra) to the more luxurious A-, B- and C-Class **hotels**, also on the main street. Book in advance for the better hotels, especially in high season – they're often packed with tour groups. Among the best-value cheaper hotels, of which there are plenty, is the D-Class **Heraeum**, just a few doors up Odhos Kondhili from the youth hostel.

FOOD AND DRINK
Eating and drinking present few problems in Olympia. You won't find any outstandingly good restaurants, and prices are predictably a bit higher than at most of the beach resorts, but there are plenty of places to eat, including a sprinkling of mediocre fast-food joints on Odos Kondhili.

AROUND OLYMPIA

Only 20 km from Olympia are the beaches of the western Peloponnese, with numerous campsites and rooms to rent in a string of villages. The nearest to Olympia are **Samiko, Kaiafas** and **Zaharo,** all of which are close to the sea but of no other real interest. Inland, the pretty little hill village of **Langadia** is an alternative place to stay while visiting Olympia. Built on a steep valley-side, it has sweeping views down to the plains, a handful of tavernas and one C-Class hotel, the Langadia (tel: 43202).

THE EASTERN PELOPONNESE

CORINTH

Gateway to the Peloponnese from Athens, Corinth is a low-key little town which has been repeatedly levelled by earthquakes, most recently in 1981. Its most noted landmark is man-made, the vertiginous cleft of the **Corinth Canal,** built in the 19th century to link the Gulf of Corinth with the Aegean. You can gaze into it from the road or rail bridges you will cross coming into Corinth on the main route from Athens.

Corinth's main glories are the site of ancient Corinth and the medieval fortress of Acrocorinth on the hilltop above it. Most of the site of **ancient Corinth** is Roman, not Greek, except for the seven columns of the 550 BC Temple of Apollo, a heavy Doric structure which lacks the grace of its Athenian contemporaries. It is easier to imagine the ancient city as it was under the Romans, who built its first century AD Agora, theatre and Odeon: a bustling, secular, commercial centre of a Roman province rather than a great Greek power.

But Corinth was more than this. It was the heart of the cult of Aphrodite – Venus to the Romans – whose temple on the crag now occupied by the fortress of Acrocorinth was staffed by hundreds of temple prostitutes. The most striking remains of the city are the huge marketplace, the seven columns of the Temple of Apollo, and the Roman Fountain of Peirene.

Above the site of the Greek-Roman city – and by contrast sparsely visited – the medieval fortress walls of Acrocorinth surround a 575 m crag. Byzantine, Frankish, Venetian and Turkish builders contributed to its massive complex of fortifications, but none succeeded in making it impregnable. Like all such sites, it is both forbidding and a little ghostly even on a bright spring day. There are heartlifting views, though, in all directions from its highest point. Range after range of blue mountains march off south-west into the heart of the Peloponnese, the chipping of stonechats in the ruined walls is the only thing which breaks the absolute quiet, and eagles spiral overhead. The steep walk from ancient Corinth is forgotten, though on the way up you pity the unfortunate Sisyphos who was condemned in legend to roll his rock to the top of this peak forever.

TRAVELLING

By Road Frequent buses from Athens, Patras, Tripoli and Sparta, and Nafplion. Buses run every half hour from the centre of Corinth to ancient Corinth (Arkio Korinthos).

By Rail Trains to Athens and Patras.

WHERE TO STAY

Hotel Belle Vue, B-Class on the waterfront, mid-priced and pleasant. For cheaper accommodation, try the C-Class **Acropolis**. At Arkio Korinth, there is a good but expensive A-Class **Pension Xenia**.

Olympia and the Games

Olympia seems to have been a sacred site as early as the turn of the first millennium BC, but by classical times Zeus had become the dominant deity. The myths say that Hercules himself planted the trees around the site which marked his father's domain, and the games were initiated as an offering to the chief of the immortals.

The first games of which records remain were held in 776 BC but there is evidence that contests were held at least two centuries earlier. It wasn't until the first quarter of the sixth century BC that they became a pan-Hellenic event, held every four years and attracting competitors from the whole wide Greek-speaking world. They lasted for four months, from June to September, with five days of games each month around the time of the full moon, and the contests were at first mainly athletic. The main event was the Pentathlon, which included discus, javelin, jumping, running and wrestling events. Wrestling — the Pancratium — more closely resembled no-holds-barred prizefighting than the Saturday-night sport we see on TV: contestants frequently suffered grievous bodily harm and sometimes died of their injuries.

A truce was declared and by and large honoured among the rival Greek cities for the duration of the games, which thus came to take on a broader political and economic importance than that of a simple athletic contest. It persisted throughout the classical era, hardly ever broken even during the thirty savage years of the Peloponnesian Wars.

With the decline of the city-state system and the advent of Roman rule, the games declined in importance, becoming once again a simple sporting spectacular.

Commercialization and trickery crept in; new events were introduced, and the games reached their lowest ebb when the loony Roman emperor Nero not only introduced several special new events but also rigged them to be declared victor. Nevertheless, they continued in one form or another until the end of the fourth century AD, when the Christian emperor Theodosius I banned them as a vestige of pagan tradition. Thirty years later his successor Theodosius II had the temples pulled down, and over the next 200 years earthquakes and floods finished the job, tumbling the ancient walls and burying them under the sands of the river Alfios. German archaeologists began the work of rediscovery in 1875.

FOOD AND DRINK
Fast food souvlaki and gyros are available from several good little places at the bus station; you'll find more substantial meals in restaurants along the waterfront. There's a handful of basic cafés at **Arkio Korinth** and one pleasant restaurant-bar at the end of the steep tarred road to **Acrocorinth**: worth it for the view alone.

MYCENAE

Between Corinth and the pretty seaport of Nafplion on the Argolic Gulf lie Mycenae (Mikines) and the other cities of mainland Greece's first civilization.

Modern Mikines is a cluster of guesthouses and restaurants servicing the ancient site and is about three kilometres from the main Corinth-Argos road and railway.

From his kingly seat in the palace which crowns the hill of ancient Mycenae, Agamemnon and his forebears were rulers of all they surveyed – a mighty kingdom of fertile plains stretching all of 15 miles in any direction, ringed by mountains. More than this, they controlled an empire of neighbouring mini-states in the Argolid of which Argos and Tiryns were the most important and were the main force in the Peloponnese. Further afield, their influence touched that of the Minoan empire and they were known to peoples as remote as the Hittites of Asia Minor.

Mycenae, on a low hill commanding a pass between higher peaks, may have been as much a ceremonial site as a defensive one. Despite its massive walls, it is overlooked by higher slopes, not an ideal location for military purposes, but by the time of Mycenae's golden age the need for a functional fortress may have lapsed. Greece was far less populous than in classical times and the Mycenaean microstates had little need to jostle for living-space. Indeed, from the site of the Royal Palace at Mycenae one is reminded that beyond the surrounding mountains much of the mainland may have been uninhabited, unexplored and covered in virgin forest. No wonder the Mycenaeans and later Greeks peopled the wilds with centaurs, satyrs, and all the other half-human creatures of their mythology. It is even conceivable that small groups of pre-Mycenaean European aborigines, semi-nomadic hunter-gatherers using stone tools and weapons, survived in the wilds and were the originals for such stories.

The site of **historic Mycenae** is about half an hour's walk from the modern village and concealed from sight by a fold in the hillside. Ancient Mycenae is one of those places where one is very conscious of the weight of centuries. Like some other Greek sites, it has the power to make legend suddenly real. In its great reception hall, Agamemnon called his allies to the war against Troy, and standing where the halls of the Royal Palace once stood it is easy to believe in the flesh and blood reality of Homer's royal heroes.

Entering the site the visitor is at first struck by its massive construction. Mycenae's walls are built of huge blocks and slabs which led later Greeks to believe they were the work of a race of giants. The way in is by the Lion Gate, whose gigantic pillars support a slab on which are carved two great lions, probably the arms of the kings of Mycenae.

Immediately inside the walls, grave circle A marks Schliemann's discovery of the royal cemetery. The gold "mask of Agamemnon" found here, together with the rest of the richest archaeological find discovered in Greece, are in the National Archaeological Museum in Athens.

On the crown of the hill, flagstoned floors and surviving low walls mark out the ground plan of the Royal Palace which like all the Myceaean palace buildings was built around a Great Court. The rectangular Throne Room and the grand Megaron or reception hall are connected to smaller rooms which would have been the royal apartments. In one, a red stucco bath has been excavated. It is impossible to resist imagining it as the very one in which Agamemnon was murdered by the axe-wielding Clytemnestra.

Clytemnestra and her lover Aegisthus were believed by Schliemann to be buried in two chamber tombs in grave circle B, outside the Lion Gate. Nearby, several streets of merchants' houses have been excavated, indicating that a lower town of common folk stood below the walls of the royal city. Tablets found here show that this trading city may have been wealthy, substantial, and involved in trade throughout the Aegean.

The massive walls of the **Treasury of Atreus**, opposite the main site (same ticket) are another awesome demonstration of the Mycenaean way with stone. Huge dry-stone blocks make up a giant cone, entered by a 15-metre corridor. Two enormous slabs of stone above the chamber door support

The Mask of Agamemnon

The German archaeologist Heinrich Schliemann achieved the biggest coup in 19th century archaeology by finding the site of ancient Troy. Schliemann was the first to guess that Homer's epic tale of the ten-year siege of Troy by a Mycenaean-led alliance might be more than a myth — might indeed be a dramatized version of real events. Most of his contemporaries thought Schliemann's search for the real Troy was a wild goose chase and were dumbfounded by the discovery of the site.

For an encore, Schliemann went on to find and excavate the site of ancient Mycenae. He believed the gold royal mask he discovered there to be the face of Agamemnon himself, but here he let himself get carried away. The mask and other burial treasures found in what Schliemann believed to be Agamemnon's grave belong to a time around 1600 BC, several centuries before the Trojan War.

The Mycenaeans were an Indo-European people who began to arrive in Greece around 2100 BC. By around 1600 BC they had created a world of little, elaborate Bronze Age kingdoms centred around large palaces which were ringed by crude but imposing walls of massive stone blocks. The best known of these is Mycenae (Mikines) itself, but there are other palace sites at Tiryns and Pylos. After the fall of Minoan civilization in Crete, the Mycenaeans moved into the power vacuum there and many inscriptions in Linear B, the earliest known Greek writing, have been found at Knossos as well as on the mainland. Mycenaean civilization crumbled quite suddenly around 1200 BC, for reasons unknown, to be followed by a Dark Age which lasted almost two centuries. Excavations show several generations of squatters using the sites of the Mycenaean palaces during that time, before the iron-using Dorians — speaking another dialect of Greek — began to trickle in and settle much of the Greek world around 1050 BC. By the time they settled the former Mycenaean heartlands, Mycenae and its kings were shadowy legends, and it came to be believed that the massive walls of their palaces had been built not by men but by the one-eyed giants called Cyclops.

the main structure: you can almost feel gravity, as well as the millennia, pressing down.

WHERE TO STAY
Hotel Petite Planete, midway between the ruins and the modern village (B-Class, closed Oct. – April); **Agamemnon** (C-Class) and **Pension Dassis**, both on the main (and only) street, are cheaper options.

FOOD AND DRINK
Take pot luck at the sprinkling of cafés and restaurants on the single main street. A van sells drinks, snacks and ice cream at the car park by the archaeological site.

ARGOS, TIRYNS, EPIDAUROS, NAFPLION

Midway between Mikines and Nafplion, the village of **Argos** gives little hint of its Mycenaean heritage. Though it was one of the major Mycenaean centres, its principal ruins, about one km. from the centre in the direction of Tripoli, are Hellenistic and Roman. The huge theatre – one of the biggest of the ancient Greek world – held more than 20,000. Not as evocative as Mycenae or Tiryns, but nevertheless worth a look, as is the medieval castle on a crag above the modern town, built by the Franks. Argos is said to be the longest-inhabited settlement in Europe, and these ruins – spanning almost three millennia – drive that point home.

On the central square, the Argos Archaeological Museum is useful for filling in the Mycenaean background of the region.

Altogether more impressive is **Tiryns**, midway between Argos and Nafplion. Once the great seaport of the Mycenaean Argolid, it has been left high and dry by the receding coastline. If you are visiting in summer and find Mycenae too crowded for comfort, Tiryns may give you greater space for contemplation: few of the coachloads of visitors make it this far.

Tiryns' walls of Cyclopean boulders are even more impressive than those of Mycenae, though the massive gateways are less well preserved. Like Mycenae, the heart of the site is the royal palace complex, with its arcaded court, central great hall with royal apartments leading off it, and a ruined tower with a secret staircase – either a back way out during a siege or serving some religious function. Also like Mycenae, nothing of the place survives but the floors and foundations, and the imagination must fill in the colours of the palace frescoes and the walls of baked clay.

The southern gateway to the Argolid is **Nafplion**. Overlooked by twin Venetian-Turkish castles and retaining some of its older buildings from an era when it was one of the most important towns of newly-independent 19th-century Greece, this cheerful seaport is one of the few larger Peloponnesian towns with real charm and character. The older part of town, with its shaky-looking balconies and red pantile roofs, is one of the better-preserved examples of pre-reinforced-concrete Greek town planning. As in other Greek towns which have survived the ravages of the 20th century, Nafplion displays random mementoes of its various occupants. Three converted mosques – one now the church of Ag. Giorghios, another a cinema and the third disused – stand around the central Syntagma square. A Turkish fountain is let into the wall of the cinema.

Nafplion's Archaeological Museum, with a good Mycenaean collection which includes frescoes from the palace at Tiryns, is good to visit either before or after seeing the sites, with displays which help the visitor to picture the ancient palaces.

Three great fortresses – the Acronafplion and the Palamidi castles above the old town and the fortified island of Bourtzi – made Nafplion one of the great strongholds of Venice in the Peloponnese until the final eviction of the Serene Republic by the Turks in the 18th century. Less than a hundred years later, during the War of Independence, the Turks in turn were besieged in this massive complex of fortifications.

No two sources agree on how many steps lead to the fortress – the NTOG says 857, others say as many as 900. In any case, the climb is literally breathtaking. At the summit, three smaller castles stand within the main curtain walls, all with the Lion of St Mark, the symbol of the Venetian Republic, prominently displayed. On a crag to the west, the twin castle of Akronafplia – part Venetian and part Turkish, built on the remnants of an ancient Greek acropolis – is more ruined and less eyecatching. Offshore, the island fort of Bourtzi commands the harbour and can be visited by small boat in summer.

Built in the fourth century BC, the great theatre of **Epidaurus** is the best preserved and grandest of all the ancient Hellenic theatres and is the venue each summer of a major festival of drama featuring the works of ancient Greek playwrights such as Aeschylus, Euripides and Sophocles, whose plays are performed in modern Greek. Though performances give you the chance to appreciate the theatre's amazing acoustics – the slightest sound carries clearly from the stage to the highest tiers of seats – the best time to explore Epidaurus at leisure is off-season, in spring or autumn, when the site is uncrowded. It is hard to believe at first that the enormous arena could have remained undiscovered for so long – it was excavated only in the late 19th century – and its design is one of the most striking examples of the ancient Greek architect's talent for merging man-made structure with the surrounding terrain.

Epidaurus was a centre of healing dedicated to Aesclepius, and his sanctuary, on the scale of Delphi, is often missed by visitors intent on viewing the better-known theatre. A small museum is a useful guide to the ruins on this section of the site, which are much less well-preserved than the theatre. They include remnants of a Temple of Aesclepius, baths, a gymnasium and the foundations of an athletic stadium as well as hospitals and dwellings for the priests of the healer-god. The tholos, a circular building designed by Polycleitus, holds an inner labyrinth. In this lived the sacred snakes of Aesclepius, and this snake pit may have been part of a rite of healing.

TRAVELLING
By Road   Frequent buses from Corinth to Argos and Nafplion.
Mikines is about half an hour's walk from the bus stop on the main road. Tiryns is just off the main road, midway between Argos and Nafplion. Argos, not Nafplion, is the main bus terminus for the region. For Epidavros, there are four buses daily from Nafplion.

By Sea   Nafplion has ferry and hydrofoil connections with Piraeus and the Saronic Islands.

WHERE TO STAY
Nafplion   Plenty of C-Class hotels including: **Hotel des Roses**, Leof. Argou 42; **Victoria**, Spiliadou 3; **Nafplia**, Navarinou 11; **Alkyon**, Leof. Argou 43; **Elena**, Sidiras Merarchias 17; **Galini**, Sidiras Merarchias 37.

Epidavros Most hotels are on the beach at Palea Epidavros, 15 km from the site. C-Class hotels include: **Aegeon, Aktis, Apollon, Verdelis Inn,** and **Christina.** The closest accommodation to ancient Epidavros is at Ligourio, 5 km away, where there are two C-Class hotels and some rooms.

Argos Hotel Mycenae (C-Class), Ag. Petrou; **Telessila** (C-Class), Danaou 2.

FOOD AND DRINK

Argos The usual variety of restaurants and snack places, none outstanding, surrounds the central square.

Nafplion Waterfront restaurants on Odos Bouboulinas and Odos Miaoulis are the best bet. Cheaper but less attractive restaurants are around the bus station on Singrou.

Epidavros There are seasonal beach restaurants at Palea Epidavros, but none at the site itself.

THE CENTRAL PELOPONNESE

A mixture of rugged, barren mountains, dusty valleys and commercial centres supplying the surrounding farming country, the heart of the Peloponnese is country most visitors choose to pass through on the way to the greater attractions on the peninsula's fringes.

Main routes between Patras and Sparta (roughly north–south) and from Kalamata in the south and Pirgos and Olympia in the west to Nafplion cross at **Tripoli,** a modern administrative and commercial city with no claims on the visitor except as a transport hub. The other major town of the central Peloponnese is **Megalopoli** – once "the great city" of the region, now unexciting but with a little-visited archaeological site nearby at Ancient Megalopolis. The site, two km from the city in the direction of Krestena, is only partly excavated, showing the first few tiers of ancient Greece's largest theatre. The rest of the huge city, built by the Thebans in the fourth century BC to hold Sparta in check, is a maze of mounds and hummocks where the soil has swallowed the remnants of streets, squares and temples. For all its grandeur,

Megalopolis thrived for less than two centuries before being deserted.

THE SOUTHERN PELOPONNESE

Dominating the south of the Peloponnesian peninsula, the highest peaks of the **Taigettos massif** shoot up to 2400m. Snow-covered as late as June, Taigettos dominates the skyline of much of the south and the summit looms on the horizon even from faraway Kithira.

From the body of the Peloponnese, three fingers – **Messinia, Mani** and **Malea** – poke south into the Mediterranean. None too accessible unless you have your own transport, this southernmost part of mainland Greece remains little afflicted by mass tourism even in high season, though holiday hotels are beginning to crop up around the region's only charter airport at Kalamata.

MESSINIA PENINSULA

The main attractions on this westernmost of the three southern fingers are the medieval citadels of Methoni and Koroni and – on the western shore of the Messinian Gulf – some good beaches on what the Greeks have taken to calling the Messinian Riviera.

Methoni's grim ramparts look far to the west and south from their headland. Below them is a rag-tag little town with no focal point and little character; it's as if modern Methoni is still cowed by the medieval stronghold. Many of the older buildings are ramshackle and deserted, and the town is in the throes of a tourism building boom which will make it a much bigger holiday centre in the near future. There's an excellent sandy beach facing east, below the castle; but if you're looking for a picturesque Greek fishing village, this isn't it.

Midway between Methoni and its twin fortress, Koroni, is **Finikounda,** a pleasant little fishing port with a handful of seafront restaurants on its single main street. Finikounda has a half-mile of fine sandy beach. There's another sandy beach about 1.5 kilometres round the headland to the east, where there is also a summer-season restaurant-bar with a kids' playground.

Koroni is much more immediately appealing than its western twin. It's by no means unaffected by tourism, but there is a more vital local atmosphere, with a feeling of hustle and bustle on business other than tourism. A sprinkling of traditional ouzeri-bars have not yet been turned into smart holiday cafés – there are plenty of those – and Koroni's capped and bewhiskered senior citizens foregather in them to discuss affairs of state and the price of fish. And while beach-boredom might begin to set in quite quickly at Methoni, you could spend quite some time at Koroni without getting sand-happy. Along Koroni's wide esplanade, looking east across the Messinian Gulf to the coast of the Outer Mani, palm tress have been planted. They're only about three feet high at the moment, but in a few years' time Koroni will have a gracious palm-lined seafront for its evening volta.

Koroni's castle, on a crag above the town, for some reason feels less forbidding than Methoni's. Perhaps its higher, more naturally defensible site allowed the builders to make its walls less massive. From the ramparts, you can see why it was one of the Eyes of Venice – the eye sweeps from the Messinian plain and the western slopes of Taigettos off to the north round to the shores of the Mani and the passage round Cape Matapan to the south and east. No hostile fleet could avoid being spotted by vigilant sentries here.

Inside the castle walls there are a number of older white-walled, green-shuttered houses and the grounds are green and shady with olive trees and potted geraniums. There are also several churches and the town's old graveyard.

Koroni's beach is uncrowded, long and sandy, separated from the town by the castle crag and with a few temporary tavernas only in high season. It's a half-hour walk from the town restaurants and bars, so take food and drink if you're planning a full day there.

Overlooking the plateia is a grandiose church of Aghios Dimitrios with a tall campanile, arcaded front and marble steps.

From Koroni north, the road runs through fertile coastal

lowlands along the western shore of the Messinian Gulf before curving west across the shallow valley of the Pamisos river to modern Messinia and Kalamata. There are rooms, beaches and campsites along this coast at little villages such as **Ag. Andreas, Nea Koroni, Kalamaki** and **Petalidi,** popular resorts for Greek holidaymakers and a sprinkling of foreigners in summer, most of them with their own transport.

Modern **Messinia** is a no-account inland market town, and you won't want to spend time here. The ancient site which bears the same name is about 20 km away near the village of Mavromati. In its time, the Pamisos valley had not yet silted up and the ancient city would have been much closer to the sea than its site is now.

Built in the fourth and third centuries BC, the city – capital of a city-state liberated from the Spartans after their defeat at the hands of Epaminondas of Thebes – was ringed by a nine-km wall. Four of its great gates remain. The biggest is the northern Arcadia Gate, where the remains of a marble-paved road still show the ruts of ancient chariots. The centre of ancient Messinia lay where the modern village of Mavromati now stands. From the village, you can also take a stiff hike to the summit of Mt Voulkanos, where there's a convent with Byzantine frescoes of the Cretan School and a monastery with a famous ikon of the Virgin. If you're here in August, the monastery of Voulkano is the focus of loud celebration of the Panaghiria (Ascension), when the ikon is paraded from the monastery to its original home in the mountain-top convent.

Beyond modern Messinia the flat countryside is dull, as is **Kalamata,** a dusty modern town not improved by having been hard hit by an earthquake in 1986. If you do have to stay here, make the most of it and remind yourself that life in a town like Kalamata, with its industry and commerce but little tourism, is a far more authentic expression of "the real Greece" than the picturesque island villages beloved of brochure and postcard photographers. File under "gritty but real".

TRAVELLING
Kalamata is the main transport hub not just for Messinia but for the southern Peloponnese.

By Road Frequent buses to Tripoli, Corinth and Athens, north and west to Patras, east to Sparta and Areopolis. Car hire available.

By Rail To Patras and west coast points between.

By Air Daily to Athens.

WHERE TO STAY

Methoni shuts down almost completely from around the end of September until late April or early May, when finding a place to stay or eat can be a problem. However, once open for the summer there are plenty of rooms, one A-Class hotel and several smaller ones.

Finikounda has a good-value new C-Class hotel, the **Hotel Finikounda**. In summer, there are also rooms to rent.

Koroni has plenty of places to stay – though, as at Methoni, many room-renters shut down in winter and you may have to hunt around a bit. Just off the town's main square, Plateia Aghiou Dimitriou, the **Hotel Diana** is probably the cheapest hotel in town. The smaller, traditional cafés are in and around this part of town, the newer, smarter and inevitably costlier ones along the sea-front.

Messinia has plenty of accommodation, mainly in B-, C- and D-Class hotels, should you arrive late and be forced to spend a night here.

FOOD AND DRINK

Methoni Limited choice of limited restaurants.

Finikoundas Some good fish restaurants along the beachfront main street, one atop the hill at the east end of the beach.

Koroni Heaps of choice, from pizzeria-cafés and pubs on the esplanade to a host of little traditional kafeneions and psistaria in and around the plateia by the church.

Messinia There's a plentiful choice of cheap and basic restaurants and fast food joints catering to locals not tourists.

SPARTA

Looking east from drab Kalamata, the jagged teeth of Taigettos on the near horizon are a reminder that better things are in store. The road to Sparta goes via a spectacular switchback pass through the Taigettos and a series of heart-stopping bends with huge views back over Messinia before you emerge suddenly from the pass to look east over the flat, olive-covered plain of the Evrotas valley and Sparta.

Modern Sparta has only the most tenuous of links with its illustrious – or notorious – ancestor. Modern Athens is still dominated by its ancient Acropolis, and one is always stumbling over yet another memento of its ancient glory, but of its old rival not a lot remains. Unlike the Athenians, the Spartans didn't place much stock in big public buildings or in city walls, and their capital seems to have been a much less grandiose place than Athens. Traces of the ancient city include the theatre carved out of the side of the tallest of the hills on which Sparta was built. There are some remains from Roman times at the Sanctuary of Artemis Orthia just off the main road to Tripoli. A small archaeological museum in a neo-classical building in the centre of town houses exhibits salvaged from these sites, neither of which is fenced in.

Modern Sparta is a commercial centre and market town for the fertile farmlands of the surrounding Evrotas plain, but the biggest attraction for the visitor is the nearby mountaintop site of medieval **Mistra**, a fairytale castle and fortified town straight out of a sword and sorcery movie. Mistra was the capital first of the Frankish Villehardouins, who carved out their micro-kingdom in the southern Peloponnese after the debacle of the Fourth Crusade, then of the Byzantine Despotate of the Morea. From the highest ramparts of its castle, you look down on what were once crowded streets of shops, churches and houses.

The site is in good repair and the architecture quite different from any other historic site in Greece. The arched doors and windows with their decorative brickwork make the surviving buildings light and airy. Because – by Greek standards at least – the site is so recent, you feel a stronger connection with the Franks and Byzantines who walked these steep cobbled streets than with the people who built ancient Sparta. It's hard to imagine the thoughts and feelings of someone who lived more than 2,500 years ago, but Mistra is less than 800 years old – just yesterday compared with Sparta, even more so in comparison with the Mycenaean sites.

Walking Taigettos

From Sparta, Mistra or Githion the snow-topped peaks of the Taigettos massif are a temptation to keen walkers. The walk to the top of Profitis Ilias takes about five hours, starting from the village of Poliana, 12 km from the main Sparta/Githion highway. There is a very basic summer taverna at Poliana, but no other source of food or drink.

The Hellenic Alpine Club has marked the route to the summit and maintains a refuge on the saddle below Profitis Ilias, about three hours' walk from Poliana, where there is room to camp. From here there are wonderful views over Sparta and the Evrotas plain. Persevere for two more hours and you reach the stone chapel on the peak. The feast of Profitis Elias is celebrated here on 20 July: there are eagle's-eye views down to the Gulf of Messinia and north into the ranges of the Peloponnese.

Mistra is much more gracefully built than the purposeful, massive fortifications the Venetians built at Methoni and Koroni. Despite its complex and imposing walls, it was far more than just a garrison-fortress. Allow at least half a day to explore not just the hilltop castle but the churches and streets of the once-bustling lower town: the best way to do this is to go in by the highest entrance, the Castle Gate, and walk down to the main entrance and main carpark. It's a steep walk; living here must have kept you fit. From its peak, a sentry commanded the key mountain passes and the fertile plain of the Evrotas, and it's easy to see why the Villehardouins, then the Byzantines, chose the site. And a visitor today, looking north and east to the mountains or over the olive-covered plain of the Evrotas valley, is rewarded by a tremendous play of light and shadow over this huge panorama.

Opening times: 08.00 to 18.00, Saturday and Sunday 08.30 to 15.00; small entrance fee.

TRAVELLING

To Sparta Frequent buses from Athens and main Peloponnesian towns.

To Mistra Several buses daily; taxis; car hire available in Sparta.

Ancient Sparta

Athens put its faith in its citizen army, its fortifications and its fleet. Sparta staked all on the near-mythical prowess of its élite infantry. For almost two centuries — until the Theban strategist Epaminondas smashed them at Leuktra in 371 BC — they seemed invincible.

Dorian invaders first settled in the Evrotas valley around 1050 BC and created a static, conservative and hierarchical society which prized military virtues. Young Spartans endured a regimen which makes modern special forces training look like a picnic. Cunning and stealth were valued as highly as strength and courage. Ritualized stealing was part of the training, with a severe beating for those caught: there is a grisly fable of the Spartan boy who stole a pet fox and — after hiding it in his shirt — let it eat out his heart rather than cry out and be detected.

Those who survived this training became Spartiatai, full warrior-citizens who were sworn to fight to the death for Sparta. They also had a reputation for tough one-liners. "Good," said the Spartan king Leonidas, when told that the Persian army facing him was so vast that its arrows darkened the sun. "We will fight in the shade."

Spartans chose co-kings from two royal families, each of them claiming descent from Herakles. Five ephors were elected each year to preside over an assembly of citizens and a council of elders. They had immense power.

A servile class called the periokoi and a slave-caste of helots worked the land owned by the Spartan squirearchy. Helots might be killed at will by the Krypteia, a secret society of youths which may have worked like modern death squads, murdering charismatic or courageous malcontents who might one day challenge the status quo.

Even for the ruling class life was ... well, Spartan. Their culture despised luxury and glorified simple living, but Spartans abroad were easily tempted by the luxuries of more relaxed city-states. The Spartiatai married late and their strict lifestyle allowed them few children. The biggest Spartan army ever fielded — at Plateia against the Persians in 479 BC — totalled just 5,000 men.

In this totalitarian world, women had greater status than in other Greek states, but had to conform to the warrior ethos. Girls underwent a milder form of military and athletic training alongside their brothers.

WHERE TO STAY

There are numerous hotels in B-, C- and D-Class in Sparta, but it's much more pleasant to stay at **Nea Mistra**, the modern village below the pinnacle of the old city. It's about half an hour's walk to the lower gates, an hour to the Castle Gate. Rooms are available in the village, which also has a C-Class hotel, the **Hotel Byzantio**.

FOOD AND DRINK

There are half a dozen small restaurants and cafés in **Nea Mistra**. **Sparta** itself is well supplied, with plenty of restaurants catering to local people rather than tourists.

MONEMVASIA

The walled town of Monemvasia, tucked out of sight of the mainland on a steep rock linked to the shore by a road causeway, is one of the gems of the Peloponnese and if you're travelling this way it should not be missed; in fact, it's worth a trip in its own right and is easy to get to by sea from Piraeus (Zea), the east coast of the Peloponnese and the Saronic islands.

The town marked on the map as Monemvasia really covers three towns. The modern town on the mainland, which the locals call **Gefira** (Bridge), is a quiet and unassuming village with a decent shingle beach and a small fishing harbour, three or four small hotels and a number of rooms to rent, plenty of restaurants and cafés, and several well-stocked "supermarkets" catering to the well-heeled Athenians and foreigners who in summer occupy holiday homes in the old town.

This old town, 20 minutes' walk from Gefira, is called **Kastro** (the castle). Though entirely dedicated to tourism, it's a delight to visit or stay in, with streets full of tall Venetian houses, many now converted into holiday apartments, others still ruined. On the single main street there are three restaurants, two of them quite pricy, and a couple of smart café-bars.

Though tourism has completely taken over the Kastro — which had become almost completely ruined and uninhabited until the early 1970s — this hasn't spoilt it. Strict building

Mistra

Mistra was by far the most important of three castles built by the Latin princes of the Morea to guard their 13th-century mini-state from savage Slav tribes settled in the Taigettos mountains.

By the beginning of the 14th century, the resurgent Byzantine Empire had ousted the Latins and garrisoned Mistra. In 1348 it became a fief of the Imperial family, whose princes, called Despots, ruled the Peloponnese from its castle peak.

Kevin Andrews, in *The Flight of Ikaros*, writes: "In a hundred and fifty years they gradually drove back the Franks, Angevins, Catalans, Florentines, Navarrese and Knights of Rhodes to a small region around Patras and finally out of all of Greece, except for the Florentine Dukes of Athens, who hung on there until the Turkish Conquest, and the Venetians, who held on for 40 years after that in their trading stations on the coast, doing good business. While the East Roman Empire was shrinking all the way up to the walls of Constantinople itself, this provincial Greek Despotate expanded and its court here at Mistra had a certain twilight fame as a centre of scholarship and metaphysics, like a flickering reflection of the Renaissance across the Adriatic."

But Mistra was a guttering candle about to be snuffed out: the Despotate held out for seven years after the fall of Constantinople to the Turks, but in 1460 it too knelt to the Sultan. The Turks moved in for two centuries, were ousted for a while by the Venetians under Morosini in the 17th century, and the city was sacked in the abortive Greek rebellion of 1770 and again, during the War of Independence, in 1825.

regulations ensure that houses are rebuilt in traditional style, vehicles can't enter through the iron-bound gates which give access through the medieval walls and even in high season it's possible to wander through lanes full of high-walled ruins and wild figs without meeting a soul. The mainland and the modern town are hidden from view on the other side of the rock, adding to the magical feeling of isolation. A Venetian campanile, a rusting cannon and a historic church built by a Byzantine emperor dominate the dusty little square looking out to sea over the Kastro's ramparts.

The many churches, most of them now ruinous or disused, are an indication of how populous and wealthy the town once was. Touchingly, there's usually a lamp burning in front of the icon in the little church of Aghia Anna, on the way to the Hotel Malvasia, even though the church is just an arched shell lacking much of its roof and large portions of wall.

Just above the main gate, an old pink-stucco house was the birthplace of Yannis Ritzos, Greece's leading leftist poet. In summer, when the south-facing walls soak up the sun's heat all day, the walls radiate an almost tropical heat late into the night, but inside the dark old buildings it's pleasantly cool. You can swim from the rocky quay just outside the walls – follow the signs to "Portillo" where a small arched gate pierces the seaward wall.

To see what Monemvasia was all about, though, you have to climb the steep and zig-zag staircase which leads from the

lower Kastro to the walled top of the rock — **Pano Kastro,**
"the High Fortress". In its Venetian/Byzantine heyday, this
clifftop city had as many as 30,000 inhabitants, but since
early this century no-one has lived up here. The only intact
building is a well-preserved church of Ag. Stefanos on the
north-east peak; it's open and has some interesting frescoes.
Elsewhere, the site is a sea of thistles and thorns with reefs
of masonry — stubs of walls and ruined arches — emerging
from it. There are many cistern-pits hewn into the rock —
Monemvasia had no springs or wells and relied on rainwater
— so watch your step.

TRAVELLING

By Sea   Frequent hydrofoils from Piraeus via the Saronic islands and
the east coast, onward to Kithira. A weekly ferry runs from Piraeus
to Monemvasia and onward to Kithira, Githion and Kastelli in Crete.
In 1991 there were plans for a ferry service linking Monemvasia with
Serifos in the Cyclades.

By Road   Buses to Sparta and Molai. In Gefira, Peter Derzotis at
Malvasia Travel can arrange transport tickets, accommodation, car
and motor-bike hire.

WHERE TO STAY

There are rooms to rent and several hotels in **Modern Gefira.** The
Hotel Akrogiali, run by the Sofos family, is the cheapest of these, an
old-fashioned D-Class hotel with light, clean, high-ceilinged rooms,
balconies and (not always reliably) hot water. The **Hotel Aktaion**
and the **Hotel Minoa** are more expensive, modern and soulless but
comfortable. Some 3.5 km out of town on the road to Nomia and
Neapolis there is a good campsite, **Camping Paradise.**

In the Kastro the best choice is the expensive but lovely little
Hotel Malvasia, tucked away in two separate old mansion-houses
five minutes' walk from the little main street. Room rate includes —
remarkably edible for Greece — a good continental breakfast of rolls,
honey or jam, tea or coffee and orange juice. You can also stay at the
Hotel Byzantio, similarly shoehorned into an old building overlooking
the square. Apartments can sometimes be found by asking around in
the Kastro — expect to pay roughly as much per person as you would
in a good hotel.

Note: Finding accommodation in either Gefira or the Kastro during
the **Greek Easter** is almost impossible unless you have booked well
in advance; don't turn up without a booking and expect to find
a place to lay your head. Accommodation is also very tight in
July and August, when the place can be unpleasantly crowded and
blisteringly hot.

FOOD AND DRINK

There are plenty of good restaurants in **Gefira**, most of them clustered around the harbour front.

In the Kastro, **To Kanoni** is the most expensive restaurant – it even takes American Express. Next door, the family-run **Matoula** is a bit less costly, serves excellent food and has a beautiful terrace shaded by figs and vines and looking south over the ocean. Just across the street, **Marianthos** is friendly and cheerful and quite a bit cheaper than the other two.

Bar Angelo is the smartest place to drink in the Kastro, despite the charming and multilingual Angelo's refusal to serve beer, ouzo or retsina. His iced drinks, fruit punches and vodka cocktails are superb and pack a punch – so do his prices.

MANI

The Southern Tip of Europe

This southernmost part of mainland Greece – indeed of mainland Europe – is profoundly weird. From its savage, near-desert landscape, the towers of fortified ghost towns spring up straight from the rock. The Mani proper is a tiny enclave, yet its huge mountains and the enormous northern peaks of Taigettos combine with a peculiar clarity of air to make it seem far larger, and – virtually unconquered throughout the years of Turkish rule and the forcing-house for the final war of liberation which began at Areopolis in 1821 – it has a peculiarly large role in modern Greek history for such a small area of land.

Mani is littered with history, but its most interesting feature is the unique architecture of its tower villages, built by Maniot clan-chiefs not so much for defence against Turkish invaders as for strongholds against rival clans. Most of these villages are now deserted or lived in only by a handful of old folk, and it doesn't take much imagination to feel a heavy air of melancholy hanging over the peninsula. It's a land whose time has passed.

Traditionally, **"Deep Mani"** – the Mani proper as opposed to the "Outer Mani" coast and hill-slopes between Areopolis and Kalamata – begins south of the ruined Turkish castle at Kelefa, built to bottle the rebellious Maniots up inside their

Malvasia's Golden Age

Monemvasia was Mistra's seaport, though it began building much earlier than Mistra, when mainland Greeks fleeing the Gothic and Slavic invasions of the fourth century AD started to occupy and fortify the rock. Its name derives from the Greek *mono emvasis*, meaning "only one way in", and certainly no invader could, or did, take it by assault throughout its thousand-year history. Successive besiegers — Turkish, Venetian and Greek — had to wait until thirst and hunger forced the defenders to surrender. Not just a fortress, Monemvasia became an important city in its own right, almost as large as Mistra itself, with perhaps 30,000 people living on top of the rock; the lower Kastro, where the hotels and restaurants now are, was a district of churches, warehouses and ship chandlers. When Mistra fell, Monemvasia passed not to the Turks but to Venice. It became an important part of the Serene Republic's trading empire in the Aegean and an entrepot for goods from all over the mainland and the archipelago, best known for the wine the English called "malmsey" — a corruption of the town's Venetian name, Malvasia, or of the French Malvoisie.

The Venetians ruled over a mongrel citizenry of Byzantines and other survivors of the region's frequent population shifts, including Byzantine noble families who retained their airs and graces after the conquest of Constantinople. The main business of these merchant-princes was commerce, but in the lawless medieval Aegean piracy was often just trade by more direct methods and a pirate simply a trader whose holds were empty.

The Venetians hung on until 1540, pulling out after Suleiman the Magnificent defeated them at the mainland battle of Preveza; they returned under Morosini in the 18th century, were again ousted, and Monemvasia slipped off the map. It re-entered history briefly in 1821 with the dreadful siege of its Turkish garrison by Mavromichalis and his rebel Maniots: the defenders were finally starved out. After that, it was gradually deserted. The last dwellers on the top of the rock left at the turn of the last century, and only a handful of long-standing families now live in the Kastro.

Around Monemvasia

There's a good sand beach at Ambelakia, a couple of kilometres past Camping Paradise to the south (too far to walk). Closer to town, there's a long sand and pebble beach about 25 minutes' walk from Gefira along the main Molai road. There are tavernas for food and drink at both beaches.

North of Monemvasia, there are pretty and interesting villages accessible by boat or by Flying Dolphin — Gerakas is on a classic smuggler's cove, hidden from sight by its twisting fjord until you round the last of a series of bends. Paralia Kiparissi is quiet and cool with a clean white-pebble beach and very clear water. There are tavernas at both, but very few rooms available.

If you can, take a trip to Mistra, Monemvasia's hilltop twin, easily accessible by bus via Sparta.

rebellious little hideout. In turn, Deep Mani is divided into "Sunward Mani", on the eastern slopes of the range which runs down the length of the peninsula, and "Shadow Mani" on the western side. It's the west which holds most of the most spectacular tower villages as well as a score of tiny and criminally ruinous churches holding luminous frescoes, some of which are more than 1,000 years old and few of which are adequately protected from the weather.

From **Githion** – a pretty little port and worth visiting in its own right – you approach Areopolis and the Deep Mani through a steep pass commanded by the remains of the Frankish fortress of Passava, built by the Villehardouins of Mistra. The scenery becomes steadily starker and steeper as you near **Areopolis**, but this little town and nearby Pirgos Dirou give little inkling of what is to come. Once called Tsimova, Areopolis was renamed in honour of Ares, god of war, in honour of its role as the starting-point of the War of Independence. There's swimming nearby at the tiny harbour of Itilo, a steep half-hour's walk away or – if you have transport – at a sweep of good beach further north along the coast, and Areopolis has one tower of its own, now an NTOG guesthouse. But sitting in its dusty little plateia you may wonder what is so special about Mani.

Mani
The Towers of Vendetta

Family feud and fierce pride dominate the history of the Mani. Like Sfakia in western Crete, this rocky peninsula — a natural fortress ringed by cliffs and cut off by mountains — was never completely conquered by the Turks. Instead, they left local clan chiefs in power, asking only that they kept piracy and banditry down to a dull roar and paid a tribute, an agreement which was broken more often than not.

In 1821 the Maniot chieftain Petrobey Mavromichalis raised the rebel banner in his capital Tsimova — now Areopolis — and the Niklian aristocracy and their followers exploded out of their little world to spread rebellion and terror across southern Greece.

For centuries, the Niklian families in their crowded hills feuded over land, rents, and real or imagined insults. These feuds were not only between village and village but between neighbours. Each family home was a little fortress and families would blaze away from their towers or send sharpshooters to bushwhack members of the rival family. Truce could be called to meet an outside threat from the Turks or at harvest time: it was a highly codified form of war in miniature, like a paintball game with real bullets.

Maniots were great pirates and wreckers, terrorizing shipping and ranging far abroad to take slaves — Muslim or Christian — to be sold to all comers in their slave market at Itilon. Maniot traditions included the miroloya, a dirge in rhyming couplets improvised by professional mourning-women. Niklian families prized only their sons — the "guns" of the family — and daughters were regarded as chattels.

Though full-scale feuding went on well into the 19th century, Greek independence gave Maniots the freedom to live elsewhere and people began to drift away to find work or land elsewhere. Most of the tower-villages are empty or almost empty, though well-off foreigners have begun renovating them as holiday homes. But some echoes of the fierce old Mani remain. Not long ago I was told in all seriousness by a Greek architect involved in the EOT traditional settlements programme that there had been death threats over the transformation of the Vathi village towers into government-run guest rooms.

Head south, to Kitta and beyond, and you'll see. **Pirgos Dirou**'s main claim to fame is its underground lake in caverns discovered nearby. There are conducted tours through the spikes and pinnacles of the caves, but for much of the year you'll have to wait your turn while coachloads of tour groups troop through.

THESSALY AND EPIRUS
The Northern Mainland

The northern mainland of Greece is dominated by rugged mountain ranges which separate the western province of Epirus from the lower hills and plains of Thessaly in the east. Other mountain massifs, including Mount Olympus itself, cut Thessaly off from Macedonia in the north. Thessaly is a farming region of rolling hills and fertile plains, and is the route of least resistance into the heartland of Greece from the north. From Mardonius's Persians to Hitler's Panzers, every invader in Greek history has had to march and fight through the dusty foothills of Thessaly.

Though its fields are spattered with red, yellow and purple wildflowers during its brief spring, the onset of summer quickly turns Thessaly into a cauldron of monochrome grainfields. The region's small towns and farmlands are of no great interest to the visitor and the province is notably short of first-division ancient sites. It does, however, have some of Greece's most awe-inspiring mountain scenery in the cloud-capped peaks of Mount Olympus; some of the loveliest and least-changed traditional villages on the leafy slopes of the Pilion peninsula; and for connoisseurs of weird beauty, the fantastic monastic fastnesses of the Meteora.

THE PLAIN OF THESSALY

The colourness Thessalian plain — enlivened occasionally by a nesting stork — whets the appetite for what is to come. Heading north-west, the roads lead to the cliff-perched monasteries of the Meteora and onward into the empty peaks of the Pindos range, the spine of the western mainland.

To the north-east, the National Road runs through the historic pass of Tembi to Mount Olympus and Macedonia, while to the east the forested peninsula of Pilion juts into the Aegean like a finger pointing to the Sporades.

Lamia, where Thessaly meets Attica, is the southern gateway to the province. For more than 2,000 years its location at the crossroads of main routes north to the plain of Thessaly, south to Athens, west to Epirus and east to the sea has made it a town of some importance, but successive conquerors have left nothing to catch the eye.

From Lamia the main north-south artery, the National Road, skirts the Aegean coast before heading inland to the commercial centre and road/rail junction of Larissa, thence north to Macedonia.

Volos, some 26 km off the main highway, a grubby port and cement exporting town, is the jumping-off point for the hillside villages of Mt Pilion and for sea-travel on to the Sporades. At the head of the almost landlocked Pagasitic Gulf, Volos is ringed by tremendous mountain scenery but has little to recommend it. Hotels are on the noisy main street, Leof. Dimitriados, or overlook a busy waterfront, Od. Argonavton. There is a long string of restaurants and cafés, ranging from grimy old-style ouzeris to flashy modern bars, along the waterfront.

Larissa, the hub and capital of the province, is a prosperous, bustling commercial centre with little to show for an exciting past. Like Lamia, its location gave it a central role in Greek history but helped to ensure that not much would remain as successive waves of invaders washed over it. The leader of the Thessalian cities in classical times, it was a Macedonian, Roman, Byzantine and Turkish capital and these occupiers quarried its ancient buildings for new works. Only traces remain of its ancient Acropolis, temple and theatre.

Trikala, like Larissa, lost most of its ancient buildings to quarriers, but this smaller metropolis still has a few streets of 19th-century traditional houses, a Turkish-Byzantine castle, and a handful of churches to provide contrast to its modern buildings. Trikala too is a riverside town, standing on the banks of the Letheos.

TRAVELLING
By Road Frequent buses from Athens (5 hours from Larissa) and Thessaloniki (3 to 4 hours from Larissa), via the fast National Road, stop at all towns. Several buses daily from Larissa and Trikala to Kalambaka, Metsovo, Ioanina and Kozani. Several buses daily from Volos to the main Pilion villages. Car hire available in Volos.

By Rail Several trains daily on the Athens–Thessaloniki line stop at Volos and Larissa. A restored narrow-gauge steam railway runs between Volos and the main Pilion villages.

By Boat Ferries and hydrofoils daily in high season from Volos to Skiathos (connections to other Sporades and Evia).

WHERE TO STAY
Trikala The C-Class **Hotel Palladion**, Od. Vironos 4, is small, cheap and adequate. The B-Class **Achillion** is larger, fairly expensive and comfortable but dull.

Volos **Hotel Aegli**, 24 Odos Argonauton: comfortable, old-fashioned medium-price hotel next to ferry dock; **Hotel Iason,** corner of Odos Mela and Odos Argonauton, is cheap and equally convenient for boats; **Hotel Argo**, 165 Leof. Dimitriados is small, new and cheap but noisy.

Larissa   Plenty of hotels in all categories. **Pension Edelweiss** is a pleasant mid-priced pension.

FOOD AND DRINK
Trikala   Plateia Vassileos Ghiorghios, the town's main square, over-looks the river and is lined with cafés and restaurants.

Volos   Athenaiki taverna, Od. Venizelou 1, is cheap and pleasantly old-fashioned. Equally handy for those awaiting a ferry or getting off one are **Kafeneion Pagasitikos**, **Ouzeri-Mezedzitiko to Delphini**, and **Kafeneion 1 Akropolis**, next to each other on the corner of Od. Argonavton and Od. Kartali. All are cheap, cheerful and old-fashioned. Further along Argonavton are a string of modern but mediocre restaurants at higher prices.

Larissa   Well provided with gyros and souvlaki snack-bars, modern microwave joints and traditional restaurants. The pleasantest are those beside the Pinios River which runs through the town centre.

PILION

This mountainous peninsula – the home of the mythical centaurs – is thickly cloaked with woods of plane and chestnut and watered by abundant streams which keep it cool and green in high summer, a fine refuge from the baking heat of the Thessalian plains.

The peninsula – shaped like a curly-toed boot with the toe pointing in towards the mainland – is roughly 60 km from north to south, but its prettiest and most interesting villages are on the mountain slopes no more than 20 km from Volos. Houses on Pilion are distinctive mansions with half-timbered upper stories overhanging the lower floors and elaborate painted woodwork within; many of the finest mansions have been restored as part of the National Tourism Organization's traditional settlements programme and are open as guesthouses. Typically, these villages cluster around one or more broad plateias shaded by the leaves of enormous plane trees and looking out over the sea.

Makrinitsa is where the lush woods of Pilion give way to the dry country of Thessaly. The slopes behind the village are well-watered and thickly wooded, but looking west the country turns bare and dry within a few hundred metres of the village.

Traditional Settlements

The 20th century has not been kind to Greece's more out-of-the-way communities. Four years of occupation and four more of civil war saw many remote villages razed by occupying troops, ELAS guerrillas or government or paramilitary forces.

Depopulation has worked more slowly but even more effectively. Many communities have been feeling its effects for generations as younger people trickle away to Athens or to foreign cities in search of work and a better standard of living.

In almost any village you will see houses — some of them grand, some modest, but all of them part of a rich and very varied vernacular culture which cannot be replaced — which are gradually slumping into ruins. Many of them belong to families who have emigrated, others to people who have built a new home nearby and left the old family house to crumble.

In a commendable effort to save some of these — and to bring some of the cash benefits of tourism to remoter communities — the National Tourism Organization of Greece has since the 1970s been acquiring and renovating such properties as up-market guesthouses. Once these are established, the original owners have the option of taking over the operation from the NTOG. It can be a sweet deal for the owners, who get a going concern in exchange for a pile of rubble. It also inspires imitators to rebuild and conserve older buildings, rather than tearing them down to build a modern guesthouse in the prevalent cement bunker style.

Some of the most impressive of these ventures are in the grand landowners' mansions of the Pilion villages. In Mani — not without resistance from the fiercely conservative locals — the tower-village of Vathi has been taken over almost completely, as has Ia on Santorini, whose precariously perched houses were abandoned by their inhabitants after the volcanic eruption which shook the island in 1957. For a full list of the traditional settlements, and to book a room, contact NTOG offices in Athens or abroad.

Makrinitsa is the most developed of the Pilion mountain villages as well as the closest to Volos. The views from its flagstoned plateia, shaded by three huge plane trees, are marred only slightly by the urban sprawl of Volos, about 14 km away but seeming almost directly below. The square is full of café tables and graced by an elaborately-carved fountain and an arcaded church of St John Prodromos, John the Baptist.

If your time is limited, Makrinitsa is the closest village to Volos and the easiest to get to, with plenty of places to stay, but even prettier and much less visited are **Milies** and its neighbour **Vizitsa**, three km apart and about 30 km from Volos. Both have huge, shady balcony-plateias and beautiful old mansions and each has an imposing church beside its main square. On a summer afternoon when not a soul is in sight it is hard to believe that the plateia is the heart of village life, but by evening every chair will be taken, locals will be hopping from one table to the next and the inevitable games of tavli (backgammon) will be in full swing. Now is the ideal time to try Pilion dishes such as rabbit casserole or sausage stew, strong red wine from the cask or tiny bottles of the even stronger local spirit, tsipouro.

About eight km below Milies – too far to be within comfortable walking distance – the fishing village-cum-resort of **Kala Nera** is very popular with Greek families and has several small hotels and plenty of good restaurants (in season) spread out along a nondescript, pebbly beach. Six km further south, **Alissos** is a smaller, quieter village with a shady plateia and quayside restaurants where you may be entertained by three busking musicians – violin, tambour and clarinet – playing the nasal, oddly jazz-like music of the northern mainland.

After Alissos you have a choice. You can head south, through increasingly barren mountain country, through the hillside villages of **Argalasti** and **Lafkos**, where the road divides again, taking you south to **Platania**, a quiet village with good beaches and a handful of little restaurants, or east to **Milina** – which has a campsite and a beach – and **Trikeri**, a somnolent hilltop village overlooking a natural harbour.

Centaurs

The half-horse, half-human centaurs of Greek legend are among the most appealing of the mythical creatures of the Hellenic world. The ancient Greeks had a thing for human–animal hybrids — the horned and goat-footed satyrs and fauns, snake-tailed lamia, and bull-headed minotaur — but the centaurs sometimes have an intelligence and nobility that these lack. Some — like Chiron, who was the tutor of many heroes — had wisdom and magic which they had learned from the gods themselves. Centaurs could also be rude and barbarous, with a taste for strong liquor and rape. At the wedding of Hippodameia, princess of the Lapiths, the drunken centaur Eurytion and his clan tried to abduct the bride but were thwarted by the hero Theseus.

Centaurs lived in all the high mountain ranges of the Greek mainland but especially in the forests of Mount Pilion. Mythologists believe the originals of the myth may have been cattle-herding, horse-riding people from northern Greece whose customs were alien to the settled southern and island Greeks.

Or you can follow the road which loops spectacularly round the main Pilion massif, winding through beech forests and gorges choked with semi-tropical jungles of creepers and undergrowth, and back to Volos, passing on the way through more of Pilion's cool, scattered villages.

The best of these are **Tsangaradha**, around 60 km from Volos, and **Makrirahi**. Less quaintly refurbished than the villages of the western Pilion, they are still working communities which owe little to tourism. Each has several plateias, above and below the main road and connected by rambling stairlike streets.

TRAVELLING

By Road Buses from Volos several times daily to Makrinitsa, Milies, Tsangarada, Makrirahi and Portaria, and the west coast resort villages. Elsewhere, buses are not reliable. Car rental is available in Volos.

By Rail The narrow gauge steam railway between Volos and Milies is being restored and is planned to reopen at least partly by 1992. Not to be missed, if available.

By Sea Hydrofoils and day-trip boats (one way journeys possible) connect Trikeri and Platania with Skiathos several times a week in high season.

WHERE TO STAY
Several fine mansion houses – "**archontiki**" – once belonging to the Pilion squirearchy in **Makrinitsa**, **Milies** and **Vizitsa** have been saved from ruin by the NTOG and converted into comfortable though expensive guesthouses. They are by far the pleasantest places to stay in Pilion and among the nicest in Greece, and it is worth visiting one of these villages just to stay in one. Book ahead with NTOG offices abroad or in Athens, or check availability at the NTOG office in Volos.

In Makrinitsa, **Archontikon Diomidi**, **Archontikon Mousli**, **Archontikon Sicilianou**, **Archontikon Rapana** and **Archontikon Theophilos** are all within 40 m of the main street and plateia and clearly signposted. All are medium to expensive.

Cheaper are the mid-priced **Hotel Achilles**, a modern hotel in traditional style overlooking the plateia, and the **Hotel Pilioritiko Spiti**, mid-priced with a sunny terrace above Makrinitsa's main street.

On the west coast of Pilion, there are plenty of beds in cheap to mid-priced if undistinguished hotels at Kala Nera and Afissos. There are a number of reasonable **campsites** close to Kala Nera.

On the east coast, accommodation is hard to find except at Agios Ioannis, which has a clutch of small hotels, rooms and apartments, all of which are surprisingly expensive, and at Horefto, where there are a few rooms to rent fairly cheaply.

FOOD AND DRINK
Makrinitsa Restaurant Pantheon, whose outdoor tables take up much of the plateia, is a cavernous traditional building whose dark wooden interior is vaguely Teutonic. Nearby, the **Café Ouzeri Diamanti** overlooks a bubbling stream and steep stairway-path to the lower village.

Milies Has one traditional plateia restaurant which seems to be nameless. Open in the evening only, it serves excellent Pilion food. At nearby **Milies**, there is a small family-run restaurant under a vine canopy on the main street and a traditional kafeneion on the main plateia.

There are good fish restaurants, catering to a Greek tourist clientele, on the waterfront at Kala Nera, at Afissos and at Aghios Ioannis, and a couple of very basic tavernas at Damohouri. Seasonal tavernas cater to day-trippers at Platania and Trikeri in summer and there are plateia restaurants at Tsangarada, Zagora and Portaria.

Pilion Beaches

Pilion's east coast beaches are pebbly but clean and for much of the year uncrowded and extremely enticing from the bird's eye viewpoint of Tsangaradha or Makrirahi. From either village, you can walk down cobbled donkey-tracks to the sea. The walk is steep and takes at least two hours, passing through thick woods and past several derelict mansions. The last kilometre or so is a zig-zag stairway over cliffs and crags. The reward is a string of beaches and villages starting at the pretty hamlet of Damouhori and leading to Agios Ioannis, which has long sweeps of clean pebbly beach and is a mini-resort popular with Greek holidaymakers.

A steeply winding road connects Agios Ioannis with Makrirahi and the main road back to Volos via the uninteresting village of Hania (which in winter becomes one of Greece's few ski-resorts) and Portaria, a tourist crossroads mainly composed of shops and restaurants but with an attractive plateia-restaurant and an antique lion-headed spring gushing water even in high summer.

Alternatively, take the turning north for the mostly-modern hill village of Zagoria, backed by the higher ranges of northern Pilion with splendid views of the sea, and go on to Pouri. This little balcony village surrounded by Pilion's jungle-like woods is very much the end of the road. Below it there is a good sandy beach at the quiet village of Horefto.

MOUNT OLYMPUS (OLIMPOS, OLIMBOS)

Almost 3000 metres high, Olympus dominates the northern coast and the hinterland of Thessaly and Macedonia. Its peak, almost always cloud-covered, can be seen from miles out to sea and from far inland. Rising from the low hills and plains with no nearby mountains to rival it, it is easy to see how the ancient Greeks peopled it with gods. From an aircraft en route to or from Athens or Thessaloniki the peak of Olympus can often be seen rising out of a carpet of cloud when the surrounding countryside is out of sight beneath it. It feels faintly blasphemous to be looking down on the home of the gods . . .

Covered in fir and beech forests, Olympus is a challenge to keen walkers though only the toughest and best-prepared should attempt the six-to-seven-hour ascent.

Litochoro, 5 km from the main National Road on the lowest slopes of Olympus, is a natural starting point for walkers. For those who just want to gaze at the summit from a comfortable distance, there are beaches at Limenas Litohorou, Plaka and Paralia Skotinas, all of which are rather marred by the nearby highway.

Dion, on the mountain's lower northern flank, is the site of an ancient Macedonian temple-city. City walls, sanctuaries of Aphrodite and Demeter, and later Christian churches have been excavated. The city, inundated by mud in an earthquake 1,500 years ago, is well preserved and has some fine mosaics. It is open daily in summer.

TRAVELLING
By Road Buses to Litohoro and Dion from Athens, Thessaloniki, Volos and Larissa.

By Rail Slow trains on the main north/south line stop at Leptokaria, 9 km from Litohoro. Buses run between village and station.

WHERE TO STAY
There are comfortable **campsites** at Plaka and Limenas Litohorou. In Litohoro the **Hotel Myrto** is cheapish and reasonable. On Olympus itself, the **Spilios Agapitos** refuge hostel is a large and comfortable hostel, the **Giosos Apostolidis** refuge more primitive and less busy. Book ahead for Spilios Agapitos (Tel: 0352 82 300).

FOOD AND DRINK
In **Litohoro**, a handful of basic taverna restaurants on the main street. On the mountain, bring your own — and remember to take your rubbish back with you.

THE METEORA

The clifftop monasteries of the Meteora are among the world's strangest places. Nothing in the low-lying landscape of Thessaly prepares you for the impact of this valley of bulbous plugs of rock — like something Salvador Dali might have painted — each crowned improbably by its rickety monastery. Only five of the two dozen are now lived in —

the monasteries of Great Meteoron, Agia Triada and Varlaam and the nunneries of Agios Stefanos and Roussanou and all but for Agia Triada and Agios Stefanos are museums rather than working monastic houses. A sixth, Agios Nikolaos, has been restored and is open as a museum but unlived-in.

Kalambaka, four km from the valley of the Meteora, and **Kastraki,** about one km from the mouth of the valley, offer a wide choice of places to stay, eat and drink while visiting the monasteries.

Kalambaka is the larger of the two, a mostly modern medium-sized market town and road junction. Most hotels are on the busy main street. Kastraki, about 3 km away, is smaller and quieter, an old-fashioned village ringed by modern campsites and hotels. The rocks of the Meteora loom directly above the village.

The Olympian Pantheon

The Greek gods are endearingly human. Up on Olympus they drink, squabble, scrap, screw around and misbehave on a grand scale. Their meddling in mortal affairs is usually disastrous for the mortals, who end up blind, dead, lost or transformed into plants. The Greek gods had their own notions of fun and fair play, and they could be rather rough.

To the ancient Greeks, destiny was more important than good or evil, and the gods themselves were subject to its unalterable rule in the form of Moros, son of Night. Sensible Greeks – who could see the home of their gods from a vast distance – made the appropriate sacrifices and hoped to avoid divine intervention in their lives.

The gods were related by blood as well as marriage and it is interesting that the ancients felt incest to be such an immense sin – look what happened to Oedipus – despite the frequent brother-sister marriages between deities.

ZEUS, greatest of the gods, overthrew his father, Kronos, and freed his siblings whom the giant had swallowed. After marrying Metis, goddess of wisdom, Themis, goddess of law and a Titaness called Mnemosyne who bore him the nine Muses, Zeus married his own sister Hera, but continued to play the field with goddesses, nymphs and mortals. His most famous sanctuary is at Dodona in Epirus.

HERA, the oldest daughter of Kronos, bore Zeus two sons, Ares and Hephaestos. The centre of her cult was at Argos.

ATHENE, daughter of Zeus and Metis, was born full-grown and armed from her father's forehead after Zeus swallowed

VISITING THE MONASTERIES

With a car you can visit all the monasteries in one day. A new tarred road runs the length of the valley of the Meteora – but on foot you'll need two or three days. It's worth it – not only for an insight into Greece's deep Christian roots, often overlooked by visitors more interested in the pagan ancient world – but also for the views. From each pinnacle you can see for miles over the patchwork plain of Thessaly and off to the slopes of the Pindos. In few places in Greece does the sky seem so close and the horizon so far off.

Metis to prevent her bearing children who might overthrow him. A warrior-goddess, she protects peace and art and represents wisdom as well as courage. She is also the original girl who can run faster than her brothers, and adept at defending her chastity against randy male Olympians.

APOLLO, her half-brother, represents the sun principle, though the lesser sun-god Helios does most of the day-to-day work. He is the god of archery, divination and prophecy, sudden death and healing. The great sanctuary at Delphi was his most important shrine.

HERMES is Zeus's messenger and the god of journeys, commerce, eloquence, gambling and profit, whether dubious or legitimate.

ARES is a simple war-god. His province is dumb courage, carnage and the fury of battle. His brother **HEPHAESTOS**, the lame blacksmith and armourer of the gods, is the patron of smiths, skilled craftsmen and mechanical ingenuity. He is married to **APHRODITE**, the flighty goddess of love, marriage and sex, who cheats on him with Ares, Apollo and anything in trousers.

POSEIDON, Zeus's brother, matches the power of the earthquake with Zeus's thunderbolt and controls rivers, seas and navigation. Their third brother, **HADES**, rules the shadowy underworld. With his wife Persephone, daughter of Demeter, and the night-goddess Hecate he keeps his own court in the land of the dead.

HESTIA, goddess of the home and the hearth, appears only rarely in the main myths but in everyday life she must have been a most important deity, as was **DEMETER**, goddess of fertility and farming.

One can only wonder at the fervour – not to mention the sheer cussedness – of the first monks to claw their way to the top of the smooth-sided crags. It must have taken a very powerful faith to attempt the climb.

Unassuming on the outside, inside the monasteries are richly and elaborately decorated with frescoes, ikons and altar screens. Not an inch of the interior is unpainted and each scene tells a story, often grisly, of martyrdoms and crusades, sanctifications and torments. Here a group of sinners roast in torment; there a six-winged seraph guards the gates of heaven while the archangels select those to be admitted.

Of the five, the finest view is from **Great Meteoron**, though much of the monastery is off-limits to visitors. **Agia Triada's** lovely church of St John the Baptist teeters on the brink of its pinnacle. **Varlaam** has some of the finest frescoes in its Church of All Saints; they are the work of a painter of the Cretan school, Frankos Castellanos, painted in the 1560s and restored in 1870. If time is limited, **Agios Nikolaos**, whose rock is the lowest in the valley and the closest to the village of Kastraki below, is the most accessible and is richly decorated and uncrowded.

Opening times: 08.00–13.00, 15.00–17.00. Opening times may vary during holy days and religious festivals. *Entry fee for each monastery.*

Each house has a strict dress code: long trousers for men, skirts for women, and long sleeves for both. All are the target of throngs of coach tour visitors in the holiday season. These tend to arrive from around 10.30 onwards, but if you make an early start you will be among a mere handful of visitors.

TRAVELLING
By Road   Buses from Lamia, Larissa, Trikkala, Ioanina.

WHERE TO STAY
The A-Class **Motel Divani** is Kalambaka's most expensive hotel and in high season often fully booked. The C-Class **Aeolikos Astir** and the C-Class **Odyssion** are mid-priced alternatives and there are a number of other C-Classes, all much of a muchness, on Kalambaka's main street and central square.

Camping Kastraki and **Camping Meteora** in Kastraki are both clean, modern and efficient with swimming pools and constant hot water showers. At around half the price of the cheapest rooms, they are a good alternative for those with camping gear.

Virtually every house around the main plateia in Kastraki, within easy walking distance of the first of the monasteries, seems to offer **rooms to rent** at high prices in summer.

FOOD AND DRINK
A limited choice of run of the mill restaurants on Kalambaka's main plateia and more basic kafeneion food in the centre of Kastraki. The restaurants at the campsites – open to outsiders – are as good as any.

EPIRUS

The Backbone of Greece

The great mountain ranges of Epirus and Pindos, Greece's westernmost region, run from the Gulf of Corinth to the Albanian border, climbing steadily. These mountains were the heartland of some of the fiercest resistance to Turkish conquest and the bloodiest battles and atrocities of the Civil War. Like so many of Greece's remoter regions, they have gradually become depopulated and villages and towns are few and far between. The scenery, especially of the Pindos range, is wild and beautiful. White-water rivers carve their way through kilometre-deep canyons and snow lies year-round on peaks above the tree-line. Melting snow waters pastures of spring wildflowers here as late as July, long after the sun has parched the lowlands dry, and snow lies year-round in pockets on the highest peaks.

The Vlach and Sarakatsan nomads who once grazed their flocks in the high pastures have settled down and lost most of their distinctive sub-cultures in the past two generations, but there are still wolves, bear and lammergeier vultures in the remotest regions. Hardly touched by tourism, these mountains are one of Europe's last pocket wildernesses.

METSOVO

Perched 1,160 m above sea level, Metsovo is the eastern gateway to Epirus. It is an attractive village of restored traditional houses with breathtaking views down into the foothills south and west. Dominating one of the key passes of the Pindos range through which the main east-west highway passes, it was founded by the Romans as a strategic fortress. Many of its inhabitants are Koutsovlachs, former semi-nomadic herders whose language has Latin roots. Their local costume – black or dark-blue baggy pants, shirt and embroidered waistcoat with heavy wooden clogs each bearing a red pom-pom – is worn only on festivals.

Attractive though it is, Metsovo is dedicated to tourism – every second building on its main street seems to be a souvenir store peddling goat-bells, rugs and faded traditional costumes – and can feel a bit museum-like. Indeed, it has a fine local museum: the 18th-century Tositsa Mansion, deeded to the town by its owners as a Museum of Popular Art, and well worth visiting for an insight into Epirot customs, costumes and history.

TRAVELLING
By Road Frequent buses from Athens, Kalambaka, Trikkala and Ioanina.

WHERE TO STAY
Pension Flocas is a comfortable, B-Class pension with ten rooms, the best-value accommodation in Metsovo. The C-Class **Galaxy** is a comfortable mid-priced hotel and there are a number of other C-Class establishments including the **Olympic** and the larger **Egnatia**, which is the biggest hotel in town. The A-Class **Diasselo** is the most expensive, but smaller and less anonymous than many.

FOOD AND DRINK
No great choice: two or three adequate restaurants on the airy main square, all of the microwave and grill school of cuisine.

IOANINA
The lakeside capital of Epirus has more going for it than many of Greece's regional towns. Ringed by mountains and overlooking Pamvotis, one of Greece's largest lakes, Ioanina retains a handful of historic buildings from its turbulent past under the Turks. Its surviving mosques have lost their pointed peaks and are nesting sites for storks, but the walls and bastions of its fortress, the Frourio, are a reminder of the power of Ali Pasha, the 19th-century bey who ruled Epirus.

The oldest and most interesting streets are those in and around the Frourio, built between the 14th and 17th centuries. Ali's wooden palace was destroyed during the siege of 1821/22 but the Fethiye Mosque, built in 1430, survives, though badly neglected, within the walls of the inner citadel. The Frourio is surrounded on three sides by water, and opposite the Fethiye Mosque at its northern tip the Mosque of Aslan Pasha is now a Museum of Popular Art with a serendipitous collection of Epirot odds and ends.

Outside the walls, the old bazaar quarter with its narrow lanes of ramshackle workshops, cafés and barbers has seen few changes this century apart from the appearance of motor vehicles and electric light.

Boats leave from the small quay on the north shore of the fortress promontory – beside Plateia Mavili – for **Nisi**, the pretty island in the lake whose 17th-century village, built by exiles from the tumultuous Mani region, is protected as a traditional settlement. Of the six little monasteries on the island, two are worth a look: Filanthropinon has fine 16th-century frescoes and Agios Panteleimon, where the Sultan's troops finally assassinated Ali Pasha, is an interesting tiny museum of the period.

TRAVELLING
By Air Daily flights from Athens.

By Road Frequent buses from Trikala, Kalambaka, Metsovo. Several daily from Athens and Igoumenitsa. Car hire available.

WHERE TO STAY
Hotel Metropole, Od. Krystali 2, offers the cheapest decent accommodation. **Hotel Tourist**, Od. Koletti 18, is a mid-range C-Class and the nearby **Astoria** a cheaper C-Class **Hotel Bretania**, on the central Plateia Dimokratias, is the most expensive, a fine old-style provincial hotel which can be noisy until the traffic stops. There is an excellent lakeside campsite at **Camping Limnopoulo**, about ten minutes' walk along the lake shore from Plateia Mavili.

FOOD AND DRINK
Plateia Mavili, just north of the Frourio, is the best place to eat and drink. Take your pick from half a dozen lakeside cafés and restaurants offering lake fish, grills and traditional dishes. Patronized almost entirely by locals, the plateia restaurants bustle every night and the food is excellent.

For aficionados of the traditional Greek kafeneion the **Hotel Bretania** has a cavernous old café on its ground floor, while the big café **Ellas** on Pl. Dimokratias is an old-fashioned ouzo, tavli and cards venue, full of rickety tables and an almost equally rickety clientele.

THE ZAGOROCHORIA AND MT TIMFI

North of Ioanina lies some of Greece's most spectacular mountain scenery. A handful of distinctive hill villages huddles below Mt Timfi in the Zagoria region, around 45 km from Ioanina. Below them is the Vikos Gorge, a winding canyon roughly 18 km long and more than 1000m deep in places. The Vikos-Aoos National Park is one of Europe's last regions of near wilderness and the whole region is a delight for lovers of wild landscapes and solitude.

More than 40 villages – known as the Zagorochoria – are scattered around this wild and desolate region. The easiest to get to are **Monodhendri**, at the southern end of the Vikos Gorge, and the twin villages of **Mikro Papingo** and **Mega Papingo**, at the northern end. Like so many traditional Greek settlements — until recently built entirely of local materials — these villages look as if they have grown, like coral or swallows' nests, out of the bedrock. Walled and roofed with slabs of mountain granite, the houses of these villages merge with the rocky outcrops around them and they are hard to spot from a distance. They would be worth visiting just for their dizzying alpine views and remarkable vernacular architecture, which has not yet been marred by philistine new building, but they are also natural base camps for anyone planning to walk the Vikos Gorge or hike Mt Timfi.

Monodhendri is a spread-out village whose main plateia, dominated by a solidly-built church and a giant plane tree, is some distance below the main road. Balanced on the lip of the Vikos Gorge, it has splendid views of the huge peaks of Pindos to the east and is surrounded by mixed woods of fir and beech. Makro Papingo, at the other end of the canyon, has an even more spectacular location under the huge crags and peaks of Mt Timfi.

TRAVELLING
Infrequent buses from Ioanina. The best way to explore the region is by car: the roads connecting the villages with the main road from Ioanina are good, though steep and winding.

WHERE TO STAY
Several guesthouses are part of the NTOG traditional settlements programme and can be booked through the NTOG. **Monodendri Pension** (Tel: 0653 61233) has good, mid-priced rooms in a traditional building on the main road. Across the road, **Pension Astir Pallas** has good, slightly cheaper rooms in a modern building. At **Megalo Papingo** there is an NTOG traditional guesthouse (expensive) and lovely old-fashioned rooms rented by Kalliope Ranga in an old family house. If both are full, try asking at the café-bar on the main street run by the Christodoulou family.

FOOD AND DRINK
Choice is limited but the food good. Pleasant café by the plateia at Monodhendri, and the **Pension Monodhendri** has a snack-bar restaurant. Kalliope Ranga serves meals and drinks to guests in her courtyard. Ioannis Christodoulou runs a small café-bar-cum-shop on the cobbled main street and a small restaurant opposite.

The Lion of Ioanina

The Turkish-Albanian warlord Ali Pasha — "The Lion of Ioanina" — was one of the most colourful figures of pre-independence Greece. Nominally a vassal of the Sultan, Ali was a valued general of the Ottomans who seized control of Ioanina in 1788 and made it the capital of a tiny state which was only nominally subject to the Grand Porte. His ruthless crushing of the Souliot Greeks of the mountain villages did not prevent Britain and France dallying with Ali, and in 1817 Britain sold him the port of Parga which it had acquired during the Napoleonic Wars. At the height of his power, Ali controlled the mainland west of the Pindos, held uneasy sway over the klephts of the high ranges, and through his equally ambitious sons had a say in the affairs of much of the Peloponnese. Byron, who visited Ali's court, paints an engaging picture of an oriental princeling with all the charm of a king cobra. Less easily hypnotized than some of Ali's more gullible Western guests, Byron knew of his capacity for little unpleasantnesses such as the drowning of his son's Greek mistress, who refused to sleep with the old ram, the murder by torture of the klepht-captain Katsandonis and more. Even by the undemanding standards of Ottoman Turkey, Ali Pasha was not a nice man. Ironically, it was Ali's overweening ambition which laid the ground for the successful risings of 1821 and the War of Independence. By 1820, the Turkish Sultan had had enough of the uppity Pasha and Ioanina was besieged for more than a year by a huge army led by the Grand Vizier. Ali was eventually hounded down and shot dead on the lake island not far from Ioanina. While the Turks were at each other's throats, revolt swept through Greece and on March 25 1821 — a date commemorated by street names in every Greek city — Bishop Germanos of Patras and the Maniot chief Petrobey Mavromichalis raised the banners of rebellion in the Peloponnese.

THE IONIAN COAST

The coast of Epirus, facing west to Corfu and the Ionian Islands, is rugged for much of its length and there are few beaches, villages or approaches to the sea. **Igoumenitsa**, the northernmost town of any size, is of interest only as a ferry port for boats to Corfu and Italy. Rebuilt after severe war damage, it is charmless but functional. There are plenty of hotels should you have to stay the night while waiting for onward connections.

TRAVELLING
By Sea Several ferries daily to Corfu; frequent ferries to Paxi, Ithaki and Kefallonia. Daily international ferries to Brindisi and Ancona in Italy.

By Road Frequent buses to Ioanina and points east and southward to Arta and Mesolonghi.

WHERE TO STAY
Hotel Jolly, Hotel Oscar, Hotel Tourist and **Hotel Astoria** are all adequate C-Class hotels conveniently close to the waterfront and ferry docks.

FOOD AND DRINK
Plenty of pizza, burger and Greek-style fast-food places on the waterfront.

PARGA

Roughly 50 km south of Igoumenitsa the charming seaside resort town of Parga is one of the pleasantest places to stay on the Ionian coast, despite an influx of package holidaymakers from June onwards. With its tall, stucco-fronted houses, pantiled roofs, narrow hilly lanes and little squares, Parga might almost be in Italy. On the promontory to the north of the lagoon-like harbour, the Venetian Kastro is all that remains of the Italian connection.

Parga is built around an island-studded crescent bay with an excellent, if crowded, beach immediately in front of the town. Even better beaches at Valtos, two km north of the town and Lihnos, three km south of Parga, add to its appeal. In the tourist season, motorboats shuttle between the beaches and the little pier midway along the Parga waterfront.

Though Parga becomes crowded in high season — and nine

Walking in Zagoria

Zagoria is Greece's best walking region, blessed by splendid scenery and cool air.

The Vikos Gorge offers one of the finest gorge walks in Europe. From Papingo to Monodhendri it's a stiff eight hours for a fit walker, over a path which frequently loses its way among pebbles and boulders. You may not see another soul, and it is not advisable to go alone: even a sprained ankle would be a disaster. But it's worth it for the silence, the bare cliffs soaring hundreds of metres above green woods, streams and pools full of trout and tiny yellow-bellied toads, and if you're lucky the sight of a lammergeier soaring high above. Roughly midway between the two villages a clear, cold stream enters the gorge, forming icily refreshing pools. The last hour to Monodhendri is the real sickener: the path zig-zags steeply up near-vertical slopes and only the inspiring knowledge that there is cold beer waiting in the plateia keeps you going.

Zagoria's other accessible walk, to the saddle of Mt Timfi, also starts at Papingo. Also known as Gamila, the mountain peaks at 2497m. Like the Vikos, it is stiff but practicable for any reasonably fit walker and is well signposted and marked (with red painted dots) by the Greek Mountaineering Society (EOS) which also runs a mountain refuge on Timfi. Allow a full eight hours for the round trip, or stay overnight at the refuge, taking sleeping bags and food: the keys are kept at Mr Christodoulou's café on the main street in Papingo. The refuge perches on a ridge immediately below the craggy summit of Timfi. The views in all directions can only be described as awesome, with wheeling lammergeiers above the crags as a grace note. Below the refuge, a shepherd family herds flocks in summer in a lush, swampy valley. Descending into this and climbing the slopes on the far side – heading for the stone cairn you can see on the horizon – you come after an hour's walk to a crystal clear tarn called Drakolimeno, "the dragon lake". At the very lip of a dizzying drop into the Vikos Gorge, it is indeed just where you would expect to find dragons. The lake is infested by tiny alpine newts, very like minute dragons with vivid flame-coloured stomachs: local legend holds that they were once real dragons, turned into their present harmless form by some forgotten saint or hermit. Standing by the cairn at the cliff's edge, with nothing but peaks on all horizons, you might be in any century; and that alone is worth the walk.

out of ten fishing boats have acquired the canvas sun-awnings which indicate more tourists than fish – it is a good base for exploring the region as well as for a beach holiday. The ancient sites of Efyra, Kassopi, Nikopolis and Dodona are within easy reach and local tour agencies operate boat trips to Paxi and on the Aheronda river delta nearby.

TRAVELLING
By Road   Buses from Igoumenitsa and Preveza. Car and moped hire available.

By Sea   Daily caique to Paxi in high season.

WHERE TO STAY
Accommodation can be hard to find from July to September, when most hotels are block-booked by tour companies. Off-peak, try the C-Class **Alcyon, Avra** or **Olympic**, all small, comfortable and reasonably priced. For those with a tent, **Camping Parga** on the southern edge of the resort is quiet, friendly, well-run and shaded by olive trees.

FOOD AND DRINK
The Parga waterfront, Od. Arxartisias, is lined with good restaurants. For good value seafood, try **Restaurant No. 2. Souli**, next door, is a pleasant traditional grill restaurant. About 50 m away from the waterfront, on the little square at Od. Ag. Kosma, **Restaurant Oi Psarades** is a slightly cheaper fish-restaurant.

The **Island Music-Bar** is a cheerful roof-terrace bar looking over the bay to the spotlit churches on Parga's little island. **Rudy's Bar** is another rooftop drinks place with a pleasantly ramshackle air.

SOUTH TO MESOLONGHI

Beyond Parga the coast and countryside are uninteresting and the towns mainly modern, with little to catch the visitor's eye. The most obvious feature on the map is the Amvrakikos Gulf, a shallow, narrow-mouthed lagoon fringed by saltmarsh, but its stagnant-looking waters are a disappointment to anyone hoping for exotic beaches and sheltered swimming.

Preveza, on a promontory at the mouth of the gulf, is an unspectacular town with few facilities for the visitor. Ferries shuttle across the gulf to **Vonitsa**, whence there are buses for points south and over the causeway to the nearby island of Lefkada.

Inland, the main road runs through **Arta**, the second biggest town in Epirus. A riverside site by the Arahtos,

Dodona

Dodona, one of ancient Greece's holiest sanctuaries, remains so empty and unvisited that it has the wonderful impact of a personal discovery. No other great site has such tranquillity, ringed by bare mountains and miles from the nearest town. Goats graze around the ancient ruins, storks stalk through the surrounding fields, and with luck you may have the site to yourself. Originally an oracle of the pre-Olympian Great Goddess, Dodona may be Greece's oldest. It became a shrine to Zeus after the arrival of the Dorians around 1300 BC, and its barefoot priests interpreted the god's messages in the sound of wind in the oakleaves or a metal whip blown against a brass bowl. Ancient though the site is, the best-preserved buildings are more recent: the foundations of a temple and the sacred house of Zeus are less impressive than the large arena built by the Macedonians in the third century BC and used by the Romans for drama and contests.

The sanctuary became a Christian basilica — whose foundations can be seen — in the fourth century, but a Gothic raid in the sixth century removed Dodona from the map until its rediscovery by a Greek amateur archaeologist in 1876.

a larger than usual complement of Byzantine and medieval buildings, and a fine arched bridge — the oldest in Greece — make it one of Greece's most attractive provincial towns.

The 13th-century Church of Panagia Paragoritissa is a unique blend of Western and Orthodox architecture and is now an archaeological and medieval museum. With its collection of domes, it looks vaguely like a miniature Kremlin: inside, the main dome is supported by a system of cantilevers and beams whose complexity can lead one to suspect that the architect's experience in episcopal geometry was limited. The city's rulers — the Despots of the Angelos family, who ruled here after the fall of Constantinople itself to the Latin Crusaders in 1204 — built their riverside fortress in part from fragments of earlier classical buildings, giving its walls and battlements a slightly haphazard air which oddly complements the makeshift eccentricity of Paragoritissa. Other surviving buildings from the 13th

Efyra and the Necromantion

The Sanctuary of Persephone and Hades, where pilgrims communed with the dead, exerts a fascination belied by its first impression. On a low hill above the Aheronda river — the Acheron or Styx which flowed into or through the underworld of the myths — the ground-plan reveals the antechambers, labyrinth and finally the underground chamber where baffled seekers received their messages from beyond.

In Homer's time the site was an island in a lake fed by the river, but the lake has dried and the Aheronda shifted in its course leaving it high and dry. The site is about 20 km from Parga and the easiest way to see it is by one of the tours run by local tour companies. The boat trip from Parga to the Necromantion via the Aheronda delta is one of the best options. Otherwise, rent a car or moped at Parga to see the site on your own, or get off the Igoumenitsa/Preveza bus on the main road at the village of Kastri: the site, five km away, is signposted.

century, when Epirus was an independent Byzantine statelet, are the churches of Ag. Theodoron and Ag. Vasilios in Arta itself and the monasteries of Kato Panagia, two km from the town, and Vlachairnon, not far away in the Arahtos valley. Richly decorated mosaic work and a flock of peacocks make Kato Panagia one of Greece's most attractive small monasteries.

South of the Gulf, the coast is unpromising and **ASTAKOS**, the only place of any size, is of interest only as the ferry port for boats to Ithaki and Kefalonia. Inland, **Agrinio**, a commercial centre and farming town, is a hub of the Greek tobacco industry and the last stop before the port of *Messolongi*. A sad anti-climax, Messolongi's uninspired modern buildings belie its romantic, Byronic past — though its steamy summer heat and penetrating damp the rest of the year are reminders of the fever which did for the greatest of the Philhellenes.

TRAVELLING

By Road Frequent buses between Preveza and points north, and Vonitsa and points south and east, and across the causeway to Lefkada; frequent buses between Messolongi and Nafpaktos and points east.

Nikopolis

Seven km north of Preveza stands Nikopolis, the "Victory City" built by Octavian to celebrate his trouncing of Mark Anthony and Cleopatra at Actium. The victory made him the undisputed successor to Julius Caesar, soon to be the Emperor Augustus and ultimately — on his death — to be declared a god. But the building of Nikopolis, much of it by cannibalizing earlier classical buildings for stone, was an act of typical Roman imperial arrogance. It never became a city of great importance, was sacked by barbarian invaders and rebuilt under the Byzantines, then finally sacked by a Bulgar army in 1040 and abandoned.

The site is sprawling and impressive. The main features are massive fortifications and a huge stadium, but Nikopolis sadly lacks the unerring sense of landscape which marks more ancient Greek sites. It is a monument to one man's ego, rather than to the culture of a whole people. In this setting, the sixth-century mosaics of the Basilica of Dometios are a welcome change from Roman military engineering. The site museum houses an undistinguished collection of Roman odds and ends.

By Sea Shuttle ferries connect Preveza and Vonitsa across the mouth of the Amvrakikos Gulf. Rio/Andirio shuttle ferries connect the region with Patras and the Peloponnese. Frequent ferries from Astakos to Ithaki and Kefallonia.

WHERE TO STAY

In Arta, the B-Class **Xenia Hotel** is the best choice for its location within the walls of the medieval fortress. The C-Class **Anessis** is an alternative.

FOOD AND DRINK

In this untouristy part of Greece, cafés and restaurants are plentiful but undistinguished: toast, pizza, burger and gyros eateries are ubiquitous.

Byron at Mesolongi

The quintessential romantic, Lord Byron, undoubtedly rendered Greece the greatest possible service by dying of fever in this undistinguished little town. Byron was no soldier, but his love of Greece led him to spend much of his fortune on arming the freedom fighters of the War of Independence. The Greek leaders showed their gratitude by making him commander of their raggle-taggle army of 5000 guerrillas, bandits, Phillhellenes and soldiers of fortune. But Byron never led them into battle. While the argumentative leaders of the rising bickered and the campaign bogged down, he caught fever in the unhealthy climate of Mesolongi and died in bed instead of going out in a blaze of glory on the battlefield as he had so ardently hoped. Nevertheless, the death of a man who was a cult hero throughout Europe mobilized opinion in favour of the independence struggle and forced France and Britain to take notice. He is remembered: Greek schoolchildren still learn about "O Lordos Vironos" along with the other heroes of Greece's long fight for freedom, streets and squares are named after him all over Greece and his heart is buried in Mesolongi beneath his statue.

MACEDONIA AND THRACE
The Far North

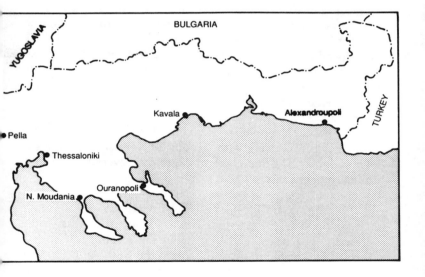

Greece's northernmost provinces border Yugoslavia, Bulgaria and Turkey. Macedonia is bounded roughly by the great ranges of Grammos in the east and Olympus in the south, and is a mountain region with a strong identity of its own. Macedonians – the descendants of Alexander the Great – are taller and fairer than the Greeks of the islands and the south, and are often blond-haired and blue- or grey-eyed.

Thrace, divided from Macedonia by the Nestos river, is less mountainous, with hills backing a coastal plain which faces south and extends east to the border with Turkey.

THESSALONIKI

Greece's second city, the capital of Macedonia, is the gateway to all of north-eastern Greece, within easy striking distance of the beach resorts of Halkidiki, the monasteries of Mount Athos, and the region's prime archaeological site at ancient Pella.

Built on a long sweep of harbour, Thessaloniki is an almost entirely modern town with a only a handful of medieval Byzantine and Turkish buildings to interest the visitor. Much of Thessaloniki's cosmopolitan character was destroyed early this century, first by a disastrous earthquake which levelled the city in 1917, then by the expulsion of its large Turkish population and finally during World War Two by the extermination under the Germans of its huge Jewish community.

Less hectic, less polluted and better looking than sprawling Athens, less flooded with groups of tourists in summer, Thessaloniki is a fine place to experience everyday life in a modern Greek city.

GETTING YOUR BEARINGS

Thessaloniki is a long, thin city, laid out in an east—west crescent. The heart of the city is in the rectangle of streets formed by Langada/Dodekanisson in the west, Ag Dimitriou to the north and Panepistimiou/Ethnikis Aminis in the east. Its south side is the city's waterfront promenade, Nikis, with Plateia Eleftheria (Freedom Square) at its west end and the White Tower, Thessaloniki's most visible historic building, at the east end.

DON'T MISS . . .

The White Tower
This round, 16th-century Turkish fortress is all that remains

of Turkish "Salonica" except for a handful of tumbledown old houses in the back streets.

The Archaeological Museum
Leof. Stratou (opposite the White Tower). The museum houses a rich collection of finds from the ancient Macedonian site at Vergina. Open daily 08.00 to 19.00.

ALSO WORTH SEEING . . .
Within the central rectangle, Thessaloniki's other buildings of note include the church of **Agios Georgios**, a fourth century AD domed building intended originally as a tomb for the Roman ruler Galerius but soon afterwards converted into a church. Its mosaics are from the time of the authoritarian Emperor Theodosius, who in the late fourth century was the first Byzantine ruler to set standards for Christian intolerance of other faiths. Its surviving minaret indicates its use as a mosque in the Turkish centuries. Nearby, close to the east end of Odos Egnatia, is the Arch of Galerius, built to commemorate this third century emperor's victories in Asia. Egnatia is part of the Egnatian Way, the Roman Empire's main east-west highway through Greece to Constantinople.

Thessaloniki also has a handful of other Roman-period sites, including what remains of Galerius's palace on what is now Plateia Navarino, and the foundations of the Roman market and stadium at Plateia Dikastirion.

TRAVELLING
By Air Scheduled flights from London several times weekly. Frequent daily flights to Athens.

By Road The fast National Road connects Thessaloniki with Athens; fast frequent bus connections to all major Greek cities of the northern mainland. There are international bus lines to main European cities via Yugoslavia and there are also international buses to Turkey.

By Rail Several trains daily to Athens and points between.
International trains via Yugoslavia are best avoided. There are also daily trains to Istanbul via Alexandroupolis.

By Sea Weekly ferries to the Sporades, main Cycladic islands and Crete and to the North-East Aegean islands and northern Dodecanese.

WHERE TO STAY

Egnatia, running smack through the centre of town, is the best place to hunt for accommodation. Like most Greek main streets it can be noisy, but you are unlikely to want to stay more than a couple of nights at most, and the central location compensates. **Hotel Aegeon Egnatia** 19; **Grande Bretagne**, Egnatia 46; **Mandrino**, at the corner of Antigonidon and Egnatia; and **Delta**, at 13 Egnatia, are all reliable C-Class hotels, and between them are a number of cheaper and scruffier D- and E-Class places.

FOOD AND DRINK

There are a host of souvlaki and fast food places on Egnatia. At the east end of Nikis, opposite the White Tower, is a clutch of good psistaria grills. The smarter café-bars are concentrated around Plateia Eleftheria and Plateia Aristotelou, two blocks east of Eleftheria facing the sea on Nikis.

WESTERN MACEDONIA

Much of the west is mountainous and distinctly off the beaten tourist trails: explorers and walkers will find enough to occupy them indefinitely. Among the less inaccessible regions, the mountains around the small regional capital of **Florina** hold some of Greece's biggest lakes. **Kastoria**, further west, is built on a peninsula on the lake of the same name: the town contains some dignified Macedonian mansion houses. Carved ceilings and shutters are a feature of these 18th-century buildings and their enormous stone hearths are a reminder that this is a region of harsh winters. Kastoria also has many Byzantine churches noted for their frescoes: Agii Anargyri, Taxiarchis, Ag, Stefanos, Ag. Nikolaos, Ag. Athanasios and Panagia Koumblelidiki are among the more lavish of more than 70 churches.

The Odos Ethnikos or National Road, Greece's major north-south highway, runs the length of Western Macedonia's Aegean coast. Though there are frequent campsites dotted along this shore, its beaches are disappointing.

For most visitors, though, the main point of coming to Macedonia is to see the key archaeological sites at Vergina and Pella. Fortunately, these are relatively accessible, within 40 km of Thessaloniki.

PELLA & VERGINA

Philip II's fourth-century BC capital is easily reached on the main road to Edessa (buses half-hourly from Thessaloniki). The site, discovered only in the late 1950s, is still being excavated. The most interesting discoveries so far are the pebble mosaics of the royal court. Three of these are still on view where they were discovered, the rest in the museum at the site.

Vergina, not to be confused with the modern village of Veria nearby, is an even more ancient Macedonian site, identified as Aigai, the Macedonians' first capital, and has been fully excavated only recently. The tombs of Philip II and other Macedonian kings have been found here. There is much less to see here than at Pella (the more recent finds are in the Thessaloniki museum and the Royal Tombs are still being excavated and are closed to visitors). The main features are the Tomb of Veryina, with marble doors and a carved throne on which the body of the entombed king presumably sat, and the cluttered remnants of the Palace.

The Jews of Salonika

When Thessaloniki fell into Greek hands in 1913 it was neither predominantly Greek nor Turkish but Jewish — a cosmopolitan, westward-looking business community with its own banks, newspapers and a railway line, financed by Jewish entrepreneurs, running north to Belgrade to connect it with the great cities of Europe.

In 1910, the city was peopled by 80,000 Ladino-speaking Jews, 35,000 Christians and 30,000 Turks. The Jews had settled in Thessaloniki in the mid-15th century, fleeing persecution in Christian Spain. In the 19th century they were reinforced by refugees from pogroms in Russia. They founded schools and newspapers and made the city the Ottoman Empire's foremost industrial and financial centre, while playing a leading role in introducing reformist and socialist ideas into the Balkans.

This unique society's golden age was doomed by the surge of 19th- and 20th-century nationalism. The ramshackle but oddly tolerant Ottoman Empire was being dismantled by former vassal-states which were fiercely Christian and looked with suspicion and hostility on other faiths. Huge numbers of Greeks flooded into Thessaloniki after the war of 1922/23, altering the balance drastically. By 1933 there were 180,000 Greeks and fewer than 70,000 Jews. There was resentment of perceived Jewish wealth and insularity. And there was the lure of Palestine, where the Zionist movement had begun encouraging Jews to return.

The Germans came in 1941. According to a witness at the trial of holocaust-overseer Eichmann, the Germans at once gave non-Jews a free hand to take what they wanted from Jewish shops. Then they herded Thessaloniki's Jews into squalid ghettoes before taking 56,000 to death camps. At the end of the war fewer than 2,000 remained. Most of these left for Israel after its founding shortly afterward. There is little to show they were ever here. Today's Austrian Chancellor Kurt Waldheim, a ranking officer in the German intelligence corps while all this was going on, says that he failed to notice the disappearance of all these people.

To get to Vergina, take the Veria bus from Thessaloniki and change at Veria, about 20 minutes' ride away.

EASTERN MACEDONIA AND HALKIDIKI

East of Thessaloniki, Macedonia's coastline plunges south like a three-fingered hand pointing into the Aegean. This is Halkidiki, and two of its three peninsulas have some of Greece's best beaches. Most of these are thoroughly developed, and the "fishermen's hamlets" enthusiastically listed by local tourist office literature have suffered the fate of most such villages and are now thriving resorts, many of them with huge campsites catering to an influx of German and Austrian families who drive to Greece in summer.

Kassandra, the westernmost of the Halkidiki peninsulas, is virtually solid with visitors from one end of the peninsula to the other, a disappointment to anyone hoping for untouched remote beaches. The busiest resorts are at Possidi and Akti Sani on the west coast and at Kriopigi and Hroussou on the east, all of which have luxury campsites. Between Hroussou, which is close to Kassandra's southern tip, and Polihrono the beaches are less crowded. To compensate for the crowds, Kassandra's beaches really are excellent and visitors late in the season will be rewarded with white sand and warm water. On the other hand, the peninsula has little to offer except beaches – its hinterland is unexciting pinewoods and its villages have largely been submerged by tourism.

Sithonia, the middle peninsula, is considerably less busy – 40 km further away from Thessaloniki, its beaches are not quite up to the standard of Kassandra's white sand, especially at Metamorfossi, the northernmost village-resort on its west coast. A little further down the west coast, though, big-scale tourism is personified in Porto Carras, a giant tourism complex. Neighbouring Nea Marmaras is a mass of campsites with literally thousands of summer visitors, so between the two there is little peace and quiet

A Turbulent Century

A century ago, Macedonia was much more mixed than it is today, people by Greeks, Slavs, and Bulgars, all of them calling themselves "Macedonians". As Turkish power waned and the empire was carved up by the emerging Balkan states, Greece and Bulgaria vied to take over the province. From the 1890s onward, a socialist guerrilla movement — the Interior Macedonian Revolutionary Organization — campaigned for an independent Macedonia. Photographs show IMRO partisans — called komitadjis — as fiercely whiskered warriors with gunbelts crossed over their embroidered waistcoats, tasselled caps and pistols and daggers thrust through their belts. They and the Greek guerrillas who favoured union with Greece spent as much time bushwhacking each other as fighting the Turks, and to make matters still more complex Bulgaria sponsored a third grouping seeking to unite Macedonia with Bulgaria. They and IMRO rose in arms in 1902 and 1903, but the crisis came in 1912, by which time Turkey was weakened by revolution. In October, the tiny Balkan kingdom of Montenegro attacked Turkey's frontier in Albania: on general principles, Greece, Serbia and Bulgaria piled in too, each determined to seize as much turf as possible, and on November 8 Crown Prince Constantine led the Greek Army into Thessaloniki, barely beating the Bulgarians to it.

The Bulgarians had done most of the fighting in the First Balkan War and they took most of the spoils, including much of Thrace. The following year, their allies turned on them, and in the Second Balkan War Greece drove Bulgaria out of Thrace and occupied almost all of the province: the frontiers between Greece and Turkey were defined after the disastrous war of 1922/23.

here. Sithonia's east coast has far fewer big beaches to offer, though plenty of smaller, secluded ones which you can reach if you have your own transport: oddly, few of the campsite holidaymakers, most of whom come by car, make the effort to do so. Sarti, midway up the east coast, has a long sand and pebble beach and has escaped the brunt of development, with rooms for rent, a choice of relaxed tavernas and little else.

THE HOLY MOUNTAIN

There could hardly be a bigger contrast between the bouncing bronzed bosoms of the Kassandra and Sithonia beaches and the bewhiskered celibates of **Mount Athos**. The monkish peninsula is an anomaly, a virtually self-governing theocracy within Greece, populated entirely by monks and lay brethren and off-limits not only to women but to female domestic animals.

Holy men began to settle the peninsula as early as the seventh century. In 885 Emperor Basil I ruled that only monks and hermits might live there, and by 1046 it was confirmed as a Holy Mountain by Emperor Constantine IX Monomachos. The monks themselves claim that some monasteries were founded by Constantine the Great as early as the fourth century AD.

Athos suffered from piracy and pillage during the break-up of the Byzantine Empire but after the fall of Constantinople was able to arrive at an accommodation with the Turkish Sultans, who placed the monasteries under their protection in return for submission. Nevertheless, like the Church elsewhere in Greece, the monasteries helped to keep the flame of national identity alight and played an important part in the struggle for independence.

Athos was never a Greek monopoly. It received monks from Serbia and other Balkan kingdoms. Russian Czars and Orthodox Balkan princes sent wealth, relics and sometimes sons to the monasteries. As the Turkish Empire began to crumble in the 19th century there was intrigue on an international scale between Russian, Bulgarian and Greek factions, and the Czar wanted Athos to become an international zone or Russian protectorate. It finally became part of Greece in 1913. After the Russian Revolution, fleeing Russian monks brought wealth and relics to Athos and swelled its numbers.

The monasteries are of two kinds – coenobitic, in which shelter, work, food and prayer are communal, and idiorrhythmic communities, in which the monks pray and live together but eat and work separately. Coenobitic houses are more strictly organized, and ruled by an abbot and a council of elders elected by the monks; idiorrhythmic monasteries are governed by a council of superiors elected for life and two or three trustees appointed each year.

Some 20 monasteries are still lived in. Athos has a larger number of chapels, hermitages and little outlying communities of monks, each of which is dependent on the bigger monasteries.

Sketae are loose communities of monks chiefly occupied with farming and handicrafts; the kellion is a chapel-farm with its own small piece of land, lived in by three or four monks from a parent monastery; similar is the kalyve, a chapel-community of a few monks living and working together.

A kathsisma is a one-monk chapel close to the parent monastery, while a hesychasterion is an isolated hermitage, often a remote cliff-cave, lived in only by monks who seek the greatest austerity. All are ruled by a Holy Assembly of 20 meeting at Karyes twice a year, and by a Holy Community of 20 – one from each monastery – which is elected annually.

Around 1300 monks live on the mountain, and after years of decline there has been something of an influx of new members in recent years.

Athos is closed not just to women but to anything female. Men can visit the mountain, but must apply for a special permit from the Northern Ministry in Thessaloniki . . . You can, however, stay at **Ierissos**, an east-facing beach village just north of the isthmus which is the frontier of the holy mountain, and from which there are summer boat tours round Athos. If women are on board, they must stay a minimum of 500 m offshore.

Kavala, a modern town, is unexciting, though a Byzantine-Turkish citadel above the harbour relieves the monotony. Its older harbour-front, too, is busy with boats and pleasant enough. However, if you are here you almost certainly passing through – either to **Thassos**, only 17 km away, or to the Roman-Byzantine archaeological site at **Philippi**, scene of Octavian's victory over Brutus and Cassius in 42 BC.

First a Macedonian city, it was an important stop on the artery of the Via Egnatia. The archaeological site is some 14 km away from Kavala, with at least 12 buses a day. These go on to the farming town of Drama, an alternative place to stay either before or after visiting Philippi. Philippi itself has a Roman forum, two Byzantine cathedrals, and a Roman amphitheatre carved out of the hillside. The biggest and most impressive surviving building, however, is the Roman latrine, with 50 marble thrones. The site is overlooked by a Byzantine fort.

TRAVELLING
By Road   Buses from Thessaloniki to all major towns. Limited choice of car rental in Thessaloniki.

WHERE TO STAY
Halkidiki   Resort hotels, pensions, campsites and rooms to rent at virtually all beaches on Kassandra and Sithonia peninsulas.

Florina   Hotel Antigone is a reasonable C-Class; there are a number of more expensive B-Class hotels.

Kastoria   Kastoria has a large choice of B- and C-Class hotels but is short on cheaper pension-style accommodation.

Kavala   Vournelis is a decent B-Class pension; **Acropolis, Esperia, Europa, Nefeli** and **Panorama** are C-Class hotels. Accommodation in Kavala can be tight in summer.

Drama   Pension Anessis is both the cheapest and most pleasant place to stay at Drama if you have just come from Philippi; otherwise there's the big B-Class **Xenia** and an equally big C-Class, the **Marianna**.

THE IONIAN ISLANDS
Seven of the Best

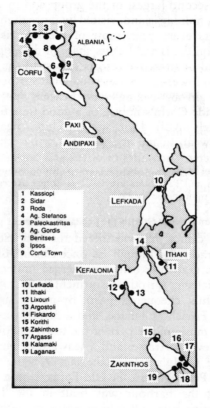

1	Kassiopi
2	Sidar
3	Roda
4	Ag. Stefanos
5	Paleokastritsa
6	Ag. Gordis
7	Benitses
8	Ipsos
9	Corfu Town

10	Lefkada
11	Ithaki
12	Lixouri
13	Argostoli
14	Fiskardo
15	Korithi
16	Zakinthos
17	Argassi
18	Kalamaki
19	Laganas

Six of the seven islands of the Ionian group lie within spitting distance of Greece's western shores, sharing a milder climate than the Aegean isles. Unlike the rest of Greece, they never became part of the Ottoman Empire, remaining in Venetian hands until the 19th century. The seventh – lumped in with the rest for administrative convenience rather than geographical proximity – lies far to the south and east, off the southern tip of the Peloponnese.

CORFU

Corfu is the second largest of the group and by far Greece's most popular holiday island, visited by more than one million holidaymakers every year, most of them British. Virtually every beach on the island has its share of development, from sprawling and unattractive resorts closest to the airport and main town to lower-key places somewhat further away. Not an island for anyone seeking empty beaches and quiet fishing villages, seaside Corfu's notion of a good time for visitors is more intimately involved with fish and chips, cheap booze and garish beachwear. Inland and into its northern hills, though, there are quieter landscapes of olives and orange groves, and tourism is less overwhelming, despite the summer cavalcades of mopeds and jeeps.

CORFU TOWN

The island's capital has weathered the tempest of tourism surprising gracefully, though its once-elegant old Italianate buildings are gradually being submerged under a tatty tide of commercialism. An odd assortment of historic buildings reflects Corfu's chequered past: Byzantine and Venetian fortresses, a French esplanade, and a British rotunda, shrine and palatial museum are part of the town's heritage.

Two medieval fortresses and a seaward defensive wall are reminders of Corfu's role as the last Venetian foothold in Greece. The **Paleo Frourio** or Old Fortress on a promontory commending the harbour was built in the 12th century under Byzantine rule and subsequently strengthened by the Venetians to meet the Turkish threat in the 16th century. A defensive canal is crossed by a causeway, but the canny Venetians hedged their bets by building a 65m tunnel which emerges inside the main city walls. The New Fortress or **Neo Frourio**, built by the Venetians in the 13th century, stands behind the modern ferry harbour.

Picking your way through Corfu Town's streets full of tourist bars and beachwear and souvenir shops, you will find most of the town's points of interest in the triangle bounded by the seafront, the Esplanade, and the crowded shopping street of Odos Nikiforou Theotoki.

The **Spianadha** or Esplanade is Corfu Town's main strolling street, a mixture of British, French, Greek and Italian which is quintessentially Corfiot. The open space was the Venetian garrison's parade ground. At its north end stands the former Royal Palace, a splendid Georgian building designed by a British military architect as the residence of the British High Commissioner. Subsequently used as a palace by the Greek royal family, it now houses the municipal library and a fine Museum of Asiatic Art.

Nearby, the British connection is marked by an Ionian Rotunda built in memory of Sir Thomas Maitland, first British High Commissioner of Corfu. The elegant arcades, houses and pavement cafés along the northern section of the Esplanade called the Liston were built in imitation of the Rue de Rivoli in Paris by Corfu's French occupiers between 1807 and 1814. The Spianadha is definitely the pleasantest place to waste time in the town.

THE EAST COAST

Corfu's biggest concentrations of battery tourism are either side of the town and its charter airport, on the island's east coast.

Heading south from town, **Benitses** is the kind of holiday sprawl described by tour brochures as "lively" — which is to say that it is noisy, very overcrowded and strictly for the party animal. Its main streets are a mass of bars, discos and restaurants and its pebbly beach hardly lives up to its reputation as a beach holiday destination. Down-market debauchery increasingly appears to be the order of the day.

Further south, **Messongi** and **Moraitiki** have blended into one noisy resort popular with young Britons. Its shingly beach is very crowded throughout Corfu's long holiday season. **Petriti** and **Boukari**, further south still, have escaped this level of development mainly because they are on rocky shores with no good beaches.

Kavos, on Corfu's southern tip, is another noisy holiday spot with a good beach and a plethora of pubs and discos.

The east coast between Corfu Town and **Ipsos** to the north is another near-solid mass of hotels and tourist bars and the beaches are nothing to write home about. Another kind of tourism is evident in the stretch of coast between Ipsos and the slightly lower-key resort of **Kassiopi** at the north-east corner of the island, where villas and self-catering apartments are more popular than big "bed factory"-style hotels.

This north-east corner of Corfu is dominated by the looming, olive-covered massif of **Mount Pantokrator** and the villages and woods of the mountain slopes are welcome escape from the frenzied hedonism of the coast resorts. It is well worth walking to the 906 m summit for the view. On a clear day you may be able to make out the Italian coast far to the west. In the opposite direction you look far into the enigmatic mountains of Albania, only a few kilometres away. The best starting point for the climb is Perithia, on the north slopes of Pantokrator.

Barbati and **Nissaki**, a few kilometres apart, are typical fishing-cum-tourism villages with small beaches nearby which become crowded during the day when hordes of trippers descend from Ipsos and elsewhere by caique.

Kassiopi, built around a sheltered natural harbour, is a pretty village despite its burgeoning holiday business. Quieter than the big east coast resorts, it is still unashamedly a tourist resort, albeit one with real character. Its shingly beach is not one of the island's best, but from May onwards a small fleet of boats plies between Kassiopi and the many small coves nearby.

THE NORTH COAST

Corfu's windy and unspectacular north coast has fallen victim to the domino effect of tourism: as hotel building sites nearer the airport and the capital have been used up, developers have sought space further afield. **Sidhari** and **Rodha** are undistinguished resorts, and Sidhari's much-hyped beaches are crowded and not very appealing. **Ag. Stefanos,** on the north-west corner of the island, and nearby **Arillas** get some of the overspill from Paleokastritsa. Their beaches can be windy, but the fertile, hilly hinterland is attractive for undemanding walks among olives and orchards.

THE WEST COAST

Corfu's best beaches and its pleasantest holiday villages are on its long west coast. While those holidaymakers who head for the Ipsos to Messongi east coast strip sometimes seem to be more bent on dedicated drinking than on soaking up Greek island ambience, the west coast is less frantic.

Paleokastritsa is Corfu's most beautiful resort, with fine beaches in a series of almost-landlocked circular bays backed by steep, wooded hills. It is a thoroughly developed resort, but hotels, restaurants and villas are less obtrusive than elsewhere, being scattered and concealed on the hillsides.

Ag. Gordis, midway down the west coast, has one of Corfu's best long sand beaches and as a result has become a very busy mainstream holiday resort with all that that implies. Further south, **Ag. Giorghios** has long, sandy (and windy) beaches nearby, though the town itself is a mixed bag of small hotels and self-catering apartments which quickly fill with package holidaymakers in the summer season.

TRAVELLING

By Air Many charter flights from British and European airports in summer. Several flights daily to/from Athens.

By Sea Several ferries a day to/from Igoumenitsa. Frequent international ferries to/from Brindisi and Ancona. Frequent ferries to the rest of the Ionian islands (not Kithira) and Patras.

Around the Island Buses run frequently between Corfu Town and points north and south, less frequently to other points on the island. Car, moped and motorbike hire available in Corfu Town and main resorts.

WHERE TO STAY

Corfu is dominated by package tourism and accommodation for independent travellers is limited. In high summer (July to September) you are unlikely to find a room unless you have booked ahead. The rest of the year accommodation in private homes is available, cheap but basic, and most flights and ferries are met by people with rooms to rent.

In Corfu Town, the room-finding service at Arseniou 43 has a huge list of approved villas and apartments to rent all over the island.

FOOD, DRINK AND NIGHTLIFE

No village on Corfu's coast is without its complement of tourist bars, nightspots and restaurants catering to the tastes of summer visitors. The signs advertising English Breakfast are ubiquitous and prices competitive.

Corfu Town **Restaurant Averof**, Proselendou, by the old harbour, is excellent value for money: traditional Greek food and pleasant atmosphere. **Restaurant Argo**, at the New Port, is expensive by Greek standards but has delicious fresh lobster and fish available daily.

Kassiopi **Calami Beach Restaurant**, a short bus ride from the village centre on the beach of the same name, overlooks the bay. Good food, on the expensive side.

Paleokastritsa **The Spiros Taverna** is the best and friendliest restaurant in the Paleokastritsa area: cheap beer and big portions of traditional Greek food at fair prices.

Moraitiki **Mayflower Restaurant**. Good food and reasonable prices; like most places here, a choice of Greek or English food and prices listed in sterling as well as drachmas. Good steak. **Cartoon Bar**. Excellent (and very potent) cocktails: cheap, cheerful and crowded, with two drinks for the price of one until 01.00.

Benitses   Marabou Restaurant, Benitses Bay. Slightly more comfortable than most, good food, worth paying a little extra for. **Babylon Disco**, Benitses harbour. Lively atmosphere, varied music and generous measures.

PAXI (PAXOS)

After Corfu's big resorts Paxi is an oasis of calm with no large hotels and only three little villages. A Venetian castle on a tiny island both dominates and shelters the harbour of Gaios, the island's main settlement, which is a charming clutter of pink and yellow stucco-fronted mansions whose colours echo the tooth-achingly sweet cakes to be found in the pierside pastry shops and tavernas.

Equally pretty is the island's second village, **Porto Longos**, with a sprinkling of tiny shingle beaches on either side of its harbour-bay. Paxi's only sand is at Mogonissi, and in summer all of the island's beaches are crowded not only with the many northern European and Italian visitors who rent villas here but with day-trippers from Corfu. Cognoscenti favour the quieter beaches on Paxi's even tinier satellite, **Andipaxi**.

TRAVELLING
Frequent boats from Corfu and the mainland.

Around the Island   Walking is a real option, as distances are short and most of Paxi's roads and tracks well shaded by olives and fruit trees. Buses connect Gaios with Porto Longos several times daily. Small boats ferry visitors to Andipaxi several times daily in summer.

WHERE TO STAY
Almost all accommodation on Paxi is in villas and apartments which are block booked by tour companies. As usual, most boats are met by a group of people with private rooms to rent, but in July and August accommodation is hard to find.

The 30-room **Paxos Beach Hotel**, about 30 minutes' walk outside Gaios, is the only proper hotel on the island. There is no accommodation on Andipaxi.

FOOD AND DRINK
Gaios   bustles with attractive restaurants, cafés and bars. Catering to

Corfu's History

Corfu and its satellite islands are the oddballs of post-Byzantine Greece. Never conquered by the Turks – though it was touch and go during the great siege of 1537 and again in 1716 – the island remained a Venetian outpost until it was taken by the French in 1807. The Union Jack, nowadays adorning the bulging buttocks of thousands of Corfu's less elegant visitors, is no stranger to the Ionian islands. In 1815 Britain declared Corfu and its dependencies a protectorate, and so they stayed until 1864 when they were finally ceded to Greece. Their villas and public buildings, such as the Maitland Rotunda, the Ionian Academy and the preposterously-named Mon Repos, the summer villa of the British commissioners, can make Corfu look like Brighton with Greek extras. The British (who else?) are credited with importing cricket, still played in Corfu Town on the Esplanade. The Ionian Academy, founded by the eccentric philhellene Lord Guildford during the British rule, was a brave attempt to revive the virtues of ancient Greece but did not survive the creation of the modern Greek state. The building stands at the north end of the Spianadha by the statue of John Capodistrias, a son of Corfu and the first prime minister of independent Greece. Sir Thomas Maitland, the first High Commissioner, is remembered for mooning at a particularly importunate petitioner for his support. And Edward Lear, the famous landscape painter, nonsense poet and limerick artist, fell in love with the island – though not with the braying of visiting British ninnies who ruined his peace at Paleokastritsa. He'd hate it now.

a higher-spending clientele than cheap and cheerful Corfu's, most offer good-quality food and drink but at prices which can seem high by Greek standards.

There are open-air bar-restaurants at **Mogonissi** and on the beach at **Andipaxi**: the latter open only during the day.

LEFKADHA (LEFKAS)

Island or mainland? Lefkas is separated from the mainland by a marshy channel a few hundred metres wide at most, spanned by a causeway and pontoon bridge, and it certainly lacks the splendid isolation which is part of the charm of a "real" island. Indeed, Lefkas owes its island status to people rather than nature: in 640 BC Corinthian settlers built a canal through the marshes to make it easier for their ships to pass.

Perhaps this is why it has not yet caught the imagination of the package tour companies who dominate its neighbours. Whatever the reason, it remains the least touristified of the major Ionian islands, with some fine clean beaches, excellent walking through fertile hills to traditional villages which see few foreigners, and an idiosyncratic if ramshackle island capital.

Lefkadha, the eponymous main town, lost its pretty Ionian buildings in the earthquakes which hit the region in 1958. No building over two storeys is allowed, and upper floors are usually built of corrugated iron – a measure which could have made them more than usually hideous but for the Greek passion for slapping a coat of candy-coloured paint on anything that stays still long enough. The harbour is popular with yachtspeople. Close to the island's northern tip, Lefkadha faces east towards the medieval Fortress of Santa Mavra – the Venetian name for Lefkadha.

The best beaches and most attractive scenery are in the northern half of the island, within fairly easy reach of Lefkadha town. **Ieropetra,** the nearest, is a long stretch of sand and shingle less than an hour's walk from town and is overlooked by a deserted hilltop monastery.

Kathisma, midway down Lefkadha's west coast, is by far the pick of the beaches but often sadly littered by campers. Close to the island's south-west tip, **Porto Katsiki** – "Goat Harbour" – is undeveloped, unusually clean and uncrowded.

The only bugbear is the west wind. When blowing strongly, it can make swimming and sunbathing unpleasant on these exposed beaches; and Lefkadha's more sheltered eastern shore is dull and marshy.

Inland Lefkadha is hilly and most easily explored on foot: a network of tracks connects the inland villages and farmhouses, but only one main road – via the hilltop village of **Karia** – crosses the island. Karia perches above a deep, fertile valley and from its hilltop you can see clear across to the mainland mountains. South and east of Karia, a series of valleys run down to the sea. This is the best part of the island for walkers, as the north and west are drier and more barren. Many of the smaller hill villages were settled by refugees from the turbulent Sfakia region of Crete who fled the Turks as Venetian power there crumbled in the 17th century. On Lefkadha's southern tip a modern lighthouse stands close to the site of a clifftop Temple of Apollo from which disappointed lovers, accused criminals and sacrificial victims plunged 70m into the sea. The poetess Sappho ended her life here, but the priests of Apollo were less suicidal – like the cliff divers of modern Mexico, they were skilled divers who managed to survive the leap.

TRAVELLING
To Lefkadha town Frequent buses from Vonitsa on the mainland. Occasional caiques to Ithaki.

Around the Island Several buses daily to Karia and around the road which rings the island, calling at all major villages.

WHERE TO STAY
Hotel Lefkas in Lefkadha is the best of a very few real hotels on the island, though there are several cheap and scruffy alternatives in town. There are good low-priced private rooms to rent at all the main beaches.

FOOD AND DRINK
Seasonal tavernas flourish on Lefkadha's beaches. In town, a well-off yachting clientele ensures the presence of a wide choice of good restaurants and bars, most quite pricy: for cheaper meals, there are plenty of less touristy restaurants and psistarias and prices decline away from the harbour.

KEFALONIA (CEPHALLONIA)

Biggest of the Ionian islands, Kefalonia is a perplexing mix of gritty functional settlements rebuilt after earthquake damage in the 1950s and attractive traditional villages which – having miraculously escaped the quakes – are now the focus of a growing tourist industry and favoured by yacht sailors. Like some of its Ionian neighbours it also has some remarkable sea caves. **Sami**, the main port, faces across to nearby Ithaki. On the opposite coast, **Argostoli** is big, boring and expensive.

On Kefalonia's northern peninsula are two much pleasanter places to stay. **Assos** is a fishing harbour just beginning to turn on to tourism but not yet completely commercialized: there is still enough life going on around the quayside to make it more than a holiday resort, for all its prettiness, its sunsets and its brooding Venetian castle to the west of the harbour. **Fiskardho**, facing east at the tip of the promontory, is even prettier and, understandably, more developed, losing some of its personality in the process. Its visitors, however, are not of the rowdy persuasion. In season, yachts can outnumber local fishing boats in its sheltered harbour and chic shops line its pastel-painted alleys.

Kefalonia's highest mountain, the 1632m **Mt Ainos**, is a national park cloaked in dark fir trees unique to the island, and much of the rest of the island is thickly wooded. The summit commands a central, fertile plain. Plagued by earthquakes throughout its history, Kefalonia is studded with ruined settlements from all eras, most of them in the south-east corner of the island.

Agios Georghios, also known as **Kastro** after its Venetian castle, is a derelict and spooky fortress-town which in Byzantine and Venetian times housed 15,000. Siege and a series of earthquakes have reduced it to a honeycomb of tottering walls and arches. At **Krani**, site of one of four ancient cities of Kefalonia, there are impressive Cyclopean walls dating from Mycenaean times. The Mycenaeans also left tombs carved into the cliffs at Mazarakata and finds from these and other ancient sites can be seen at the small Archaeological Museum in Argostoli.

Kefalonia's natural wonders are the sea caves at **Melissani** and **Dhrogarati**, on the east coast, 2 km and 4 km from Sami respectively. At Melissani a hidden grotto is filled by an underground channel which connects it with a point on the opposite side of the island, where the flow of water was used to drive mills until diverted by the 1953 earthquake.

At Dhrogarati, giant stalactites dangle from the ceiling of an even bigger cave. There is a small entry charge for each.

TRAVELLING
By Sea Frequent boats to Kefalonia from Astakos, Corfu and other isles.

By Air Charter flights from UK airports in summer. Daily flights from Athens.

Around the Island Erratic bus services. Car and motorcycle hire available at Argostoli and Fiskardho.

WHERE TO STAY
Argostoli Hotel Agios Gerasimos, mid-priced.

Fiskardho Pension Dendhrinos, low-priced and good value.

Assos No hotels but a growing number of private rooms to rent.
  Like other Ionian islands, Kefalonia sees more package holidaymakers than independent travellers and in high holiday season accommodation is hard to find.

FOOD AND DRINK
Fiskardho Plenty of good and relatively costly harbourside tavernas.

Assos Several unsophisticated but friendly fish and grill tavernas; generally less expensive.

Argostoli Like any Greek commercial town, Argostoli has heaps of fast-food places, cafés and grills, none of them remarkable. **Estiatorion Limenaki**, on the harbour, is one of the better ones.

ITHAKI (ITHACA)

Odysseus's kingdom is one of the Ionian's best boltholes for anyone weary of the relentless tourism of Corfu and its more developed satellites. Its lack of big beaches and relative inaccessibility have kept the tour companies away, but for connoisseurs of smaller islands there is a friendly, old-fashioned harbour-village, good swimming from empty pebble beaches, fine snorkelling around the rocks and plenty of well-marked walks – none of them too long and most offering a swim at the end.

Looking at the map, it seems odd that tiny Ithaki should have been Odysseus's capital, not nearby Kefalonia, which he also ruled. From **Vathi**, Ithaki's main village, it makes perfect sense. Hidden at the very end of a deep L-shaped fjord like a penny in the toe of a Christmas stocking, it's the perfect place for a pirate haven, sheltered from gales and prying eyes alike. The long quay welcomes a steady flow of cruise liners and their passengers, who keep a handful of souvenir shops in business, but after they leave it is an ideal harbour for idlers and loafers. Even more suitable for low-key idleness is **Frikes**, some distance north of Vathi, with a shingle beach, a small ferry pier and half a dozen unsophisticated tavernas.

The best beaches on Ithaki face east, on the tip of the headland which shelters Vathi from the open sea, and are accessible only by boat. Small boats run from the harbour to the beaches close to Cape Skinos in summer. Elsewhere, most swimming is from rocky coves and man-made platforms. The deep inlet on which Vathi stands almost cuts the island in two, each half dominated by a high peak. A number of coastal and hilltop sites have been claimed as Odysseus's palace. Schliemann plumped for Alakomenae, on the slopes of the low hill called Aetos. This site is now known to be too recent, and speculation centres on a location at Polis, near the undistinguished village of Stavros, where Mycenaean remains have been found. Pelikata, where a Venetian hilltop fort stood, is another possibility. All are worth walking to, less for the remains to be seen, more for the walk itself and for the views on arrival. Take a water-bottle, as Ithaki is an arid and underpopulated island.

TRAVELLING
By Sea Ferries from Astakos on the mainland and from other Ionian islands. Small boats from Fiskardho on Kefalonia in summer.

Around the Island Several daily buses round the island. Mopeds for hire in Vathi.

WHERE TO STAY
Hotel Mentor, between Vathi and its unexciting town beach, is cheap, clean and good value. Elsewhere, there are a few rooms to let privately. Some self-catering accommodation, used in high season by one or two tour companies, may be available in spring and autumn.

FOOD AND DRINK
Kantouni, by the harbour, is one of the better of a handful of Vathi tavernas. Another is **Psistaria Athinaiki Goumi**.

ZAKYNTHOS (ZANTE)

Zakynthos runs Corfu a close second in the popularity stakes, attracting several hundred thousand holidaymakers a year – most of them former Corfu devotees looking for somewhere still unspoiled.

This is understandable. Zakynthos is a lush, green island blessed with near-tropical fertility and some fine beaches. Those looking for more than a beach holiday, though, may find Zakynthos unrewarding. The main town – also **Zakynthos** – was levelled by the 1953 earthquake and its hard-edged modern buildings, though built on the old street-plan, give no hint of the glories of its past, when it was famed as the most beautiful of Venice's island possessions. Above the town a purposeful Venetian fortress, with the gloomy look common to all abandoned military works, looks over to the mouth of the Gulf of Corinth.

Laganas on the south coast is the island's biggest holiday resort by virtue of a long sandy beach which is unfortunately one of the last nesting sites of the endangered loggerhead turtle.

Alikes, on the long sandy bay of Ormos Alikon, is infinitely more appealing but is becoming the nucleus of a similar package holiday resort. **Argassi**, four km south of Zakynthos town, has a decent beach but like the other island beaches is on the brink of overdevelopment.

TRAVELLING
By Air Many summer charter flights to Zakynthos by British and European tour companies. Daily flights from Athens.

By Sea Ferries from the northern Ionian islands and daily from Killini on the north-west corner of the Peloponnese.

Around the Island Buses radiate from Zakynthos town to Keri in the very southern part and Volimes in the north. Cars and motorbikes to rent at Alikes, Argassi and Laganas.

WHERE TO STAY

Zakynthos town As usual, ferries are met by people with rooms to rent. Several larger hotels, of which the expensive 50-room **Lina** has a pool. Elsewhere, it is hard to find accommodation: most beds are block-booked by tour companies in holiday season and closed the rest of the year.

FOOD AND DRINK

In Zakynthos town, it is worth walking the 20 minutes or so to the hillside village of Bohali where a plateia-full of local tavernas is popular with locals and Greek visitors. Much better food and wine than in most of the tourist places which line the streets of the newer resorts.

KITHIRA

Rocky and remote, Kithira lies far to the west and south of the other islands of the Ionian archipelago, and its links with them are historic rather than geographic. It's a high island, visible as a dim outline on the horizon as far off as Githion, and its westward aspects have an almost Atlantic atmosphere.

Most of the island's visitors are Greek – either Kithirans returning for an annual stay or Athenian holidaymakers – and this makes for a higher standard of accommodation and other services than on islands dominated by foreign package tourists.

Kithira is a big island, with plenty to explore. High sea-cliffs thrust up to a patchwork plateau of barren thorn-pastures studded with patches of cultivated greenery. Many of the island's villages are hidden from sight in little sheltered valleys and almost all have lost most of their people to emigration, mainly to Australia. On this high table-land and even in the villages there is a powerful silence about Kithira, broken only by larks and goat-bleats.

I recommend it to walkers, cyclists and anyone looking for peace and quiet – indeed, outside the busy season which opens in mid-June and closes in late August, Kithira is so quiet that it can be a problem finding somewhere to eat.

Of Kithira's two harbours, **Agia Pelagia** is the less interesting, with a nondescript beach at the foot of rocky slopes. At the

The Turtles of Zakynthos

Zakynthos's most popular resort, the 14 km beach of Laganas Bay, is the stage for a continuing tragedy. Laganas is the last major nesting site in the Mediterrean of the loggerhead turtle (Caretta caretta), now balanced on the brink of extinction.

The number of turtles returning to the beach to lay their eggs has halved since the 1970s. At sea, loggerheads fall victim to fishing lines, nets and pollution throughout the Mediterranean. At Laganas, their nests may be destroyed by sunbathers and motorcyclists, and mother turtles maimed or killed by speedboats. The lights of the tavernas and hotels destroy hatchlings' sense of direction: struggling to find the sea, they die of thirst or starvation.

Legislation to protect the turtles is helping to change local attitudes. The nesting sites are closed at night, beach umbrellas have been banned, and seasonal restaurants right on the beach have been closed. Given that many local people now depend on tourism for their livelihood, this may be the best conservationists can expect. Whether it is enough to save the turtles is in doubt.

other end of the island, **Kapsali** has clean beaches in two small bays overlooked by a frowning Venetian castle and the white houses and churches of **Hora**, the island's capital. Two flash bars, Bikini Red and Bananas, are a sure giveaway that the island has an Athenian clientele. Opening in late April, they're frequented by the Athenian post-hippy ponytail set and are a good place to go for rock retrospectives – the Bikini Red DJ favours the more outré tracks of the mid- to late- 1970s. Who would expect to hear the Sensational Alex Harvey Band in a place like this?

Hora is one of Greece's most attractive island towns, its tall white houses with their blue shutters a blend of the Italianate architecture found in the Ionian with a hint of the Cyclades. Apart from the occasional cruise ship, it's empty of tourists for much of the year.

Above the white-painted cubist clutter of Hora, the island's Venetian castle looks down over the twin bays of Kapsali and out to the craggy offshore islet of **Avgo** (Egg). This, according to the Greek myths, is where Aphrodite was born from the sea. Further off on the horizon you can see the silhouette of **Andikithira**, Kithira's barren and almost-uninhabited twin. Beside the fortress's church, there are half a dozen rusting iron cannon of Napoleonic vintage, and it comes as a surprise to see that three of them carry the familiar broad-arrow mark of the old War Office and the English royal insignia – presumably they were spiked and abandoned when Britain ceded Kithira, along with the rest of the Ionian, to Greece after its half-century of occupation.

In the north of the island, **Potamos** is a more lively and busy village with affairs of its own, a grandiose silver-domed church and an idiosyncratic taste in paintwork – the terrace-café in its plateia is a cool pastel eau-de-nil while the nearby Kafeneion Alexandras is a grandiose traditional kafeneion from the last century which has been restored to its former glory with gilt mirrors and panelled ceiling in shades of mauve and purple. Potamos also has a substantial bridge spanning its deep ravine, though the river from which the town got its name has vanished completely into irrigation conduits. This part of the island is green and fertile, giving little hint of the harsh landscape of Kithira's windswept highlands, where there is little to see but low thorny scrub. Villages are hidden oases in sheltered valleys. The prettiest is **Milopotamos**, where a small stream runs through the centre of an almost-deserted village. Many of the houses are crumbling away, beams gradually sagging, roofs falling in and walls cracking. There are two restaurants, one in the village's shady plateia, another in a cool green grotto where a small waterfall tumbles into an emerald pool – this one the brainchild of the owner who decided to convert a local beauty spot into a nice little earner. Both open only in high season. Just outside Potamos, caves with Byzantine frescoes are touted as a tourist attraction – check with one of the travel agencies in Hora for guides and opening times.

TRAVELLING
By Air   Daily flights to Kithira from Athens by Olympic.

By Boat   Ferries to Piraeus, Monemvasia, Githion, Neapolis and Kastelli on Crete from the island's two ports, Ag Pelagia and Kapsali. Hydrofoils from Piraeus via Monemvasia in summer.

Around the island   Rudimentary bus services. Motorcycles and cars to rent in Hora and at Kapsali.

WHERE TO STAY

Can be tricky. Outside high season, many places are closed; in high season, many are full. Kapsali in particular gets very crowded from mid-June to the end of August, as does Hora. If you plan to visit Kithira at this time of year, book ahead. Casual camping is not welcome.

At **Kapsali**, George Kalligeros rents two-bedroom apartments with a fully-equipped kitchen: mid-priced, excellent value. It's the house with the green shutters and lifebelts outside, one street back from the Kapsali waterfront. In **Hora, Pension Kitty** is well spoken of. Try asking in the two or three cafés and restaurants or the supermarket for rooms — there's an efficient word-of-mouth referral system for accommodating homeless arrivals. The most expensive accommodation in town is the **Hotel Margarita**, a very pretty building with views over the terraced valley below Hora. It's an expensive Class-A.

There are rooms, too, at **Aghia Pelagia**, though you'll only want to stay here if catching an early-morning boat.

Most of Kithira's best accommodation is self-catering. The bigger of Hora's two supermarkets is the better supplied, but there is no bakery — for fresh bread you have to go to Livadhia, four km away.

FOOD AND DRINK

Like accommodation, this can be a problem outside the main summer season. There are two basic restaurants at **Kapsali**, both of them closed except in summer, and a couple in **Hora**, again open only in spring and summer. **Zorba's**, on the main street, is the best of these and opens earlier in the year. Above the plateia at Hora, a new café sells the ever-popular toasted sandwiches, tiropitta and burgers.

THE ARGO-SARONIC ISLANDS
The Playground of Athens

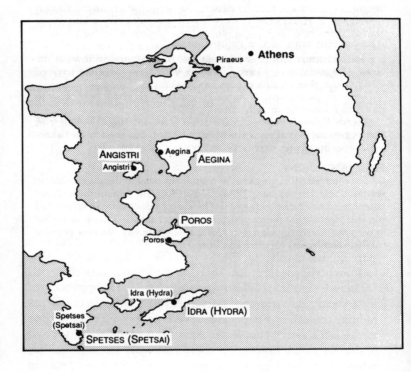

Though only a short hop from Piraeus by ferry, hydrofoil or yacht, these islands are far closer to the visitor's ideal of an untouched holiday isle than many of those in the further reaches of the Aegean. There are few or no vehicles, the little harbours with their steeply climbing ranks of white sea-captain's houses are the subject of a thousand posters, and the insistent pounding of last year's dance hits is gratefully absent – at least outside high season.

Their postcard prettiness is, on closer inspection, not so much unimpaired as retouched, and their low-key charm the result of an alliance of foreign and Athenian holiday home owners who have resisted the kind of tourism influx which has swamped less prosperous communities. That is not to say that tourism has not reached these islands: far from it. Easy to reach and a delight to the eye, Egina, Angistri, Poros, Idra and Spetses are a fine sampler for Greece's island delights and ideal places to tan, swim and relax after visiting Athens or touring the ancient sites of the Peloponnese.

Immediately south and east of Athens and the southern peninsula of Attica, the Saronic Gulf is Greece's busiest stretch of sea, criss-crossed by cruise liners, ferries, yachts, merchant vessels and hydrofoils. The Corinth Canal connects it with the Gulf of Corinth. The Akti peninsula, at the top of which most of the great Mycenaean sites are clustered, separates it from the Argolic Gulf.

AEGINA (EGINA)

The biggest of the islands and closest to Athens, Aegina is slap in the middle of the Saronic Gulf. Surprisingly, it is less involved in tourism than its neighbours, with fertile farmlands and a still-thriving fishing harbour supplemented by a steady day-trip traffic from Athens. Outside the Greek holiday season its main village reverts to its own pace as soon as the last day-trippers leave. **Agia Marina**, on the east coast of the island, has however become a crowded package holiday resort. The island has few historic sites; its strategic location made for a turbulent history in which successive invaders from Perikles to Barbarossa, the Venetians and finally the liberation fighters of the War of Independence fought over it.

On the north-east tip of Aegina stands the Doric Temple of Aphaia, protectress of women and believed to be a local avatar of Artemis. Most temples in the islands have been considerably knocked about but despite Aegina's repeated conquests Aphaia's retains most of its 32 columns. From here, the island seems to be ringed by land and on a clear day you may be able to see as far as the Acropolis and Cape Sounion. The fifth-century BC Temple of Apollo on a site in Aegina town has been less lucky: only one of its 36 columns still stands.

The hilltop village of **Palaeohora**, midway between the Temple of Aphaia and the port, is ghostly and sad. Once the island's capital, built in the ninth century AD as a refuge from pirates, it was abandoned after independence in the 1820s and all that remains is a crumbling maze of church walls half-buried in thorn bushes.

Perdhika, the small village 8 km south of Aegina town, has the best beach on the island, though it is fairly small and gets crowded. For less busy places to swim and sunbathe, the neighbouring island of **Angistri** with one village and a clutch of small holiday hotels is a better bet.

TRAVELLING

By Sea Very frequent ferries and hydrofoils from Piraeus and Zea Marina and onward to the other Argo-Saronic islands and Nafplion and Porto Heli on the mainland. Several small boats daily to Angistri from Aegina harbour.

Around the Island Frequent buses round the island; mopeds and bicycles for hire.

WHERE TO STAY

Can be tight, especially in high season. The B-Class **Pension Pavlou** is the best value for money. Most accommodation is in C-Class holiday bunkers, virtually all pre-booked by tour companies. Some private rooms to rent.

FOOD AND DRINK

Lots of good restaurants on Aegina harbour testify to a strong Greek clientele with excellent Greek food at prices to match. Also some smaller local places – as always, the rule is that prices drop the further you are from the harbour.

POROS

Tiny Poros, with its single pretty harbour village and few kilometres of road, could be claustrophobic were it more remote, but since it is separated from the mainland by a mere few hundred metres of water it has the advantage of easy access to the ancient sites, beaches and hinterland of the Akti peninsula and the Peloponnese. It is also within "commuting" distance of Athens, making it an attractive option for anyone interested in visiting the capital but unwilling to stay there.

The multi-coloured pastel village of Poros is on a promontory separated from the rest of the island by a narrow channel crossed by a causeway. There is an all-day bustle of ferries and hydrofoils throughout the summer season, when the island is packed with tourists and Athenian weekenders, and the waterfront shops and restaurants cater to the holiday market. This veneer of tourism is only a few streets deep and the narrower streets and alleys away from the quayside are quieter. **Kalavria**, the main body of the island, has only the 18th-century Zoodhodos Piyi Monastery and the skimpy remnants of a Temple of Poseidon – a couple of columns and some foundations – to offer the sightseer. There are no recommendable beaches.

Explorers and sightseers will find the mainland opposite more rewarding. The village of **Galatas**, immediately opposite Poros town, is of no interest, but if you visit the mainland in spring or early summer give your nose a treat with a visit to the vast citrus plantations at **Limonodhassos**, where tens of thousands of lemon trees perfume the air when in flower. The ancient Mycenaean site of Troezen and the Sanctuary at Epidavros are also within easy reach.

TRAVELLING
Several ferries and hydrofoils daily from Piraeus/Zea. Small boats shuttle between Poros and Galatas.

WHERE TO STAY
Pension Epta Adelfia, Tombazi 1 and **Pension Theano** are good B-Class pensions; the C-Class **Manessi** is a reasonable small hotel. Furnished apartments such as the C-Class **Possidonion** may be available in low season before the package tourists arrive.

FOOD AND DRINK

The waterfront is solid with a variety of tavernas and bars catering to the holiday visitor; cheaper estiatorions and kafeneions used by locals tend to be in the smaller streets inland and uphill from the harbour.

HYDRA (IDRA)

Hydra's harbour town is one of the prettiest in the Greek archipelago. Rows of imposing whitewashed mansions rise above a port crowded with fancy yachts and cruisers as well as fishing boats, for Hydra has become the holiday resort of choice for many wealthy Athenians. At the beginning of the last century it was one of the wealthiest places in Greece, with a powerful trading fleet and a population of 30,000 thanks to a mutually profitable agreement with its Turkish masters. Hydra was freed from taxation in return for manning the fleets of the Turkish navy, but during the war of independence its captains put patriotism before profit and its fleet fought for Greek liberation. Some of the mansions (arhondika) of the great ship-owning families can be visited, notably the Koundouriotis house overlooking the harbour which is kept up by descendants of the great Hydriot admiral. Others worth a look include the Ikonomou and Votsis mansions, while the Tombazi residence is part of the Athens School of Fine Arts.

Hydra has been an artists' refuge since the '60s, though much of the work now shown by its summer painters is undistinguished at best.

Inland, the island is rocky and deserted. There are no roads outside the port – one of Hydra's endearing qualities being the absence of motor vehicles except for the town rubbish truck – and though glossy Hydra town is crowded from June onwards and at Easter, most visitors do not stray far from the bars and cafés of the waterfront. A stiff hour's walking to the island's highest point will bring you to the monastery of **Profitis Ilias**, reached by a rough footpath and with wonderful views over Hydra and the surrounding ocean.

More for lovers of harbour café society than for beach seekers, Hydra has few places to swim. Closest to the town (about 20 minutes' walk west from the harbour) is **Kamini**, a shingle beach which is busy throughout the summer. A little further on, the small rocky beaches at the hamlets of

Kastello and **Vlihos** may be less peopled. Better coves for swimming and sunbathing are on the island's south coast, around **Limioniza**.

TRAVELLING
Frequent hydrofoils and ferries to Hydra from Piraeus, the other Saronic islands, and Peloponnesian mainland points including Nafplion, Porto Heli and Leonidhion.

Around the Island There's no motor transport. Small boats run to the south coast beaches.

WHERE TO STAY
Rooms are like hens' teeth from late June to September and prices accordingly high. Good places to stay include the B-Class **Pension Kamini** and **Pension Orlof**; slightly cheaper is the C-Class **Hydra**. The A-Class **Miramare**, some distance outside Hydra town, has its own beach but is expensive. In town, the A-Class **Pension Miranda** is also pricy but well worth it if you feel like splashing out. Studios at the **Hydriza** furnished apartments are good value for money.

FOOD AND DRINK
Bars and restaurants on the flashy waterfront are the most expensive; for slightly cheaper prices try eating at Kamini, where a couple of more

modest places serve good fish and squid. Though prices on Hydra are higher than elsewhere, food is also better.

SPETSAI (SPETSES)

Most remote of the Saronic islands, Spetsai lies between the Saronic and Argolic Gulfs, a stone's throw from the mainland and the posh resort complex at Porto Heli. Hilly and covered with pine woods, it is an attractive island for not-too-strenuous walking and exploring. **Spetsai** town, also called **Kastelli**, is an attractive mix of 18th-century sea-captains' mansions and neoclassical 19th-century buildings, some of the more florid – such as the old Possidonion hotel – donated to the town by its wealthy shipowners. A small museum in one of these old mansions – formerly the home of the Mexis family – houses relics of the War of Independence, in which Spetsai played a leading part.

Among them are the bones of Laskarina Bouboulina. This Pirate Jenny of the Aegean was one of the leading captains of the war and is credited with inspiring Spetsai to become the first island to join the rebel cause in 1821. The town – virtually traffic-free – surrounds two harbours, the older fishing port and the newer harbour of Dapia, where the ferries and hydrofoils dock. Inland, much of Spetsai is covered with pine woods and is eminently walkable. There are good beaches at Agia Paraskevi and Agii Anargyri, on the opposite side of the island from the town and harbour. Closer to Spetsai town, Agia Marina is adequate but can be very crowded in summer.

TRAVELLING
Frequent ferries and hydrofoils from Piraeus, the other Saronics, Porto Heli and Nafplion. Small boats to Kosta on the nearby mainland, with a decent beach and buses to Porto Heli.

WHERE TO STAY
Rooms, hotels and pensions to suit all pockets but often choc-a-bloc in high season. For fanciers of old-style hotels, the Edwardian **Hotel Possidonion** on the waterfront is worth a try, as is the D-Class **Saronikon** on the harbour front at Dapia, the main town harbour. Pensions include the B-Class **Villa Anessis**, **Villa Christina** and **Villa Martha** and the

expensive A-Class **Akroyali**. There are two large C-Class hotels, the **Ilios** and the **Star**.

FOOD AND DRINK

Trehandiri, by the old harbour, is one of the best seafood restaurants in Greece. Cheaper restaurants and cafés are in the streets between the new and old harbours.

THE CYCLADES
A Ring of White Islands

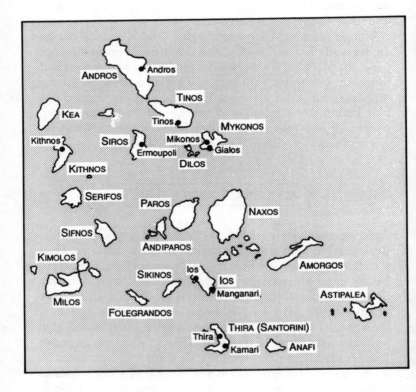

Dotting the Aegean Sea in a rough circle, the Cyclades – the name comes from the Greek word for circle, kyklos – are the quintessential Greek islands. Most are barren and rugged, and the white splash of a typical island village stands out brilliantly against the monochrome tan and ochre colours of the Cycladic landscape.

Tourism has had a powerful impact on many of the islands. Charter airports on Santorini and Mykonos funnel huge numbers of holidaymakers into these and neighbouring islands each summer. Mykonos, Paros and Ios have become holiday resorts to the exclusion of all else. Others only a short ferry-hop away from the main holiday resorts remain remarkably undeveloped, in part because ferries which stray off the central route from Piraeus through the main Cycladic islands to Crete can be unreliable.

In high summer – July and August – the Cyclades can be unpleasantly hot and windy, and the strong Aegean summer wind, the melteme, whips beaches into minor sandstorms and plays havoc with ferry timetables. One compensation for the dust-laden air is the authentic Cycladic sunset – washed-out blue fading through bands of orange and rose into a deep purple, all of it reflected in a dark blue sea. Sunset-watching is something of a ritual in the Cyclades.

MYKONOS AND DELOS

A strong contender for the Most Picturesque Greek Island title, Mykonos has been attracting visitors since the late '50s, when a trickle of artists and bohemians discovered the haphazard beauty of its whitewashed villages and blue-domed churches. Since then, these have become the visual cliché of Greek holiday brochures, but Mykonos is no less beautiful now than then – though it is certainly not the quiet island idyll you may have been dreaming of. This is one of the Aegean's liveliest islands, and its nightlife style is strongly influenced by a large gay clientele, diluted in peak season by a less colourful influx of mainstream visitors, mostly young and voraciously intent on a frantically good time.

Mykonos Town is a maze of whitewashed lanes and alleys which no map can adequately explain; getting lost is easier than in most island villages because Mykonos is built not on a defensible hilltop but on the flat, so you can't even head downhill in the hope of eventually ending up at the harbour. Wandering at random is one of Mykonos's main attractions.

You can't go far without finding a watering-hole of one sort or another. That applies to night life too – a Mykonos bar and club crawl challenges legs, liver, wallet and grasp on reality to the maximum.

The town is built on and around a promontory and a natural harbour. The remains of a Venetian Kastro on the tip of the promontory and some well-refurbished Venetian merchants' mansions in the Alefkhandra part of town south of it testify to the island's medieval owners. On a low ridge in the heart of Alefkhandra stand four white windmills, clearly visible from boats entering the harbour and one of Mykonos's long standing trademarks.

A small archaeological museum on Agiou Stefanou contains a collection of finds from Delos, worth a visit if you plan a trip to the sacred island. Also worth seeing is the Paraportiani church, on the promontory beside the Venetian castle. The oldest church on the island, it is a classic of haphazard vernacular architecture – four churches which have gradually fused into one building over the centuries, clearly the work of generations of jobbing ecclesiastical builders.

Mykonos's best beaches are on its south coast – the north is exposed to almost constant wind – and are tucked away in a series of sheltered sandy and pebbly bays, all of which turn into tourist flypaper from June to September.

Platis Gialos, about four km from town, is a fair-sized sandy beach lined with holiday hotels; neighbouring **Psarou**, on the opposite side of the bay, is less built up and prettier, with shade from trees and "Greek bamboo" reeds, but equally crowded in season. A hike over a rocky, dusty footpath takes you to the next bay and **Piranga** beach, an excellent strip of sand with several seasonal tavernas. The beaches dubbed **Paradise** and **Super Paradise** have the distinction of pioneering nudism in Greece but are no longer monopolized either by the serious hippies of the 1960s or the predominantly gay clientele of the '70s and early '80s. Both are super beaches with friendly bars and tavernas. **Elia** and **Kalo Livadhi**, the easternmost of the Mykonos beaches, can be less crowded than those closer to Mykonos town.

To the ancients, the holy island of **Delos** was the hub of the Cyclades and one of the greatest religious centres of the

Hellenic world as the birthplace of the twins Artemis and Apollo. It was also a commercial centre of the Aegean and the intertwining of religion and political power in the ancient world made Delos the prize in the long-running power struggle between Athens and its adversaries. The whole island is now preserved as an archaeological site.

Delos is one of the more melancholy ancient sites, inspiring a sense of how much has been lost rather than of what has miraculously survived. From the small landing pier which stands between the ancient sacred harbour and commercial harbour, you enter the site by the Sacred Way, no longer lined with monuments. Marble steps lead to the Sanctuary of Apollo, once thronged with statues which have long since been looted. Three temples to Apollo in varying states of decay stand along the Sacred Way. The Sacred Lake, where Leto gave birth to the divine twins, is a dry depression surrounded by an incongruous brick wall, but is overlooked by five wonderful lion-statues from the seventh century BC. Of the nine originals, one was lifted by the Venetians and is in the Arsenal in Venice. Three others have been lost.

Perhaps the best way to imagine Delos in its heyday is to head for the so-called "theatre quarter" where the overview from the dilapidated theatre helps to pull the scene together. Fragments of mosaic in the nearby House of Masks help to picture the interior detail of some of the site's buildings. For a wider view over Delos and Mykonos, climb the low hill of Kinthos south-east of the theatre.

TRAVELLING

To Mykonos
By Air   Charter flights from most UK and European airports in summer. Scheduled flights from Athens, Crete and other islands.

By Sea   Ferries from Piraeus via the northern Cyclades and to Ikaria, Samos, and Patmos.

Around the Island   Car and bike rental available. Small boats shuttle between Mykonos Town and the south coast beaches.

To Delos
Ferries leave each morning at 09.00 for Delos from the pier by the Venetian Kastro and return at midday.

WHERE TO STAY
Mykonos Town has a large choice of rooms and hotels but is very crowded from mid-June to Sepember. Crowds of room-touts meet every ferry. Hotels on the beaches are monopolised by tour companies.

   Les Moulins and **Andronikos** are B-Class pensions, quite expensive – like all Mykonos accommodation – but good value. Rather cheaper are the **Hotel Delfines** and **Hotel Apollon** on Od. Mavroyeni.

FOOD, DRINK AND NIGHTLIFE
Listing every good restaurant, bar and nightspot in Mykonos would take a book in its own right; every second building seems to have become a taverna, disco, or smart café-bar.

   Venerable institutions include the **Remezzo**, at the northern end of the waterfront, a great bar for sunset-watching; and **The Yacht Club**, *the* all-night dancery on Mykonos. But the Mykonos scene is fluid in the extreme and the only sensible way to handle it is to play it by ear.

SANTORINI (THIRA)

Santorini is simply the most spectacular island in Greece. To arrive by boat at sunset, when the cliffs which ring its natural harbour glow an ominous red, is like sailing into a

---

Body Language

How do you silence a Greek? Tie his hands behind his back. Greek is strong on non-verbal communication, with a whole range of hand, head and whole-body movements to convey outrage, agreement, helplessness or complicity.

A backward movement of the head – to British or American eyes confusingly like a nod – indicates "no". The sharper the movement, the stronger the negative. An absolute, final and non-negotiable "no" is conveyed by jerking the head back while clicking the tongue and rolling the eyes heavenward.

A rapid side-to-side headshake means "I don't understand you" or "Your question makes no sense, kindly cease wasting my time". Often used in answer to daft questions like "When does the bus to X leave?", when everyone but a silly foreigner knows there is no such bus, never has been and never will be.

An outflung hand, palm up and fingers spread, means something like "Whadda you want from me, blood?" or "Gimme a break", while the same hand, fingers spread and palm down, conveys something along the lines of "Go and do something anatomically improbable to yourself".

Another hand movement, a serpentine snaking of an open hand towards a hip pocket, means "Perhaps we can come to some mutually agreeable arrangement without the need to derange our overworked friend the tax inspector." Something along those lines, anyway.

Moving the head shoulderwards in a graceful sideways and downwards movement indicates your agreement with the sentiments expressed, while a whole thesis could be written on the complex and delicate range of shrugs available to the Greek conversationalist.

Western. This is scenery which belongs in Arizona, not the Aegean.

Like Mykonos, its blue and white villages inspire photographers to frame semi-abstract compositions of light and shade. But instead of ringing a gentle harbour, the villages of Santorini sit hundreds of feet above the Aegean in a savage volcanic landscape.

Formed by a huge volcanic eruption which blew the island in half around 1600 BC, Santorini is a rough crescent surrounding on its western or inner side a deep natural harbour studded with smaller islets. In the centre of this flooded caldera, the jagged black mass of the "burnt islands" of Nea Kameni and its smaller neighbour Palea Kameni are all that remains of the volcano, which is still active if dormant – Nea Kameni emerged from the sea in the early 1770s and grew with the eruptions of 1866 and 1925, and a minor eruption and earthquake rocked the island villages of Thira and Oia in 1956.

Thira is beautiful, with heart-stopping views and psychedelic sunsets to watch from a choice of clifftop café-terraces suspended above the 600 (or so) steps which lead achingly from the harbour immediately below the town. Only the toughest, proudest, or brokest travellers pant their way up the staircase, a hike of about 45 minutes; the muleteers who meet each boat offer an old-fashioned alternative, and a dizzying cable-car offers a cheaper and quicker way of getting to the top.

Thira's business is tourism and the village has a huge number of jewellery and souvenir shops, snack bars, and expensive places to eat and drink, all of them clamouring for the drachmas not only of the package tour holidaymakers who throng the island from June to September but of thousands of passengers from the cruise shops which call by the score. Many of the older buildings are of the barrel-vaulted construction favoured on this earthquake-prone island because of its strength, and a number of stylish medieval mansions are left over from the period of the Venetian Dukes of Naxos, who named the island after their St Irene – hence Santorini.

Oia (Ia), the island's other clifftop village, is 12 km from Thira. Close to the island's northern tip, it is equally pretty and a bit quieter, though no less touristy. In fact, the holiday business can take most of the credit for rebuilding the village. Most of its people left after the 1956 quake, which left many buildings teetering on the verge of collapse. A number of houses have been rebuilt by the ministry of tourism under its traditional settlements programme and are used as luxury guesthouses, and others have been rebuilt as holiday homes or pensions by private owners. Oia has no beach, but fitter swimmers can clamber down 200 steps to a small fishing harbour where you can swim from the cement pier. The stuff floating in the harbour is porous pumice-stone from the volcano, not (as you feared) sewage. Alternatively, there is a long and little-used beach at Mavropetra, about two km away on the north-west outer coast of the island.

THE EAST COAST

Santorini's longer, gentler east coast has fine beaches of black volcanic sand at **Kamari**, a hugely-developed resort complex which is jammed in summer and closed for most of the rest of the year. Separated from Kamari by a steep rocky headland on which stands the remains of Ancient Thira, the longer and less built-up beach of **Perissa** is a more attractive choice for independent travellers. On its seven-km stretch even the most isolation-loving sunbather can usually find a space away from the crowd. However, Santorini's popularity with holiday sunseekers owes more to the convenience of its charter airport than to the beaches themselves. Black sand soaks up the heat of the sun and quickly becomes unpleasant to lie on and – by afternoon – too hot to walk on in bare feet, and the east-facing beaches are exposed to the full oven-draught force of the summer wind.

THE INTERIOR

Inland, the island is far gentler and greener than the savage cliffs above the west coast harbours lead the visitor to expect. Dusty and unpromising though it looks, the volcanic soil is extremely fertile and Santorini is a patchwork of little vineyards and tomato fields. The vineyards are not immediately recognizable as such, because the vines are not trained on trellises but clipped into low shrubs, gathering the heat thrown back from the soil and huddling out of the force of the wind. The grapes are left on the vine until they are over-ripe and rich in sugar to produce a muscat-style wine with a very high alcohol content.

Of Santorini's inland villages, **Pirgos** – midway between Thira and the east coast beaches – is the most interesting. Like Oia and Thira, it shows the impact of the 1956

quake but unlike them it has not been refurbished for tourism and a wander through the whitewashed maze of its
steps and alleyways is a step into the world of pre-tourism
Greece.

The village is overlooked by a Venetian castle, built here
for good reason. From its ramparts you can see over all
of Santorini and its nearer neighbours, so the fort would
have provided both lookout and refuge for the Venetian
overlords against rampaging fleets of Turkish and Saracen
corsairs or Christian rivals. The view from the castle is
dotted randomly with the blue splashes of little domed
chapels, of which Santorini has an over-supply even by
Cycladic standards. Could this apparent devotion be inspired
by fear of the vampires who are said to lurk horridly among
the sulphur-scented rocks of Nea Kameni?

Close to the southern tip of Santorini, archaeologists have
found remains of a Minoan settlement which was first exposed
by earth movements after the 1956 earthquake. These had
been buried by ash when the island exploded in 1500 BC. The
excavation has unearthed remnants of three-storey buildings
decorated with frescoes similar to those of Knossos, now on
show at the Athens National Archaeological Museum, as well
as hoards of Minoan pottery, much of which is exhibited at
the Thira Archaeological Museum.

Excavation continues, but part of the site is open to the
public daily. The Greek archaeologist Professor S Marinatos,
discoverer of the site, was killed here by a falling wall and is
buried nearby.

THE CRATER ISLANDS

Opposite the village of Thira on the western side of the flooded
crater, the little island of **Thirassia** sees few visitors other than
a trickle of curious day-trippers in high season. There's not
much here – a little harbour village called Hora with a handful
of fishing boats and tavernas and two even smaller hamlets,
Potamos and Agrilia, inland. There are no beaches as such but
you can swim from the cement pier at Hora or from a few
rocky coves; the snorkelling is excellent, in deep clear water
with plenty of sealife.

In the middle of the crater, **Nea Kameni** is a sinister mass

Aegean Atlantis?

Look over the caldera of Santorini at the scattered fragments of the original island and imagine the force of the explosion which blew the heart clean out of it, leaving a bay 200 to 400 m deep – a bang to make Krakatoa or Hiroshima sound like a child bursting a balloon. And, archaeologists believe, a bang big enough to shatter the sophisticated Minoan civilization which had dominated the Aegean for more than a thousand years, and plunge the lands around the Eastern Mediterranean into something akin to a mini- "nuclear winter" of black rains, clouds of ash, gas and smoke and giant tsunamis which pounded cities into rubble.

Apocalypse indeed, and conceivably the factual origin of myths from the Biblical Flood to the sinking of Atlantis. Backers of this theory suggest that the fabled Atlantis of which Plato and Solon wrote, was a memory of the great Minoan empire, passed down in fragments to later Greeks. The Krakatoa eruption last century, the biggest bang ever recorded, cracked walls by aerial vibration more than 160 km away, raised tidal waves of 15 to 30 m and was heard more than 4,000 km away. Santorini, blowing up in the middle of the Aegean, must have wrought havoc all around and its dating coincides neatly with the destruction of many of the Minoan palaces and cities on Crete.

of tumbled, shattered black rock, all jagged points and edges. The smell of brimstone from a steaming, muddy, hot spring makes it a truly hellish landscape, a fit home for the vampires locally rumoured to infest it. Nervous visitors may like to take a crucifix, some garlic and a stout aspen stake.

TRAVELLING

By Air Charter flights to Santorini from many UK airports in summer. Scheduled flights from Athens and Crete.

By Sea Very frequent ferries call en route between Athens, the northern Cyclades and Heraklion, and less frequent ferries to other Cretan ports and smaller Cycladic islands. Daily fast catamarans from Chania and Rethimnon in summer.

Ferries arrive at any of three harbours, all on the west coast: Skala Oia, Skala Thira and Athinios. Larger ferries usually dock at Athinios. Small boats for day trips from Skala Thira to Nea Kameni and Therasia.

Around the Island Buses run around Santorini between Thira and Athinios to connect with most boats. Buses also run from Thira to Ia, Kamari, Perissa, Pirgos and other inland villages. Car and motorbike rental available in Thira and Kamari.

WHERE TO STAY

Beds in **Thira town** are expensive in season, especially those with a view over the crater. Affordable hotels include the D-Class **Hotel Lucas** overlooking the caldera and the C-Class **Hotel Gallini**, which is a little way from the heart of Thira. **Hotel Asiminia**, opposite the museum (Tel. 22034) and **Hotel King Thiras** (Tel. 22155) are affordable hotels in the centre of town.

At **Merovigli**, 2 km from Thira, the **Katerina** is quite expensive but makes up for it with fine views and self-catering facilities. Hordes of room touts meet each boat landing at Athinios and Skala Thira. Their offers are usually worth taking, if only for your first night on Santorini.

Firostefani, uphill from the centre of Thira town, has a number of excellent places to stay – quieter than town and with superb views. **Pension Gaby**, Firostefani 124, is cheap and comfortable. **Aeolos Villas**, an attractive complex of white and purple apartments, is medium. **Thanos Villas**, secluded, with multilevel private flowered terraces, is very trendy, expensive, but excellent value. **Honeymoon Villas**, a complex of typical blue/white Santorini buildings, is friendly and moderately priced. **Zodiac Apartments**, Firostefani 73, is also moderate. All of these are perched either side of the clifftop-hugging path leading to Firostefani from Thira town.

At **Oia**, many older houses have been turned into villas and apartments which can be good value, especially if you are with a number of others and arriving early or late in the season. Expensive but unique to Oia are the **Armenakis Villas** cave houses, overlooking the sea and sleeping up to six at A-Class apartment rates. Other restored traditional houses include the **Dana Villas** and **Atlantis Villas**.

At **Perissa** there is a thriving settlement of cheaper pensions and rooms.

NAXOS

The second largest of the Cyclades, Naxos sees fewer visitors than some of its smaller fellows and absorbs them more easily. From the sea, Naxos looks as barren as any island in the group, but appearances are misleading. Inland, a choppy landscape of little valleys reveals fertile pockets of cultivation growing potatoes, tomatoes, lemons and olives.

This fertility made Naxos the hub of the Venetian duchy of the archipelago and it remains one of the most prosperous of the Aegean islands, a factor which has helped to keep the tourist flood within bounds. Naxos – unlike poorer islands for which tourism is the only alternative to a bare subsistence – has affairs of its own to think about.

The island's main town, **Chora**, is a place of substantial homes, most set behind courtyards bursting with jasmine and geraniums. Though its mix of Cyclades cubism and faded Venetian elegance is similar to other island capitals, this local fondness for greenery makes the inner maze of Chora's alleys far less austere than the whitewashed purity of Mykonos or Thira.

Around the kastro, the old town alleys are gradually succumbing to the demands of the tourist for postcards, film, mass-produced copper and ceramic wares and "Ouzo Power" T-shirts, but have not yet gone belly-up to the same extent as Paros, Mykonos or Santorini. Lacking the immediate, even clichéd, visual impact of these rivals, Naxos is not a favourite with the cruise lines. As a result, even the waterfront – which in any island port bears the brunt of the holiday invasion – bustles as much with Naxian everyday life as with visitors.

INLAND NAXOS

The island's interior is well worth exploring. Its prosperous farming villages have made few compromises with tourism – few holidaymakers penetrate beyond the island's excellent beaches – and have a number of elegant medieval churches and crumbling castles.

Filoti, in the centre of the island, is the largest of the inland settlements, and though a rather mundane place – many of its inhabitants have left for the mainland – it is a good base for exploring the hinterland. Above the village, the massif of **Mt Zas** occupies the whole lower quadrant of Naxos. The highest peak in the Cyclades (1,000m) it is easily walkable from the village and the view of the whole archipelago is wonderful. Between Filoti and Chora, the peaceful village of **Chalki** lies in the middle of a wide,

The Dukes of Naxos

The heart of Chora is the kastro built by the Venetian Sanudo dynasty who ruled Naxos and the archipelago for three and a half centuries.

The first of this line of freebooters, Marco Sanudo, was a nephew of the Doge of Venice who in 1207 snatched the islands from Byzantium in the chaotic aftermath of the fourth crusade, subsequently denying allegiance to the Serene Republic and allying with the Latin Dukes of Athens.

The Sanudo dukes defied Byzantium long after the Emperor's reconquest of the mainland Latin kingdoms and their little state outlived Byzantium itself by more than a century, until the Turkish Sultan Selim the Sot drove them out in 1566. Giacomo, the last duke, led 500 men as mercenaries against the Turks at Lepanto in a final bid to win back his realm.

The long rule of the Venetian dukes has left Naxos and several other Cycladic islands with a substantial Roman Catholic minority and a Catholic cathedral stands in the centre of the Sanudo castle.

fertile valley of olives and lemons interspersed with crumbling Venetian tower-houses and little churches. The village itself has several 12th- and 13th-century churches which are worth a glance for their combination of Latin and Byzantine elements. Other historic Venetian relics include the Sanudo keep at Apano Kastro, overlooking the farmlands around Chalki. At **Moni**, a sixth-century monastery – grim-looking from the outside but with some lovely, glowing frescoes within – is open to visitors.

THE SOUTH-WEST

The fine beaches of Naxos's south-west coast are no longer a well-kept secret, but in spite of the mushrooming of larger hotels they are among the Aegean's best and surprisingly uncrowded even in summer. Between Naxos town and the headland of Prokopios, the long bay of **Ag Giorgios** has found its way into the holiday brochures and is well on the way to overdevelopment. **Prokopios**, a ramshackle development of small hotels and holiday tavernas, is taking

the overspill, but the beaches further along the coast —
south of the modest harbour of **Agia Anna** — are still relatively unspoiled. **Plaka** beach is a five-km sandy stretch with
room for all and only a few buildings at the Agia Anna
end. Further south still, **Kastraki** beach, separated from
Plaka by a jutting headland, is even emptier but is rather
littered.

TRAVELLING

By Sea Frequent ferries to Naxos from Piraeus and the rest of the
Cyclades and very frequent shuttle boats in high season between Naxos
and Paros.

By Road Buses from Chora to villages around Naxos island. Car and
motorbike rental available in Chora.

WHERE TO STAY

Chora: Hotel Panorama is a cheap C-Class; **Hotel Dionyssos** is a
dirt-cheap hostel-style hotel with dormitory accommodation; **Hotel
Anixis** is at the more expensive end of D-Class. All three are in old
buildings in the kastro quarter. Excellent value is the **Hotel Renetta**,
a good C-Class at lower than usual rates. Newer hotels in the more
modern part of town include the unfortunately-named **Grotta** (C-Class)
and **Sergis** (C-Class). Within walking distance, on the Ag Giorgios beach,
are a row of B- and C-Class guesthouses and hotels including the B-Class
Pension Aneza and **Pension Glaros** and the C-Class hotels **Nissaki, Zeus,
Akroyali** and **Iliovassilema**. These are likely to be full from the end of
June to mid-September but in low season you may be able to negotiate
bargain rates.

Elsewhere on the island there are rooms to let at **Filoti** and rooms
and pensions at **Agia Anna** and **Prokopios**.

PAROS

Bustling Paros is only a few kilometres from Naxos but could
hardly be more different. As the first stop on many of the ferry
routes from Piraeus, it quickly fills up with low-budget backpackers in summer and has acquired a two-edged reputation
as a cheap, cheerful, party island.

Paros's main town **Parikia** is also called **Chora**, like Naxos's
capital; but there the resemblance ends. Its waterfront is a solid
mass of tourist-oriented travel agencies, bars, restaurants,
and car and bike rental outlets. Inland from the harbour,

whitewashed lanes and alleys are hardly touched except for the odd "Rent Rooms" sign. The ruins of a Venetian castle, patched together from the desecrated marbles of much older Greek temples, face out to sea from the centre of the old Chora.

BEACHES

Nine out of ten visitors to Paros are drawn by its reputation for some of the Aegean's best beaches as well as its rowdy nightlife. There are small and not very distinguished beaches to the north and south of Chora, and far better ones on the east coast of the island, virtually all of them backed by a jumble of accommodation. The best of the bunch – and predictably the most developed – are around **Chrissi Akti**, also (and justly for once) known as Golden Beach, an enormous stretch of sand between the east coast village of **Drios** and the burgeoning tourist sprawl of all too aptly named **Pisso Livadhi**. Chrissi Akti is a strong contender for the title of best beach in Greece.

Around the northern village of **Naoussa**, once the island's capital and now a mass of dull holiday hotels, there are other good beaches, but the regular boats which shuttle summer sunbathers from every resort on the island to even the most remote beach ensure that the beaches around the bay of Naoussa – **Kolimbithres** and **Monastiri** to the west and **Santa Maria** to the east – also get more than their share of visitors.

Andiparos, Paros' smaller twin, has escaped some of the impact of tourism, but the ever present day-trippers have created a mini-boom in July and August and the island's population of 500 has not been slow to take advantage of it. Early or late in the season, though, Andiparos is great place to be, with a single village built in and around the walls of a Venetian castle and a scattering of blue-domed churches, good beaches nearby and isolated, semi-private beaches around Ag. Giorgios at the island's south-west tip.

TRAVELLING
By Air   Scheduled flights to Paros from Athens.

By Sea   More ferries than any other island, with connections to Piraeus and in all directions through the Cyclades and on to Crete, Rhodes, Samos and even Turkey.

Around the Island   Car and motorbike rental in Chora. Small boats to all beaches in summer and to Andiparos (from Chora) and Naxos (from Pisso Livadhi).

WHERE TO STAY

In summer, grab whatever is being offered by the small army of room renters which meets the ferry as it docks in the centre of town – it's the only way you will find a bed. In quieter spells, **Pension Dina** is cheap, clean, pretty and central.

On Andiparos, there are rooms to rent at the island's single village, called (guess what?) Chora.

FOOD AND DRINK

Parikia/Chora and most of the other beach resorts of Paros hold to the unwritten rule that as the number of restaurants catering to tourists increases, quality and quantity must decline and prices double. Exceptions to this rule are hard to find; but that said, at least there is plenty of choice.

NIGHTLIFE
Heaps of bars. At the far north end of the harbour at Parikia, a rambling structure houses an interlinked assortment of boozing barns and music bars calculated to appeal to a party-loving international audience. They include the **Downunder Bar**, the **Dubliner**, the **Scandinavian Bar**, the **Londoner** and the **Hard Rock Café**.

IOS

If you are going to Ios you do not need a guide book; you need a bottle of painkillers and possibly a psychiatrist. This tiny, barren lump of rock with a single village — composed exclusively of discos, tavernas, pensions and cocktail bars — and a single, incredibly crowded and not very good beach attracts incredible numbers of would-be hedonists, whose top priorities are drinking in its crammed cocktail bars and getting laid. In short, Ios has more in common with a drunken weekend in Blackpool than anything Greek. If there is an island in the Cyclades well worth bypassing, Ios is it. A better and more interesting time can be had anywhere else in the Aegean.

SIROS

Siros is the odd one out of the Cyclades, with an industrial seaport — one of the most important in Greece — a major shipyard and few concessions to tourism.

From the deck of an incoming ferry its port, **Ermoupolis**, lacks the immediate charm of the dinkier Cycladic harbour-towns, and the view of the moribund Neorion shipyard is not enticing.

The island's beaches are skimpy and its hinterland bleak, which helps to explain why tourism has made relatively little impact here. Many visitors are birds of passage who are just changing ferries.

If the relentless tourism development of other islands is getting you down, though, Siros is a healthy corrective,

Siros's History

Built during and after Independence, Siros was Greece's first major port while Piraeus was no more than a fishing hamlet, and only lost its prominence to the port of Athens around the turn of the century.

Siriot shipowners and industrialists made their fortunes on the import/export trade of the new state, building ornate mansions in questionable taste, lavish churches and leaving elaborate monuments to themselves in the port's cemeteries.

From 1207 until 1566 Siros was part of the Duchy of the Archipelago, ruled from Naxos, and most Siriots became Catholics. During the War of Independence, Orthodox refugees from Chios and other Turkish-held islands settled here, and the town has a mix of medieval Catholic campaniles and Orthodox blue-domed chapels.

with a welcome lack of tatty souvenir shops and "English breakfast" signs.

Ermoupolis bustles with the everyday life of an island town with more things on its mind than snacking-up the next planeload of lobster-pink Brits, and its medieval quarter, Catholic and Orthodox churches and 19th-century merchants' townhouses lend it an air of pleasantly fading grandeur.

The heart of the Catholic community in Ermoupolis is the medieval suburb of **Ano (High) Siros**, on the taller of two hills north of the harbour, topped by the Cathedral of St George. Facing it on a lower hill, the domed Orthodox Church of the Anastasis caps the Orthodox quarter of Vrondado. Both are great places to ramble, with flights of steps and cobbled streets lined with gradually crumbling mansions, many of them sadly deserted.

Around the busy harbour, Ermoupolis is a cheerfully eccentric town which would make an excellent film set for any banana republic-revolution movie, with an elaborate town hall building facing out over Plateia Miaoulis, the central square, dominated by its statue of the great War of Independence admiral. Other mementoes of past glories include the Apollon Theatre, once a grand opera house and now a venue for local theatricals. Plateia Miaoulis is the place for the evening (volta) and its café-arcades are a fine place to kill time.

Siros is not one of the Aegean's great beach islands but there is a decent stretch of sandy beach, not over-developed, at **Gallisas**, nine km from Ermoupolis on the west coast, and a small, sandy and pebbly bay at **Kini**, also on the west coast and about five km north of Gallisas.

TRAVELLING

By Sea Vast numbers of ferries from Piraeus, the rest of the Cyclades, Ikaria, Samos, Kalimnos, Kos and Rhodes. Siros is the most convenient jumping-off point for the smaller and more remote Cyclades such as Astipalia, Amorgos, Folegandros and Anafi.

Around the Island Buses run frequently to villages all over the island. Motorcycle and moped hire available in Ermoupolis.

WHERE TO STAY

Plenty of cheap rooms in **Ermoupolis** catering to those staying overnight between boats. **Apollon**, just beyond the ferry quay on the other side of Plateia Kamari, is cheap and convenient for one-night stays. **Hotel Hermes**, on Plateia Kamari, is a mid-priced B-Class hotel which is also handy for the quay but can be noisy.

Expensive, but worth it, is the delightful **Omiros Hotel** (A-Class), a restored neoclassical mansion overlooking the harbour. Two B-Class guesthouses, the **Athina** and the **Ghiannis**, offer a mid-priced alternative.

Rooms to rent are available at **Gallisas** and **Kini**.

FOOD AND DRINK

For eating and drinking, **Ermoupolis** is more like a mainland Greek town than an island capital dominated by tourism – there are fewer glossy places and more fast food, gyros and ouzeri joints. For octopus and other traditional snacks with drinks, try one of the places around **Miaoulis**. For a more expensive night out, **Tempelis**, below the Orthodox cathedral on Vrondado hill, has island dishes and a pleasant location.

TINOS

Tinos, like Siros, has escaped inundation by tourism of the secular kind – largely because it already benefits from a steady flow of visiting pilgrims visiting the shrine of the Virgin Mary at Panagia Evangelistria.

The healing icon was discovered in 1822 by a local nun and reposes in the overblown church of the same name in the town of **Tinos**, which is at its busiest when pilgrims flood in for the festivals which mark the discovery of the icon (January), Annunciation (March 25) and celebrate the canonisation of its discoverer, Agia Pelagia, (July 23) and Assumption (August 15).

The religious atmosphere tends to discourage island-hoppers in search of beaches and bohemian nightlife, and Tinos town is characterless. The island has only two beaches worth the name: **Porto**, some 10 km from Tinos town, is less developed and pleasanter than **Kionia**, only four km from town but dominated by a large hotel.

Tinos has treats in store for explorers undiscouraged by the unpromising town and shortage of beaches. The backbone of the island is the rugged massif of **Exobourgo**, and on its flanks – around the brooding walls of a Venetian fortress – cluster scores of little villages each with the fingers of Catholic and Orthodox bell-towers and of stone dovecotes like miniature castles pointing skyward. The ruined Venetian kastro atop Exobourgo is a stiff hike up zig-zagging stairway-paths from the villages of **Ksinara**, on the south-west slope of the mountain, or **Koumaros** on its south-east flank. The Convent of Kehrovounio, on a southern slope of the mountain above the village of Berdemnados, was where the location of the icon was revealed in a dream to Agia Pelagia, and is surrounded by lovely villages with perfect views. A perfect terrain for days of hillside rambling, either on foot or by moped.

TRAVELLING
By Sea   Ferries from Piraeus and onward throughout the Cyclades and to Crete.

Around the Island   Buses run efficiently to all the outlying villages from Tinos town. Motorcycles/mopeds for hire in Tinos.

WHERE TO STAY
Finding a bed in August, at Easter or during any of the island's many festivals is difficult, if not impossible. Across the board, accommodation costs more than in most other Cyclades ports. **Hotel Melteme**, close to the post office, is a reasonably priced if dull C-Class, **Hotel Aegli** a medium-priced D-Class and **Hotel Eleana** a cheaper D-Class.

FOOD AND DRINK
Restaurants are plentiful, on the expensive side but generally good as a result of a mainly Greek clientele. As usual, the chic-est and costliest tavernas are on the harbour-front. Cheaper souvlaki-stalls and restaurants can be found in and around the partly-covered market street which runs off Plateia Eleftherias Venizelou, behind the ferry pier; look out for the bandstand.

ANDROS

A favourite second home for well-off Athenians, this green (by the undemanding standards of the Cyclades) and pleasant island is the second largest (after Naxos) of the group and has a low-key, decentralized charm which takes time to grow on you. Tourism from overseas has yet to make much impact, though holiday hotels make an appearance at some of the beaches.

Easy to get to from the mainland port of Rafina, Andros is less than half a day's journey from Athens, which accounts for its popularity with the villa owners and also makes it a good alternative first stop for those jumping off into the islands from the capital. The capital of the island, called either **Andros Town** or **Chora**, has the inevitable Venetian castle, and a core of well-proportioned neo-classical shops and mansions, and overlooks a wide, sheltered bay. The port is much quieter than those of the southern islands, with their bustle of ferries to-ing and fro-ing. Andros is rather out on a limb, well off the heavy shipping of the central islands, and most of the ferry traffic goes to **Gavrio**, a dull modern harbour in the north-west facing Rafina and the mainland.

Outside town, Andros is even more low-key. Many natives have left for the mainland or joined the Greek diaspora abroad, and many villages have been reduced to clusters of holiday villas or abandoned completely. Those which remain inhabited are pleasant but unremarkable. Like Tinos, Andros is studded with the pigeon-towers, like miniature castle-keeps, built by the Venetians to ensure a continuous supply of fresh meat and eggs. Red-pantiled roofs, another memento of the Venetians, give many of the island houses an Italianate look.

One of the prettiest villages is **Palaeopolis**, suspended above the sea on the slopes of Mt Kouvara. **Vatsi,** midway along the west coast about ten km south of Gavrio, is the island's main beach resort with an attractive harbour and a growing number of holiday hotels.

TRAVELLING
By Sea   Frequent ferries to Andros from Rafina.

Around the Island   Infrequent buses between Gavrio and Chora via Messaria. Taxis.

WHERE TO STAY
There's no cheap accommodation.

Chora   **Hotel Egli,** C-Class.

Vatsi   **Pension Lykion,** medium-priced B-Class; Hotel **Chryssi Akti,** C-Class; **Hotel Karanassos,** C-Class.

Gavrio   **Pension Afroditi,** B-Class.

THE BEST OF THE REST

The Lesser Cyclades

From a vantage point on any of the more accessible Cyclades the silhouettes of other, less easily reached islands float, tempting and frustrating, on the horizon.

Preserved by erratic and infrequent ferry services from the mass influx of summer visitors, these minor islands are a magnet for travellers with plenty of time on their hands, a bagful of books to read and a taste for the simple life.

Even more rocky and uncultivable than their larger neighbours, their beauty is in the human touch – tiny unmodernized villages, eyrie-like monasteries and chapels – and in grand sea- and skyscapes.

These are islands for the flexible traveller. Some ports see the ferry only once a week and an unexpected cancellation can mean a much longer stay than you bargained for, so don't cut your schedule too fine if you have a homeward plane to catch.

KYTHNOS

The easiest to reach of the smaller Cyclades, only three hours from Piraeus, Kythnos gets surprisingly few foreign visitors, perhaps because connections with the main archipelago are so shaky. Greek holidaymakers come in large numbers in August and at weekends. **Merihas**, the main town, is a dozy port which mixes a few remaining Venetian-style tiled houses with more modern building and a couple of medium-sized hotels. **Loutra**, the fishing harbour about 12 km away on the east coast, is a more attractive place to stay, with a good beach. It also has one of the medicinal spas of which the Greeks are so fond.

There are no historic ruins, no inspiring mountains to climb and no nightlife beyond the tavernas and a half-hearted summer disco at the small **Kanalas** beach, on the south-east coast.

TRAVELLING
By Sea   Ferries from Piraeus, Sifnos and Serifos.

Around the Island   Buses run infrequently on the only two roads – from Merihas north-east to Loutra and south-east to Kavala.

WHERE TO STAY
Merihas   Some rooms but no cheap hotel accommodation. C-Class hotels **Possidonion** and **Kithnos Bay** are good value out of high season.

Loutra   Rooms available; also the expensive 50-room **Xenia Anagenissis** hotel.

FOOD AND DRINK
A handful of restaurant-bars, none outstanding, at **Merihas** and **Loutra**.

SERIFOS

Serifos sees more ferries than Kythnos but if anything gets fewer visitors. Roughly circular, the island rises to arid, low peaks inland. Half a dozen idyllic beach villages with rudimentary restaurants and accommodation are scattered round its rugged coast. The main port, **Livadi**, is a mismatched clutter of older buildings and small new hotels which have mushroomed ambitiously along its fine crescent beach. Much more picturesque is the largely unmodernized

Chora, two km inland above one of Serifos's few fertile valleys.

The best beaches are at **Ormos Sikamia**, six km from Chora on the north-west coast, **Psili Ammos** and Ag. **Giannis** on the west coast.

TRAVELLING

By Sea Ferries from Piraeus and Kithnos, Sifnos and Milos, and Ios and Santorini.

Around the Island Buses run from Livadi to Chora and Ormos Sikamia. Moped hire available in Livadi.

WHERE TO STAY

Cheapest hotel rooms are in the old-fashioned **Hotel Kyklades** (E-Class). Mid-priced and good value is the **Pension Areti**. There are rooms to let in Livadi and at Ormos Sikamia, but apparently no accommodation elsewhere.

FOOD AND DRINK

Restaurants in **Livadia**; basic places to eat and/or seasonal tavernas at **Sikamia, Psili Ammos** and the half-deserted harbour villages of **Koutalas** and **Megalo Livadi**.

SIFNOS

A pleasant main harbour, a very attractive white Cycladic kastro a short way inland, and a landscape dotted with neat patchwork fields and rivers of oleander flowers make Sifnos one of the most attractive of the smaller islands. Despite some good beaches, it has not yet become a major resort and most of its visitors are holidaying Athenians or Sifniot exiles visiting their relatives.

Kamares, the ferry port, sits complacently at the end of a deep inlet with a magnificent backdrop of chapel-crowned peaks culminating in the 900-metre Profitis Ilias. A harbour-front lined with tamarisk and plane trees and a general air of prosperity make this little fishing and ferry harbour ideal for loafers and loungers and there is a long pebbly-sandy beach.

Faros, seven km away on the east side of the island, is even quieter with a decent beach of its own and another nearby at **Apokofto**. The best beach on the island is at **Platis Yialos**, a little further south on the east coast and somewhat marred by large holiday hotels. **Vathi**, a fishing village at the end of a deep natural harbour on the west coast, is another attractive place to stay.

Inland, Sifnos offers rather more than its near neighbours. **Apollonia**, its main inland village, is a sprawling collection of spread-out settlements, archways, alleys and belltowers. **Kastro**, the medieval Venetian capital and stronghold, is three km away and is spectacularly located on a towering crag overlooking the sea.

Sifnos is also well endowed with medieval monasteries, some now abandoned, others still occupied by monks. **Moni Profitis Ilias**, on the mountain of the same name, has the most imposing location and is worth the stiff walk from Apollonia for the view alone. On the eastern flanks of the mountain, **Piges** monastery is lovely, ghostly and abandoned though only half an hour's walk from Apollonia. A further half-hour's walking brings you to the smaller church of **Ag. Andreas**, with sweeping views to the islands east of Sifnos. Midway between Ag. Andreas and Vathi is the **Taxiarhis** monastery (Taxiarhis is the familiar Greek name for St Michael; it means "the brigadier" in recognition of his rank as commander of the heavenly host). In summer, you can – if deemed respectable – rent rooms here and at the desanctified Hrissopigi monastery close to Apokofto beach.

TRAVELLING
Around the Island Good bus service from Kamares to the other harbour/beach villages and Apollonia. Moped hire available in Kamares.

By Sea Ferries from Piraeus via Kithnos and Serifos, to Ios, Santorini and points between, and to Paros and Milos, make Sifnos the most useful ferry-junction of the smaller islands of the western Cyclades.

WHERE TO STAY
Kamares Pension Kamari and Pension Myrto, both B-Class and quite expensive in season but pleasant. Rooms to rent available, but often full in summer.

Apollonia Pension Apollonia, B-Class, pricy but nice. Some rooms to rent.

Platis Gialos Several big B-Class bed factories; the D-Class **Filoxenia** is small, cheap and clean.

Faros   Pension Fabrica, in a restored Venetian house, is far and away the nicest place to stay – if there is space – and cheapish. There are cheaper rooms in the older part of town.

FOOD AND DRINK
Good choice in **Kamares** around the harbour; a bit rudimentary elsewhere. Plenty of expensive seasonal tavernas at **Platis Gialos** and good seafood at **Faros**; several nice old tavernas of the sooty grill and tobacco-stained ceiling persuasion around **Apollonia**.

FOLEGANDROS
Craggy Folegandros is a natural castle, its cliffs rising more than 300 metres making it a natural defensive site – and under some of Greece's more repressive governments in the past, a natural prison for dissidents. The same cliffs have until the last few years deterred tourism, but in summer the island attracts a determined cadre of younger European backpackers. It is an extremely dry, almost desert island with no outstanding beaches, and its biggest delight is the wonderful, hidden village of **Chora,** a largely untouched fortress-settlement with a wonderful medieval kastro and streets of medieval houses.

The only port is Karavostasi, which has seen a minor building boom since the building of an enormous ferry pier. A pebbly beach about 15 minutes' walk away at Livadhi is one of the few good places to swim on Folegandros. Other beaches are at **Angali** and **Livadhaki** on the island's west coast and at **Ag. Giorghios** on the northern tip.

Much of the rest of Folegandros is a patchwork of small-holdings. Farming has changed little for centuries, and most of these little farms scrape a living from the arid soil much as they did last century. Barley and goats seem to be the main staples.

TRAVELLING
By Sea   Ferries from Sikinos, Ios and Santorini.

Around the Island   Buses from Karavostasi to Chora and from Chora to beaches several times a day. Seasonal boats go from Karavostasi around the island beaches.

WHERE TO STAY
Pension Fani is good but expensive. **Hotel Danassis** (E-Class) and **Hotel Odysseas** (E-Class) are cheaper but not outstanding. Rooms to rent at Karavostasi and Chora.

FOOD AND DRINK

Harbourside tavernas at **Karavostasi**; a few nice old-fashioned eateries in **Chora**. Seasonal beach-side restaurants at **Livadhi** and **Livadhaki**.

AMORGOS

Like Folegandros, Amorgos is off the beaten track for package holidaymakers but well known to a loyal clientele of backpacking cognoscenti who pack the place out through July and August. This is understandable, as Amorgos has a choice of lovely old-fashioned villages and excellent beaches set in a striking landscape of cliffs and deserted countryside.

A knife-edged mountain ridge divides the island in two, and it is far easier to get from **Katapola**, the main ferry port, to the northern part of the island by sea than by land. Katapola is a bit nondescript – its major event seems to be the late-night arrival of the ferry – and the main town – called **Chora**, as always – is a much pleasanter place to make your base, a mixture of old-style village beneath its inevitable hilltop kastro and summer bohemianism.

Immediately below Chora – though a stiff walk up or down – there is an excellent beach at **Agia Anna**. Between the two, the **Hozoviotissa Monastery**, a great white eyrie whose whitewash is blindingly brilliant against the ochre cliff face, now houses only a couple of venerable monks, though it was built for more than 50. The monastery's treasury of icons, vestments, and reliquaries is a stunning reminder of the wealth of the Byzantine churches; well worth the hike from Chora.

TRAVELLING

By Sea Ferries daily from Naxos.

Around the Island Occasional (and elderly) buses between Katapola and Chora and to Agia Anna. Boats to Egiali in summer.

WHERE TO STAY

Out of high season, no problem; in high season, big problem. The summer migration means it is difficult to find a room from late June to early September. Hotels include the nice and inexpensive **Hotel Mike** at **Egiali** and the adequate **Minoa** at **Katapola**. Rooms can be rented at **Chora**.

CRETE
The Big Island

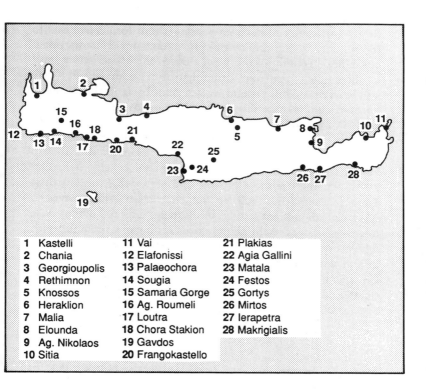

1	Kastelli	**11**	Vai	**21**	Plakias
2	Chania	**12**	Elafonissi	**22**	Agia Gallini
3	Georgioupolis	**13**	Palaeochora	**23**	Matala
4	Rethimnon	**14**	Sougia	**24**	Festos
5	Knossos	**15**	Samaria Gorge	**25**	Gortys
6	Heraklion	**16**	Ag. Roumeli	**26**	Mirtos
7	Malia	**17**	Loutra	**27**	Ierapetra
8	Elounda	**18**	Chora Stakion	**28**	Makrigialis
9	Ag. Nikolaos	**19**	Gavdos		
10	Sitia	**20**	Frangokastello		

More than any other Greek island, Crete is a country within a country, with its own history, dialects and traditions. In the mountains you'll still see many older men wearing the habitual knee-length riding boots, baggy trousers and knotted silk head-dress of the Cretan shepherd. If you take a walk in Crete's thorn-spiked hill country you'll quickly appreciate the value of the long boots to people who get about their mountain pastures either on foot or by donkey. As the pick-up truck replaces the donkey and the mule this typical garb is dying out with its wearers. Where other Greeks drink ouzo, Cretans knock back raki, a fierce spirit credited with remarkable restorative powers.

Greeks call it "the big island" and – more than 200 km from north to south – it lives up to its name. Crete is even big enough to have soaked up the massive influx of package tourism of the last ten to 15 years without total surrender to the whims of the holidaymaker. Though much of its north coast has become a continuous strip of bed factories hard to distinguish from any other Mediterranean beach, Crete still has remote hill villages, empty pebbly coves, little fishing harbours and savage mountain peaks, snowcapped in winter and searingly hot in summer.

Crete's summer heat can be African – from the south coast beaches the Libyan coast is no further away than Athens. Spring comes earlier than on the mainland or islands further north and the Cretan hills are a painter's delight throughout April, spattered with red, yellow and purple wild flowers. By May, the colours are fading; by June the reds and greens have been sun-blasted to the ochre monochrome of Cretan summer, when the mountains become a parched wilderness of thistles and aromatic herbs. In high summer, a Cretan mountainside can smell like a pizza parlour. Winter comes later than in the north and you can still swim and sunbathe happily in October and – with luck – even into early November.

Crete's major towns and its biggest package-holiday centres are all on the island's north coast, which has most, though not all, of the best sand beaches and all three of its international airports. For smaller, less brazen holiday resorts head for the harbours of the south-west which, while by no means undeveloped, are still distinctively Cretan. And for still greater privacy and authenticity, try the hard-to-get-to villages of Crete's west coast.

Most of Crete's holiday beaches and hotels are on the north coast between the island's capital, Heraklion, and Agios Nikolaos, some 70 km away. This region also has two of Crete's most important Minoan sites – the palaces at Knossos and Malia – and, not far inland, the hidden oasis-plain of Lasithi.

HERAKLION (IRAKLIO)

Crete's capital is a busy commercial harbour town of no great charm. Points of interest include the Venetian walls which encircle the old town, the remains of the Venetian arsenal by the harbour, and the Archaeological Museum which houses the artefacts and frescoes recovered from Knossos and other Minoan sites. Of these, the museum is the only must. If you have already visited Chania and Rethimnon you will find Heraklion's waterfront a disappointment, for this is a working port with none of the dinky cafés and restaurants which make Crete's other north coast towns so appealing to holidaymakers. Instead, most of Heraklion's restaurants are around the waterless Venetian fountain on Plateia Venizelou and the surrounding streets.

Heraklion's streets still have a number of older buildings in the charming – and practical – neo-classical style popular in Greece in the last century and before World War Two. Most of them are crumbling into disrepair but some are being refurbished rather than demolished. Take a look at the façade of the Commercial Bank building on Odos 25 Avgoustou, which has recently been cleaned up, and imagine what Heraklion looked like before it became the grimy collection of shoebox architecture it mostly is today.

GETTING YOUR BEARINGS

Built in a rough crescent around the old Venetian harbour, Heraklion is easy to find your way around. The town slopes down to the waterfront, Odos Makariou, which forms an esplanade. The Venetian castle on the western tip of the old harbour is a useful landmark and the sea is always to the north. The medieval walls still surround the older and more interesting part of the city. The hub of this is **Plateia Venizelou,** named after the politician who led Crete into union with modern Greece and became one of Greece's most charismatic leaders. Venizelou is linked to the waterfront by Odos 25 Avgoustou. The other hub of the city is **Platia Eleftheria**, just within the eastern walls of Heraklion and overlooking the massive concrete docks of the modern ferry harbour.

Od. Dhikeosinis connects the two, while Od Kalokerinou runs west from Venizelou to the Chania Gate in the western bastion of the city wall. Od. Evans, named after the excavator of ancient Knossos, runs south from Venizelou to the Kanouria Gate. Odos 25 Avgoustou, running between the Venetian Harbour and Plateia Venizelou, is where you'll find most of Heraklion's travel and tour offices. Odos 1866 – running off Venizelou – is the main market street.

DON'T MISS . . .

The Archaeological Museum (*Od. Pedhiados, off Plateia Eleftheria*) is crammed with the wealth of finds from Knossos, Malia, Festos and elsewhere, and gives much greater insight into the Minoan civilization than just visiting the sites can ever do. Hundreds of the exhibits – from tiny clay and bronze figurines to frescoes and the famous black and gold head of the Bull of Knossos – illustrate the Minoan obsession with their sacred animal. Pots, vases, and the double-axes – some tiny, some huge – which featured as money and as cult objects, earthenware grave-goods, weapons and coins, give some idea of how elaborate and sophisticated was Minoan civilization more than 3,000 years ago. Don't miss the exhibit of seals: the abstract symbols, mythical beasts and birds the Minoans used as personal marks are quite unlike those of any other culture and look oddly modern.

Another interesting exhibit is a game board from Knossos, a complex relief-pattern of coloured diagrams with coneshaped earthenware game pieces. Almost as ubiquitous as the bull motif is the snake goddess of the Minoans. She is believed to be their greatest deity and is depicted bare-breasted with a wriggling serpent in either hand. The busts and frescoes of Minoan rulers and deities, with their straight-nosed profiles and long curling locks are strongly reminiscent of contemporary Egyptian work, and Egypt, only a few days' sailing away, must have been a strong influence on the Minoans.

Upstairs, the surviving frescoes help you to visualize the elaborate decoration of the Minoan palaces. The fluid line and vivid colours, like so much else in the museum, seem startlingly modern. After looking at them, the much more recent Roman and Hellenistic statues and busts in the museum seem stolid and stiff by comparison.

The reconstruction of the Knossos palace is well worth a look, giving a clear idea of how elaborate the whole complex must have been. The museum is always busy, often crowded, and the best time to visit is early morning.

ALSO WORTH SEEING . . .

The Venetian Arsenal, *Od. Makariou (opposite the Venetian Harbour)* is a massive row of arched storerooms. Now open to the weather, the arches are used by boatmen for storing gear, but their huge size is a clue to the armed might of Venice in Crete.

The Historical Museum, *Makariou (opposite westbound bus terminus)* a jumble of weapons, tools, folk costumes and memorabilia in no clear order includes a room dedicated to Nikos Kazantzakis, author of Zorba the Greek.

PLUS . . .

Most of the shops and stalls on Odos 1866, the market street off Venizelou, are for local people rather than visitors, though there are a number of souvenir shops too. You'll find the ubiquitous smelly leather goods, silly hats and hideous knick-knacks, but this is still a working local market where you can get heaped fruit, vegetables and other produce – including buckets of live snails – and everyday goods. A number of shops sell packets of the herbs which make every Cretan hillside smell so appetizing in high summer, and also of the herbal teas and remedies for which Crete is famous. Saffron, at around 250 drachmas for about 20 grams, is excellent value.

ALONG THE NORTH COAST

Between Heraklion and Agios Nikolaos the Cretan coast is dominated by purpose-built holiday resorts. This strip

Knossos

Crete's best-known, most accessible and most important archaeological site is the target for thousands of coachloads of visitors each year. As with other ancient sites, the best times to avoid the crowds are first thing in the morning, late afternoon and around lunchtime. Most of the time you will, however, have to jockey your way through the coach groups. One of the reasons Knossos is so popular is that it has been reconstructed to a far greater extent than most sites, and it takes less imaginative effort to visualize it before its fall. The balance between imagination and scientific method used on the site by Sir Arthur Evans has caused hot debate ever since, and some visitors feel that the rebuilding is obtrusive and detracts from the power of the site. Its location is not quite as dramatic or evocative as some of Greece's other ancient sites. Nevertheless, with its frescoes, labyrinthine passageways and coloured columns, Knossos is not to be missed, and to get a better sense of the civilization which built this and the other palaces you should plan to visit the Archaeological Museum in Heraklion as well.

There are a few rooms to rent in the village nearby and a handful of rather over-priced café-restaurants opposite the main coach park.

Buses to Knossos run every ten minutes or so from Plateia Venizelou, in the centre of Heraklion. For those with their own transport, there is adequate free parking at the site.

has some of the best sand beaches in Crete, and there's a wide choice of accommodation and other services dedicated to the package holidaymaker. If your first priority is a Mediterranean holiday beach backed by hotels, apartments, pubs and discos this part of Crete is for you. Only some token Greek "folklore", a handful of dishes on the menu, and the day-trips to Crete's main tourist attractions differentiate these resorts from a hundred like them around the Mediterranean.

From Heraklion as far as **Limenas Hersonissou**, the beach resorts are strung out along the busy east-west highway in a succession of virtually identical shoebox towns, most of which have good beaches but are otherwise uninspiring. **Hersonissos** is rather more up-market, and the beach strip between here and the thriving resort of **Malia** has a better choice of accommodation and a bit more character than the resorts closer to Heraklion.

Malia also boasts a Minoan palace site which is far less visited than either Knossos or Festos and which, though it has not been extensively rebuilt, allows your imagination free rein. The resort has a choice of sandy beaches and is within easy reach of Knossos and the Lasithi plain, eastern Crete's main natural beauty spot.

East of Malia, the road curves inland through pleasant hill country covered by olives before hitting the coast again.

TRAVELLING

By Air Charter flights from many UK airports in summer. Flights from Athens several times a day. There are also flights to Rhodes and Thessaloniki. The airport is around 10 km from town.

By Sea Ferries go daily to and from Piraeus and at least four times a week to the main Cycladic islands in summer, two to three times a week to Karpathos and Rhodes. A fast catamaran connects Heraklion with Santorini several times a week from May to September.

Around the North Coast Buses hourly to Rethimnon and Chania, around six times a day to Agios Nikolaos and four times daily to Ierapetra and the south. Heraklion has four bus stations: double check which one you want. Buses to Chania and Rethimnon may go from the west-bound station at Od. Gazi (ten minutes' walk west from the Venetian harbour along Makariou) or from the south-west terminus on Od 62 Martirou, just outside the Hania Gate of the city wall. Buses for the south-east go from Plateia Kiprou (15 minutes' walk from Venizelou, along Od. Evans, outside the Kanouria Gate), and buses for Malia, Ag. Nikolaos and the east from the eastbound terminus behind the main ferry harbour.

WHERE TO STAY

There are many small hotels and pensions as well as more expensive B- and C-Class hotels. Rented rooms, catering to the vast summer throngs of transient independent backpackers, are plentiful but tend not to be very good value – a lot of people arrive late at night straight off the boat or plane, are too tired to be choosy about accommodation, and it's a seller's market. Quite a lot of rented rooms are rather slovenly.

Good value is offered by the D-Class **Hotel Hellas**, on Odos Kantanoleon, just behind Venizelou, and the **Cretan Sun Hotel**, overlooking the market on Odos 1866. More pricy is the **Castro**

Hotel, Odos Theotokopoulou 22, one of the city's newest hotels with an attractive, almost Art Deco exterior. Next door is the cheaper **Hotel Mirabello**, an old-style C-Class place. Theotokopoulou is rather quieter than the streets around Venizelou. **Hotel Palladion** at 16 Odos Handakos is another cheaper option for those on a budget. **Camping Heraklion**, about five kilometres west of town, is clean, cheap and has hot showers.

FOOD AND DRINK

The most expensive bars, cafés and hotels are those around **Plateia Venizelou**, catering to tourists and popular too with younger Greeks with money to spend. You'll find a street full of cheaper, less flashy places to eat in the evening between the Odos 1866 market and Odos Evans on a little street called **Odos Archimandritou Fotosaki**. A couple of blocks away, **Odos Dedalou** is another street crowded with restaurants and even has a Chinese place, the Blue Dragon. Heraklion is also a good town for stand-up eating, with plenty of gyros and souvlaki places.

AGIOS NIKOLAOS

Beloved of British holidaymakers for some 20 years, "Ag Nik" is unashamedly a good-time tourist town. Built around a natural inner harbour – almost a lake – connected to the outer seaport by a narrow channel, it certainly has location going for it, ringed by mountains and looking north and east over the Aegean.

Compulsive shoppers will find the usual run of jewellery and ceramic shops, plus a leather and T-shirt shop at the foot of Odos Constantine Paleologos (just off the inner harbour) which sells T-shirts decorated with patterns and designs from Minoan frescoes. Just across the street, hand-painted ceramic copies from ancient sites are on sale at Keramica.

For swimmers, there's a small and surprisingly clean and tidy pebbly beach in town at **Akti Pagalou** – follow Sfakianaki east from the inner harbour to get there.

TRAVELLING

By Sea Ferries twice weekly to Rhodes and Karpathos.

By Road Hourly buses from Heraklion and Sitia. Car and motorbike rental outlets on Odos Koundourou, the Agios Nikolaos waterfront, where you'll also find most of the travel and tour agencies. Adonis Bike

Rental, next door to the Avis and Budget car rental offices, claims to rent the cheapest bikes and mopeds in town.

WHERE TO STAY
Plenty of small to medium-sized hotels and pensions as well as rented rooms. Like those in Heraklion, and for the same reasons, the latter tend not to be very good value. The **Hotel Kastro** and the **Hotel Panorama**, overlooking the outer harbour, offer medium-priced accommodation. The **Hotel Akratos** and the **Hotel Du Lac** both overlook the inner harbour and are more costly.

FOOD AND DRINK
Most restaurants are around the pretty inner harbour with its moored fishing boats. There's a wide choice, from the expensive to the basic.

The **Olympia Garden Restaurant** at 11 Strategos Koraka is in one of the town's few surviving older buildings and has an attractive outdoor terrace. The **Alexandros Hotel** bar has a roof garden at 2 Kondylaki, overlooking the inner harbour,

The unassuming **Pine Taverna** on Odos Solomou is one of the better-value places to eat in this part of town. Swankier and more expensive are the outdoor terraces of the **Hotel Du Lac** and the **Akratos,** facing it across the lagoon. The **Café Zygos**, under trees on an inner corner of the harbour, is a favourite gathering spot for younger locals.

NIGHTLIFE
Nightlife, in the shape of a large number of discos and music bars, is pitched at a young and cheerful crowd of summer migrants. Thanks to them, the video bar has also come to Ag Nik in a big way, and at one bar on the outer harbour you can catch not only movies and pop videos but British sporting highlights, the evening news and even excerpts from Top of the Pops.

OUT OF TOWN . . .
Lasithi, the famous "Plain of the Windmills", is within easy striking distance of Agios Nikolaos if you have your own transport, but a bit more difficult to get to by bus. Ag. Nikolaos tour agencies run frequent coach tours to the plain. **Knossos** is the other favoured day-trip on land – about 90 minutes each way by bus – and there are plenty of cruise boats offering cruises to the offshore island of **Spinalonga** (see below), about an hour away by boat, and to nearby beaches.

About 12 km west of the noisy nightlife of Agios Nikolaos, the collection of smaller villages resorts and luxury hotels loosely known as **Elounda** offers a wider choice of generally more expensive accommodation, most of it aimed at an older, better-off clientele. There's a string of small hotels, pensions, rooms to rent and tour and hire car agencies starting at Schisma, beside the causeway which links the offshore island of Spinalonga to the mainland, and extending some five km as far as Kato Elounda, which with its sheltered harbour full of fishing boats is as near to a "typical" Cretan fishing village as you will find on the north coast. There's plenty of accommodation here, most of it rather pricier than on the south coast because it's aimed at package holidaymakers rather than independent travellers.

Above the harbour of Kato ("lower") Elounda, the village of Pano ("higher") Elounda is surprisingly untouched by tourism and has three or four round stone-built windmill towers on a ridge above the village.

Spinalonga was once used as a quarantine island for leprosy victims and is still uninhabited; it shelters the whole almost-landlocked bay of Elounda from the open sea and has a number of secluded beaches and a Venetian fortress.

About ten km east of Agios Nikolaos, **Istro** is a small resort on a little sheltered beach at the foot of steep mountain slopes, with a number of studios, self-catering apartments and a couple of larger hotels. It's pleasant enough, but a bit short on character, with the beach as its only reason for being there.

LASITHI

The mountain-ringed fertile plain of Lasithi is one of Crete's surprises, an oasis surrounded by high ranges of almost lunar barrenness. Over millions of years, topsoil has washed off the island's highest mountains, leaving sterile slopes covered with rock splinters. At Lasithi this fertile soil, instead of being carried down to the sea, has gathered in a saucer-shaped pocket some eight km across. It's one of the most fertile areas in Greece and is intensively farmed in a chequered mosaic of green fields and orchards, all the more striking because the mountain slopes all around are so devoid of life that they look almost Himalayan. Spring comes later to the fertile cup of Lasithi than to the coast, and even in late April and early May, when the sun is beginning to parch the lower hills, the fields and patches of wasteland here blaze with poppies and daisies.

Two mountain roads enter Lasithi from the coast, and the view of the plain from either pass is striking. The famous windmills whose white sails dominate most pictures of Lasithi are gradually falling into disuse. Used to draw up water for irrigation, many of them have been replaced by power-driven pumps, and the fields are full of the toppled or crazily-tilted gantries of disused windmills. If you want see the surviving ones at work, come in high summer, when a number are still used.

Lasithi's other big attraction for the large numbers of day-trippers who come by coach from the north coast resorts is the Dikti Cave, legendary birthplace of Zeus. A cobbled path leads to the cave from a car and coach park just above the village of **Psihri** where there is a steady trade in renting mule-rides and the services of "guides" to visitors.

These "guides" don't, however, appear to own a torch among the lot of them, and use stubs of church taper instead. Nor do they know much about the cave or its legends. The caverns, green with moss and full of limsetone spires and stalactites, are easy enough to explore on your own with the aid of a good torch; there's a stairway with a rather precarious handrail and the only risk is of getting your feet wet.

Cave and windmills aside, the Lasithi villages – when the coach tours have passed on – are among the parts of Crete least affected by tourism. The pick-up truck, tractor and rotavator are replacing the mule, donkey and hand-plough, but otherwise the rhythms of a prosperous small farming community have hardly been broken. Daybreak on Lasithi can be a deafening chorus of cockerels, donkeys, dogs, goatbells.

Tzermiado, the plain's main village, is the best base for exploring Lasithi and the surrounding mountains. It has two or three restaurants catering mainly to coach tours at lunchtime and in the evening to the handful of visitors who stay the night. The village is bigger than it seems at first sight, and on its old main street – supplanted by a modern through road – every other building seems to be an old-style kafeneion serving raki and coffee to a capped and whiskered clientele of local farmers. This is one part of Crete where you'll still get a lavish meze with your drinks if you ask for it. In winter – and even in spring and early summer – Lasithi can be much chillier than the coast, and these old cafés with their log-burning stoves in the middle of the room are the warmest place to be.

From Tzermiado, it's a five- to ten-minute walk to the small and less spectacular **Cave of Kronos**; follow the signs marked variously "Cave of Sanctuary" or "Kronion Cave". A narrow footpath runs off the main tarred road: where this splits, about 200m from the main road, it's marked with a splash of brown paint. Take the uphill fork for the cave. For keener walkers, following the right-hand fork will lead you through patches of terraced cultivation and olive grove and eventually to a pass through high, weathered limestone slopes where even goats find nothing worth eating. From the crest of this pass you can see, behind you, the whole of Lasithi with the mountains to the west outlined behind it. Looking north and east, the coastal hills beyond Agios Nikolaos – almost 50 km away by road – are clearly visible.

TRAVELLING
There are buses to Lasithi from Heraklion, about 50 km away, twice daily. The two main roads into the plain, from Neapoli to the east and via Potamies and Gonies in the west, are tarred and fairly wide but very steep and winding – drive cautiously. There are day trips to Lasithi from all the north coast resorts, bookable through local tour agencies and hotels.

WHERE TO STAY
Tzermiado **Hotel Idi** old-fashioned, cheapest in Lasithi; **Hotel Tzermiado**, newish, cheap.

THE EAST

Crete holds few disappointments for the visitor; and all of them are in the east of the island, beyond the isthmus – Crete's narrowest part – between the Gulf of Mirabello and the main south-east coastal town, Ierapetra.

IERAPETRA

The best you can say about Ierapetra is that it is uninspiring. Its main role is as a commercial centre for the farmland round about and to a lesser extent as a fishing harbour, but surprisingly this dusty commercial town has become quite a hit with package holidaymakers from the UK and elsewhere. It owes this success to a long, grey-sand beach which stretches for almost two miles eastwards from the town and harbour, and which is now lined with big and characterless hotels. The main package-tour bed factories are along the main beach, starting about a kilometre from the harbour. In town, there are rooms to rent and some smaller D-Class hotels. The best that can be said about them is that they're cheap. There's a functional and crumbling Venetian fort of no visual interest on the harbour and a string of pavement restaurants and cafés along the waterfront. One of Ierapetra's few plus points is that because it's still a Greek commercial centre there are plenty of non-tourist restaurants and souvlaki and gyro places where you can eat cheaply.

Fortunately, it's easy to leave Ierapetra and its dull hinterland of shabby warehouses and plastic greenhouses. Hourly buses leave for Heraklion and in the other direction buses go four or five times a day to Sitia. Cars and bikes can be rented from agencies on the waterfront.

NEAR IERAPETRA

Boat trips ply from Ierapetra harbour to the offshore island of **Chrisi**, technically a national park because of its cedar woods. You can camp and there is a small taverna.

Less than 20 km west of Ierapetra, **Mirtos** is the next beach worth visiting. You may have heard good things about Mirtos as an "untouched" beach village; forget it. Its grey sand and shingle beach is long, uncrowded and easily accessible, true. The village itself however is soulless and centreless and at an unfortunate stage in development which manages to combine all the faults of a one-time backpacker hideout – litter and a general air of lackadaisical scruffiness – with the vices of development: ugly cement blocks of rooms going up everywhere and blasting disco music. At the end of its waterfront string of cafés and restaurants, the Milky Way café is the refuge of a handful of determined Greek hippies: nobody seems to have told them the '70s are long over.

It takes about three hours to get from Ierapetra to Heraklion, which more or less rules out Knossos as a day trip. Within easier reach are Agios Nikolaos and the famed palm beach at Vai.

EAST FROM IERAPETRA

Crete's south coast heading east from Ierapetra is unpromising until you reach **Makrigialos**, which together with next-door **Analipsis** forms an unbroken strip of beach bars, cafés, discos and tour hotels along an excellent sandy bay, with smaller beaches and coves to either side. The bay is very shallow and the water warm – it's a good place for swimming in early summer, when the deeper waters around the rest of the island are still chilly.

Makrigialos retains some fishing-village character, with rooms to rent and a couple of small hotels around a quiet harbour where fishermen are still in a majority in quite a few of the cafés. About two km away, Analipsis at the other end of the fine sweep of beach is dominated by a mainly Scandinavian package holiday clientele. The huge Sunwing Hotel occupies two headlands and has two excellent, virtually private beaches. Around it are bars, restaurants, discos and supermarkets.

From Makrigialos, the main island highway curves north through hill country to **Sitia**, the north coast's easternmost port town. Like Ierapetra, Sitia attracts a substantial holiday traffic because of its good beach just outside town, a long stretch of sand which faces north and can be windswept at any time of year.

As in Ierapetra, you wonder how anyone could be seduced into spending a week here, let alone a fortnight. The town itself is ugly and dull even by the undemanding standards of modern Greek town planning. The harbour appears to have the main Sitia sewer flowing right into it, and the harbourside restaurants are mediocre and overpriced. Sitia is almost four hours' drive from Heraklion, ruling out day trips to Knossos and points west.

Perhaps this explains the enormous and I think undeserved

popularity of Vai, eastern Crete's much-hyped palm beach and "tropical lagoon". Few destinations so thoroughly fail to match their description.

The drive to the famous palm grove is through scenery which is eye-catching only in its banal ugliness. There's no grandeur here, just the barren rocky red earth and clumps of thorn bush which indicate that goats have done their worst. Vai itself consists of a quarter-mile stretch of admittedly immaculately clean sand, backed by the main attraction – a grove not of the towering Caribbean palms you have been led to expect but of the squat, North African variety you can see on most Cretan esplanades. The carpark, built to handle the dozens of tour coaches which arrive each day, is as big as the beach but not as clean (the toilets and showers, for which you have to pay a princely 30p, are a disgrace). Refreshments are available from an overpriced bar on the beach and an overpriced restaurant overlooking it. The palm grove itself is fenced off, and as the river which waters it is visibly drying up there must be some question as to how long it can survive. Over the headland beyond the restaurant, another good, fairly clean sandy cove is designated for nude swimming. But with all of Crete's beaches and other attractions to choose from, the question is surely – Vai bother?

Between Vai and Sitia, the beautiful Toplou monastery has one of Crete's most famous works of religious art, the 18th-century ikon named Lord thou art Great. For many years kept in the British Museum, it was returned to its rightful place only a few years ago.

CHANIA

Chania is one of Crete's main gateways by sea or air, and also one of the prettier towns in an island not over-endowed with urban style. There are good beaches within easy reach of the north coast and it's a main jumping-off point for the beaches of the south-west and for the Samaria Gorge.

Around its medieval Venetian harbour, beneath the walls of a small and functional fortress, tourism has transformed the old town's waterfront into an arena of café-terraces. You could spend a week here and not eat at the same place twice, though the menus are near identical in price and variety.

It's good to see that some effort is being made in Chania to renovate and restore at least some of the town's elegant old neo-classical houses, and their fresh new pink and yellow stucco and high white-shuttered windows are a marked contrast to the breeze-block eyesores which dominate so many Greek cities. It's a shame not more of these pre-war buildings have survived: they're not only prettier to look at but in high summer cooler and pleasanter within than many of the ugly new buildings.

The streets of the old town haven't quite been swamped by the souvenir industry, though in some of them it's making a gallant effort. Of all the Cretan towns, only Rethimnon retains as much of its traditional heart. These mellow, high alleys, some of them so narrow you can touch both walls at the same time, are a nice contrast to the bustling, eating, drinking and nightlife of the harbour-front, and to the modern, commercial Greek life of the new town a few blocks behind. They're full of patches of greenery, flowers in pots or rooftops shaded by vines.

GETTING YOUR BEARINGS

The heart of modern Chania is **Plateia 1866**, named for the abortive nationalist rising against the Turks in that year. This square is lined with cafés and fast food places and has a number of modern tourist hotels, the main National Bank branch and other banks and – hidden away on the fourth floor of the National Bank building – the tourist office. If it's shut, which it frequently is, the travel agency on the same floor is very friendly and helpful and arranges excursions, car and bike rental, accommodation and onward travel from Chania and from Crete. There's also a second-hand English-language bookstore on Plateia 1866.

Odos Halidhon, between the square and the harbour-front a couple of minutes' walk away, is lined with car and bike rental places and ticket and travel agencies.

DON'T MISS . . .

Many streets of Chanias's **Old Quarter** are still crumbling and half-ruined and the older buildings have clearly been built and rebuilt, added to or half-demolished over centuries. Chania's Venetian fort, overlooking the harbour, has little more to see than its walls. There's a small pension inside the walls where you can rent rooms. On Odos Michali Dalaioannis a disused mosque, now a garment factory, is a reminder that until Cretan independence in 1913, Chania, like the other towns of Crete, was almost as much Moslem as Christian. The minarets of several other disused mosques can also be seen on the skyline of old Chania.

On **Odos Halidhon** is Chania's Archaeological Museum. Its collection is much the same as Heraklion's, but on a smaller scale. Chania's museum doesn't attract hordes of visitors – as Heraklion's does – and much of the time you can wander around alone and undisturbed. The collection ranges from Minoan to Classical and Hellenistic times. It gives an interesting sense of how Knossos and its empire existed not in isolation but with close trade links with the Mycenaeans and with Italy and ancient Egypt – part of a much greater Mediterranean civilisation. On a hot summer day the old museum building is also delightfully cool.

Odos Skridlof and Odos Karaoli, running off Halidhon, exude the aroma of recently-cured leather which always indicates a Cretan souvenir-shopping street – leather bags, high boots, jewellery and Cretan rugs are the mainstay here and the rugs are far and away the best buy.

ALSO WORTH SEEING . . .

Between the old and new towns, a five-minute walk from the harbour, Chania's big **produce market** in a neoclassical building with wrought-iron gates is well worth visiting early in the day when things are in full swing and vast quantities of fish, fruit and vegetables are on sale. What there is to see depends on the time of year but it's always interesting. The market is opposite the Hotel Kidon on Odos Nikoforou Phokas.

OUT OF TOWN . . .

Heading West

There are crowded and rather scruffy beaches within 15 minutes' walk of the centre to the west. These improve the further you get from Chania in the direction of **Agia Marina**, about eight km away, and there are more and still better (though unserviced) beaches between this village and **Tavronitis**.

Heading East

You can find swimming and sunbathing on the north coast of the **Akrotiri peninsula**, at Horafakia. This suburban beach is crowded in summer. Avoid the **Souda Bay** coast, east of Hania – it's a huge naval base. The little resort of **Georgoupolis** (see box), 32 km away, has a superb beach. Chania's also within easy striking distance of Knossos, which you can see either with a guided tour, bookable through hotels or

Chania agency, or independently, using KTEL buses or your own transport. It's a longish day trip from Chania, involving about six hours on the tour coach, and even longer by KTEL – most independent travellers will prefer to take two days, staying overnight at Knossos or in Heraklion.

Heading South

Chania is a good base for exploring the spectacular mountains of south-west Crete, the Samaria Gorge walk and others (see box). If you're keen to explore further into the hills and mountains of the west, Jonni Godfrey's *Landscapes of Western Crete* is a must (see page 19). The Samaria walk can be done in a day trip from Chania, with a boat ride from Agia Roumeli to Chora Sfakion thrown in. Book at the agencies on Halidhon.

Offshore: The volcano island of **Santorini (Thira)** has recently become accessible as a day-trip from Chania using fast, Norwegian-built catamarans. The unearthly land-and-seascape of the Santorini caldera, with its garishly coloured cliffs and archetypical white cubist village above, makes the trip worthwhile.

TRAVELLING

By Sea Daily ferries connect Chania with Piraeus in summer. As elsewhere, boats are less frequent in off-season. In summer, too, there's a fast catamaran service several times a week to Santorini. It's aimed mainly at people who want to take a day-trip, but can also be used one-way. Tickets for both services are sold by agencies at the harbour and on Halkidon and Tzanakakis.

By Road Buses connect Chania with Kastelli in the west (hourly), Rethimnon, Heraklion and intermediate points to the east (half-hourly), and Palaeochora and Chora Sfakion on the south-west coast (each four times a day).

By Air Olympic Airways operates several flights daily to Athens. In summer, numerous charters from UK airports.

WHERE TO STAY

There are rooms to rent and small pensions throughout the old town and a number of small hotels overlooking the Venetian harbour. More modern rooms and pensions can be found on Odos Tzanakakis, and there are number of medium sized A-, B- and C-Class hotels on Plateia 1866 and on Nikoforou Fokas.

FOOD, DRINK AND NIGHTLIFE
There's masses of choice down by the harbour, which remains lively late into the night.

GEORGOUPOLIS

A long sweep of sandy beach – one of the best in Crete – is this little resort's big attraction. That, and a good selection of new little hotels, pensions, rooms and self-catering apartments make it a happy find for a relaxed beach holiday. Nightlife centres on eating and drinking rather than raving, though Georgoupolis does have a couple of summer discos. The village is set some distance back from its beach, at the mouth of one of Crete's few rivers, which forms the village's harbour. Thick reed-beds stand between the long beach and the village. Georgoupolis is dominated by package holiday business, and in high season independent travellers may have trouble finding accommodation. There's little trace of the original Cretan village on which the resort has been built – just a handful of old boys more or less permanently established in one of the cafés on the little plateia. The big stands of bamboo, the presence of so much fresh water – unusual for Crete – and the deafening racket of hundreds of frogs calling at night are an eloquent warning that Georgioupolis can be troubled by mosquitoes in high summer – most rooms have electric deterrent devices but this is somewhere you may need repellent.

The long beach is increasingly being dominated by big package tour hotels such as the Hotel Gorgona, and there are large hotels scattered along the length of the fine beach. If you're looking for a good holiday hotel on one of Crete's best beaches, Georgoupolis is for you. It's also within easy reach of Rethimnon, Chania, Knossos and the Samaria Gorge, and of the airports at Chania and Rethimnon. It's no more than an hour from either airport.

RETHIMNON

This seaport, with its Venetian harbour, huge fortress, maze-like old quarter and excellent beach, may well be Crete's most attractive town. It's busier – both with tourism and local commerce – than Chania, and can be noisy at night; but its long beach, running the length of its waterfront, makes it very appealing.

Like Chania, Rethimnon was built and fortified by the Venetians to consolidate their hold on Crete against Turkish and other rivals. Its huge fortress – far bigger than Chania's modest job – is the biggest and best-preserved medieval building in Crete. It looms over the pantiled roofs of the old quarter and is well worth the hour it takes to explore. From the fortress, you have sweeping views of old and new Rethimnon and of the coast east and west into the far distance.

GETTING YOUR BEARINGS

Odos Venizelou, Rethimnon's harbour-front esplanade, is lined with palm trees which add to the town's almost Middle Eastern atmosphere.

DON'T MISS . . .

Rethimnon's beach aside, the town's **Old Quarter** is its most attractive aspect. You can wander for hours in its narrow streets, many of them overhung by rickety-looking wooden balconies and, though the prolific souvenir and jewellery shops are an indication of Rethimnon's thriving holiday trade, the quarter hasn't been totally swamped by tourism – everyday life goes quietly on.

There's a busy little market area with produce stalls, fishmongers and bakers selling their heaped wares just inside the medieval **Guora Gate**, one of the remnants of the Venetian walls: waiters run in and out of the nearby cafés with glasses of raki and coffee for the shopkeepers. Around here, too, there are a handful of little kafeneions and restaurants patronized by local traders and workmen.

Several minarets testify to the fact that this, like Chania, was once as much a Turkish town as a Greek one. One of these, just off **Plateia Petihaki**, is open to the public (11.00 to 14.00) and from its turret you have a bird's eye view of the old quarter, the harbour and the castle as well as of the less appealing concrete sprawl of modern Rethimnon.

Rethimnon's main harbour has a sandy beach popular in

summer with sunbathers, though the water here smells decidedly off-colour and there are unpleasant black streaks in the sand. There is better swimming and sunbathing on the longer beach which starts just east of the modern ferry harbour, which is lined with hotels and restaurants and stretches almost as far as the eye can see. It's Rethimnon's main attraction.

TRAVELLING

By Air   Frequent scheduled flights to and from Athens.

By Sea   Ferries to Piraeus and the Cyclades. Fast catamaran to Santorini.

By Road   Buses run half-hourly to Heraklion and Hania, at least four times daily to the south coast resorts including Plakias and Agia Galini.
   Car and motorbike rental available. There are excursions by coach to Samaria Gorge, Knossos, and the south coast beaches.

WHERE TO STAY

Plenty of places to stay in pensions and rooms to rent in the maze of pretty little streets behind the harbour, in the old quarter. Generally, the further you can get from the harbour the better — Rethimnon's moped cowboys and their tinny machines can make the streets close to the waterfront hideous with noise into the early hours. There are pensions and rooms to rent right on Venizelou, but these are noisy and overpriced. The main package tour hotels are strung out along the sweep of sandy beach west of the new harbour. On Od. Tobazi, in the old quarter, there are a number of places advertising rooms to rent, a youth hostel and a self-service laundromat.
   At the top end of the price range, Rethimnon's newest hotel, built in 1987, is its best. The **Hotel Fortezza**, on Odos Melisinou, is a Class-B hotel which deserves to be an A-Class. Located on the fringe of the old town below the castle, it has a swimming pool in the courtyard and very well appointed rooms. If your budget will stand it this represents excellent value for money.

FOOD AND DRINK
The most attractive place to eat and drink is around the little Venetian harbour at the east end of the waterfront, a long esplanade called **Eleftherious Venizelou**. Excellent seafood, but you pay a high premium for location and quality. Venizelou itself is an uninterrupted strip of cafés, restaurants, fast food joints and ice-cream parlours. Scruffy by day, it's brightly lit and lively by night and is prime volta territory as the youth of Rethimnon stroll about in newly-fashionable denim. You'll

The Venetians in Crete

The Venetians first began to cast a foxy eye on the rich pickings of the Eastern Mediterranean in the 12th century, and as Byzantium crumbled they were always there to pick up the crumbs. Crete was the jewel of their Aegean empire, and they built a chain of massive harbour forts — Chania, Rethimnon, and Candia (Heraklion) to defend it. On the mainland, similar great fortresses at Kroni and Methoni, Nafplion, Monemvasia, Rio and Andirio guarded the trade routes to Venice.

From the fall of Constantinople, Venice was locked in a long and complex struggle not only with the Turks but with rival Christians — the Genoese, the Franks and the Knights of St John — as well as the mongrel Corsairs.

Venice made opportunistic alliances with any and all of them, and there was plenty of scope for double-dealing. Connivance, bribery, betrayal and sea-power were the stock in trade of a brilliantly devious and cynical foreign policy.

The Venetian fleet was supreme until the 1500s, and though the Sultan's armies held most of the mainland by then, the Venetians could garrison and supply their fortresses freely.

But by 1500 Turkey — with the aid of the expert Greek shipbuilders of the Bosphorus keelyards — was a naval power too, and the Venetians lost Methoni, Koroni, Navarino and Lepanto, though they won back Kefalonia and Levkas. In 1534 the Turkish admiral Barbarossa besieged Corfu. Though unable to take the city, he destroyed the Venetian fleet and forced Venice out of Nafplion, Monemvasia, Paros and Siros. In 1571 the Turks took Cyprus and flayed the Venetian commander Bragadino alive, and were only stopped by a Spanish, Papal and Venetian fleet, led by Don John or Austria, at Lepanto. The loss of 25,000 men and 180 ships held Turkey back for 70 years.

The Lion of St Mark flew above Crete for almost a century after Lepanto, but the last act began in 1645. The final conquest took almost 25 years. Chania and Rethimnon fell in the first year, but Candia thumbed its nose at the besiegers until 1669, when it fell after two years of bombardment.

eat much more cheaply in the smaller psistarias and restaurants a few blocks back from Venizelou.

There's another clutch of restaurants at **Plateia Titou Petihaki** in the heart of the old town. They include a fresh fruit and vegetable-juice bar, the **Vita Bar**, which also sells fruit, salad and icecream. Just around the corner, by the remains of a Venetian drinking fountain on Odos Digenis Moshoviti there are still more cafés – a good place for breakfast, snacks or lunch.

Just around the corner from the Hotel Fortezza, on Odos Xanthoudou, the restaurant and bar **Avli** has a verdant old courtyard with jasmine and orange trees and dining indoors or out. Opposite, the **Old Tavern** is another smart restaurant bar.

PALAEOCHORA

The main north-south road to the laid-back resort of **Palaeochora**, almost on Crete's south-west tip, is a good one with impressive views. Over the last few miles you glimpse the sea and the promise of Palaeochora's fine beach, a promise which is for once kept – the sand is golden and clean and the water clear, and the beach is big enough to make room for all except in the little resort's most crowded weeks in August.

Palaeochora is a favourite with independent travellers, some of whom bemoan the fact that it now attracts greater numbers of ordinary holidaymakers. In fact, the town with its two beaches and little harbour copes very well. There's still enough remaining of the original village life to satisfy purists. Chickens and goats live in ramshackle coops between the new pensions and studio apartments – one old lady's tiny cottage has become part of the ground floor of a modern pension built around and above it – and at siesta time in the late afternoon clutches of older people emerge as if from nowhere to gather in twos and threes on their front steps or on chairs in the street. While some of Palaeochora's cafés and tavernas have been taken over by a multinational bohemian crowd in the spring and summer – you might call it the funny haircut capital of Crete – others are still refuges for groups of craggy, worry-bead clicking farmers and fishermen who've lost the ability to be astonished by these odd invaders. Though there are now a couple of modern hotels at Palaeochora, they're fairly small and not too obtrusive. The OTE, tourist office and a periptero with international direct-dial phone and English books and newspapers are all on the main street, as is the National Bank.

BEACHES

Palaeochora's sandy beach faces west, ten minutes' walk from the little main street. Walk ten minutes in the opposite direction, along the south-facing coast, and you'll find a less crowded beach of clean pebbles with some patches of sand. Still further away – about half an hour's walk along the track which runs parallel to this beach – is another pebbly beach favoured for nude swimming and sunbathing.

TRAVELLING

Buses from Kastelli and Chania, where you change for Rethimnon and Heraklion. Boats in summer between Palaeochora and Chora Sfakion (often just called Sfakia) on the other side of the White Mountains, calling at Sougia, Aghia Roumeli and Loutro. There's no road along this coast, though some of the little beach villages are connected by steep donkey-tracks. By far the easiest and pleasantest way of hopping along the south-west coast is by boat.

WHERE TO STAY

Big choice of accommodation, from the most basic of rented rooms – plenty of these – to a couple of comfortable new hotels. **Savas**, who owns the restaurant of the same name on the main street, has rooms to rent and speaks good English. At the other end of the scale, the new **Hotel Aris** is bright and comfortable with south-facing balconies looking out towards the island of Gavdos. There are also a number of self-catering studio apartments which are excellent value for money – try **Studios Artemis**, on the same street as the Hotel Aris about five minutes from the harbour. It's clean, bright, quiet and very friendly. The **Palaeochora Club campsite**, about a quarter of an hour's walk out of town along the road to the south-facing pebbly beach, is well equipped and has its own snack bar-café.

FOOD, DRINK AND NIGHTLIFE

Apart from its excellent beaches, Palaeochora's main attraction is its unstructured, bar-hopping nightlife. The town's waterfront esplanade is lined with new cafés, cocktail bars and restaurants. The town's older main street, one block back from the waterfront, has another collection of generally cheaper and unpretentious cafés and restaurants. Here you'll find the glitzy **Coconuts** cocktail bar, which may be the last word in sophistication in Palaeochora but which – with its chrome, mirrors and old film-star photos – wouldn't look out of place in a London suburb. Prices vary wildly – a beer in one of the flash ocean-view places can cost three times as much as in one of the main street cafés.

AROUND PALAEOCHORA

You can buy tickets for excursions from the town's several travel agents such as Syia Travel or Palaeochora Travel, which also sell tickets for ferries onward from Crete's main ports. Palaeochora is an excellent base for exploring the mountain walks, beaches and offshore islands of this most rugged part of Crete. The towering peaks of the **White Mountains** are one of Europe's last pockets of wildernesses, the home of eagles and the last flocks of Cretan wild goat called "kri-kri". Serious hill-walkers will find plenty of challenges on peaks such as Gingilos, but even uncommitted strollers should not miss the famous Gorge of Samaria, which is reached from Palaeochora by boat. Walkers – with plenty of energy, plenty of water and tough footwear – can get to **Soughia** (see below), the next lazy beach spot on the south coast, in about six hours. From Sougia, only the determined (and experienced) should attempt the gruelling and easily-lost track which runs on to Aghia Roumeli and the foot of the Samaria Gorge, then onward to Loutro and Chora Sfakion.

You'll see a number of ancient sites marked on some maps in this area, but there's very little, if anything, to see at any of them and they're not worth making a special detour.

Palaeochora sits on a little peninsula pointing south into the Libyan Sea. On the horizon is the hazy outline of the tiny island of **Gavdos**, the southernmost point of Europe. There are a handful of people living here with some rooms to rent and a simple taverna – determined solitude seekers can go to Gavdos off-season with the Monday morning mail-boat, which takes 12 passengers. In summer, there are day trips from Palaeochora and from the other south-west coast ports.

The tiny islet of **Elafonisi**, just off Crete's west coast and a couple of hours' boat ride from Palaeochora, is graced by a shallow lagoon of brilliant blue water and sandy beaches. Well worth the boat ride, though the mainland side of the lagoon is sometimes littered with greenhouse-plastic and soft drink cans – those arriving by boat get a better impression of Elafonisi than others via the unbelievably bad road through the hills.

SOUGHIA

With its long clean pebbly beach and a handful of rooms to let as well as a couple of restaurants, Soughia is for those who want peace and quiet, plenty of beach space and not a lot else. There are rooms to let – indeed what was once a tiny fishermen's hamlet is now given over entirely to renting rooms and feeding their occupiers. Try Pension Lissos, just back from the beach and overlooking the dry river-bed, which has balconies and a pretty little garden full of jasmine, honeysuckle and hibiscus. There's also a branch of Syia Travel for arranging onward travel, and in Crete's busy summer season it's worth phoning them to book accommodation in Soughia. Soughia's sole hotel is drab, dim and stuffy. Soughia is for relaxing, not for whooping it up – there's one open-air music bar called the Alabama set on its own behind the beach, but otherwise nightlife consists of conversation, a bottle of wine and a game of backgammon. Take plenty of books and a close friend. The village has a well-supplied little general store for food, drink and odds and ends, but no bank or OTE.

From Palaeochora a rough road – surfaced in erratic patches – heads north along Crete's mountainous west coast. There's very little, if any, public transport on this road, and it's certainly not for the inexperienced moped-rider. If driving a hire car, proceed with caution. Where the road descends to the sea there is good swimming, especially at **Falasarna**, about ten km from Kastelli.

A string of hamlets – Sfinari, Kambos, Keramoti and Vathi – cling to the hillsides above and below the rough road. In spring and early summer they are conspicuous oases of cultivated greenery against the thorny slopes. In summer they show up as splashes of white on the grey-and-ochre background. They offer only the most basic refreshments, in little kafeneons catering to a clutch of leather-featured locals, but **Vathi** has some rooms to rent. Built in sheltered valleys, these villages look west to the empty Mediterranean – great views, but you'd have to be a serious solitude-seeker to want to stay long. Note that though distances don't look great on the map (only 35 km from Kastelli to Elafonisi at the end of the road) this road is very rough and winding and can't be driven safely at more than about 20 kph. You don't want to have to drive it in the dark.

Kastelli, at the end of the road, is Crete's westernmost major town, a gateway for ferries from Piraeus, the Peloponnese and Kithira and a jumping-off point for the remote and rugged west coast. It's a nondescript town with no good beaches or points of interest nearby, though rooms and hotels are there if you are forced to stay overnight. Confusingly, you'll find Kastelli marked on some maps as Kisamos. Don't worry – they are the same place.

ALONG THE SOUTH COAST

Chora Sfakion, often called simply "Sfakia" – properly the name for the whole region of south-west Crete dominated by the White Mountains – is a pleasant, dozy little town whose permanent snoozing is interrupted only by the horns of countless tour coaches collecting contingents of walkers arriving from Aghia Roumeli after the Samaria hike. After they've passed through, it drops back into its slumbers. Like Palaeochora, it's a good base or start-off point for exploring its hinterland, with plenty of rooms, a campsite and a couple of small hotels. There are boats daily in summer to Palaeochora and points between, and to Gavdos, visible on the horizon. Chora Sfakion doesn't however have Palaeochora's active nightlife.

Nearby **Loutron**, in its sheltered lagoon, is even quieter –

just a strip of tavernas overlooking a pebbly half-moon of beach. On the hill above, there's a ruined Turkish fort, and there's more swimming at the cove below the taverna on the other side of the peninsula – follow the signs to Finix.

You can walk to Loutron from Chora Sfakion via the excellent pebbly "Freshwater Beach", popular with nudist campers because of its trickle of drinkable water. It takes about an hour and a half to two hours of scrambling, and it's much easier to take the boat which runs several times a day from Chora Sfakion. You can also walk to Loutron from the village of Anopolis, on the high plateau above, but again it's a long hike on a steep zig-zag path and is only for determined masochists, though the view over Loutron and the sea makes it worthwhile for some.

The Samaria Gorge

Crete's biggest natural attraction is so supremely hyped that one goes expecting the inevitable disappointment. But for once there's a pleasant surprise: the soaring cliffs and pine-wooded slopes of the gorge are everything you could ask. True, the days are long gone when you could make the hike from Xiloskalo at the top to Aghia Roumeli at the bottom and meet only a handful of others, but with a little attention to timing you can still miss most of the hundreds of visitors who are bussed in each summer day from the big beach resorts. Almost all of these start from the upper end of the gorge and walk downhill to Aghia Roumeli, where they are then taken by boat to Chora Sfakion to meet their waiting coaches.

One way of avoiding the worst of the rush is to walk in the opposite direction, uphill from the sea. Another is to wait until around 11.00, when most of the coach tours will have left from the Xiloskalo trailhead, before setting off. The best time of year for the walk is undoubtedly early summer, shortly after the gorge, which is a national park, opens. This is usually late April, but depends on the amount of water running through the gorge — when the stream is in full spate the narrowest part, the Sidheresportes or Iron Gates, becomes impassable.

The walk, one-way, takes about four hours. It's not a demanding hike, even uphill, though good shoes will make it easier. At the beginning you'll be given a numbered ticket which is collected at the other end. This is to make sure everyone who has entered that day leaves before the park is officially closed at sunset, as camping in the gorge overnight is not allowed.

Agia Roumeli, the beach village at the seaward end of the Samaria ravine, has a good pebbly sand beach, rooms to rent and a bunch of restaurants, all catering to people who for one reason or another aren't pushing on immediately after arrival. It's a nice enough place to stay a few nights, though during the day a continuous stream of visitors flows through. From here, you carry on by boat to Loutro or Chora Sfakion to the east or Soughia or Palaeochora to the west. You can also walk out along the coast in either direction, but I don't recommend the tough hike to Soughia. The walk to Loutro, which runs for much of its length along excellent beaches, is a much better bet. It takes about five hours.

From Xiloskalo at the top of the Samaria Gorge, determined walkers can carry on to the 2,100-metre peak of Gingilos, a walk of about four hours' round trip.

FRANGOKASTELLO

From Chora Sfakion, Crete's south coast becomes less mountainous, though the roads linking the villages of the coast and the hillsides are narrow and winding enough to stop even the most lackadaisical driver's mind from wandering. Even Cretan coach drivers take these roads with a modicum of caution, and for the uninitiated a bus ride along roads suspended between soaring hillsides and plunging precipices can be hair-raising. The view is always exhilarating and the air – even in summer when the coastal villages are simmering and shimmering in the heat – has a special coolness and purity. Mass tourism has yet to make much impact on this coast, though little resorts have sprung up wherever there's a decent beach. The mountainside villages like Rodakino and Mirtos, though they have rooms to rent, move to a traditional rhythm rather than the disco beat of the beaches.

About 15 km east of Chora Sfakion, there's an uninspiring rash of small-time development at **Frangokastello**, a medieval Venetian or Frankish (sources differ) fort overlooking a double crescent of sandy beach about a quarter of a mile long. There's a ghost story attached to the fort – on a certain day in May, armed warriors are said to march from the sea before vanishing into the fort. As to who they are or were – Cretan rebels, Frankish crusaders or Byzantine knights – there is no consensus. The fort and the beach aside, Frangokastello is a curiously dispersed community, consisting of half a dozen places renting rooms scattered over a wide and rather depressing patch of flat scrubland below the mountains. There's no village as such, and though it's worth visiting for a look at the castle or a change of beach if you're staying at Chora Sfakion, it's not somewhere I'd choose to stay for any length of time. There are no shops or other facilities, and it's not particularly easy to leave or to get to, though several buses a day connect Frangokastello with Chania and Rethimnon.

From Frangokastello the road becomes steadily more demanding on both driver and vehicle, switchbacking through a handful of tiny villages which cling to the hillside above and below the road, where the big event of the day is the arrival of the Rethimnon bus or a tourist with a flat tyre.

PLAKIAS

Tourism development here has been fast but low-key. Self-catering studios, pensions and small hotels far outnumber the two or three larger properties. The little resort runs the length of one of southern Crete's best beaches, a mile-long stretch of very clean sand and shingle. Behind, the mountains are at their most beautiful. There are spectacular sunsets over the jagged summits of the headland west of Plakias. As the sun sinks behind them, the ranges shade from charcoal grey to the blue of tobacco smoke as they recede one after another into the distance, and the bare peaks are so high that they are sunlit long after the sun has slipped behind the lower ridges.

Behind Plakias, you can see that these hills have been terraced for cultivation almost up to the tree-line where people scratched a bare living out of the most recalcitrant terrain.

There's little trace left of the fishing hamlet Plakias must once have been, although a small flock of geese occupy its harbour and in spring you'll see them leading their fat furry goslings along the beach. But to date development is on a manageable scale and it has nothing like the crowds of Crete's north-coast beach strip. It's a busy little tourist town, but a very pleasant one – the location's beautiful, the beach is good and the clientele sympathetic. A smallish disco, the Hexagon Club and a sprinkling of other music-bars add variety to a nightlife that otherwise centres on cafés and restaurants.

Although there's little here that is "authentically Greek", it has everything to recommend it. As with a number of other Greek resorts where development has come a little late, accommodation is often better designed and built and maintained with more attention to detail and quality than in the resorts thrown up in the '60s and '70s.

You could spend a happy fortnight at Plakias, enlivening your stay with expeditions east and west of the resort. The Samaria Gorge is within easy reach. Good beaches within commuting distance include **Damnonia** (45-minute walk), and **Preveli**, where a little river fringed with palms runs through a clean sandy beach cut off by steep cliffs. The Preveli beach – once the last redoubt of the summer-hippy tribe, the remains of whose teepees you can see by its little church – is by no means deserted, as there are boat trips several times a day from Plakias, but it's still favoured for nude sunbathing and swimming. There's a small, seasonal bar serving drinks and snacks. Don't try to take anything but a four-wheel drive vehicle down the steep and very rocky track which leads off the tarred road to Preveli below the hilltop monastery of the same name, and if you value your life don't attempt the rough track over the cliffs from the next bay east – it's near-suicidal in at least one place. Take the boat.

A day-trip boat, the Cutty Sark, goes to Preveli from the Plakias pier as well as operating day-trips to other south-coast resorts and offshore islands. And if you're looking for the "real Greek" experience there are little hill villages like **Mirtios** within easy walking distance.

TRAVELLING
Buses connect Plakias with Rethimnon four times a day and take about one and a half hours; Chora Sfakion is about an hour by bus in the opposite direction. Mopeds, more powerful bikes, cars and mini-mokes can be rented from several competing agencies on the waterfront.

WHERE TO STAY
One of Plakias's big plus points is its very wide range of accommodation. Hotels include the sea-front **Hotel Lybikon** and **Alianthos Beach**. Most of the more recently built rooms and studios, as well as the up-market hotels, are geared to package tourism, and finding one of these in high season if you haven't booked an all-inclusive holiday can be a problem. In spring and early summer, before the package holiday flood starts, these rooms and apartments are on offer to independent travellers at bargain rates – from £7 to £10 for a double studio with kitchenette. For cheaper rooms catering for independent travellers, look in the older part of the village, west of the quay. There's also a quite pleasant youth hostel a little way out of town on the main road.

AGIA GALINI

This one-time fishing harbour has all the ingredients beloved of holiday brochure writers – steep streets and flights of steps leading up from a harbour bobbing with brightly coloured boats, cats dozing in the sun, nets drying on the pier and tiers of dazzling white buildings against a backdrop of dramatic mountain scenery. Enclosed in a grand and sheltered bay ringed with cliffs, its nearby pebble beach is adequate if not exciting. It comes as no surprise, then, to find that most of those white buildings are pensions and hotels built in the last ten to 15 years and that Agia Galini has given its heart and soul to the holiday business. This process wasn't accomplished without a few hiccups – some years back, Agia Galini's facilities were still geared to a low-budget, independent traveller clientele and were not up to handling the flood of package holidaymakers who asked for better standards. New building, too, made the town a bit of a building site for some years.

All that is in the past, and Agia Galini is now a friendly little resort, accommodation is generally good and the harbourfront restaurants cheerful and reasonably priced. It will look even better when they finish work on the pier and remove the huge cement blocks now blocking the view of the harbour. There's a thriving, disco-bar based nightlife, bars and cafés on the beach as well, and plenty of watersports and excursions. In short, Agia Galini is for anyone unashamedly looking for a cheerful, beach-and-bar holiday off the shelf.

By and large it appeals to a younger clientele, especially in high season, and is not popular with independent travellers because almost all accommodation is contracted to British and European tour operators. Car and bike rental are readily available, which is a good thing because public transport isn't up to much – four or five KTEL buses a day to Rethimnon, but travelling east or west from here towards Sfakia or Matala means a number of changes.

Agia Galini's beach is east of the harbour and reached by a cement walkway; on the way you'll pass the village's sole point of historic interest, a World War Two German gun emplacement tunnelled into the cliffside, now – judging by the pong – used as an informal toilet. The beach is pebbly rather than sandy and in places heaped with dry seaweed; as a result, there's a thriving trade renting sunloungers by the day. Cross the rickety bridge spanning Agia Galini's river if you want to get a bit further away from the mob.

Excursions from Agia Galini include boat trips to the **Paximadhi** islets. You can see their jagged silhouette on the horizon. (The name likens the shape to the tooth-breaking paximadhia rusks favoured by Greek shepherds and farmers for long storage or journeys. You can see them on sale by the kilo in any artopolion – you have to soak them in water, then dunk them in olive oil. They're surprisingly good with a bit of garlic or lemon juice rubbed in). Boats also range far and wide taking people to better and less busy coves and beaches.

For historic interest, there's **Festos**, one of the key Minoan sites about 15 km away, and **Gortys**, a Hellenistic-Roman site, about 20 km beyond that.

MATALA

Like Agia Galini, Matala has cheerfully abandoned itself to the holiday business. In the '60s and early '70s this sandy bay with its cliff-caves at one end and tiny village at the other was favoured by long-haired riff-raff from all over Europe (I know because I was one of them), camping on the beach and in the caves.

In summer, its campsite is still popular with budget travellers, but the tiny village has become a fair-sized holiday resort with accommodation mainly in newly-built rooms and some smallish hotels. Some hardliners bemoan this inevitable transition, but in practice Matala, though now in the holiday mainstream, is a pleasant, laid-back resort with a lively young beach-and-café clientele and the rock and pop of three decades providing the background score. In high season the beach, which is clean and sandy but only about half a mile long, gets very crowded in the afternoon, when busloads of day-trippers from the big northern resorts are dumped here for lunch and a swim after visiting the nearby Minoan site at Festos. Both beach and resort are much smaller than Agia Galini, which has grown far faster.

Matala has plenty of places to eat and drink on and behind the waterfront, though price, quality and variety are much of a muchness. Nightlife consists of a handful of music bars and Zorba's Disco, a five-minute ride from the village. Zorba's runs a minibus shuttle to and from Matala, but it's within easy walking distance unless you are totally tanked up.

Lacking the imposing mountain scenery of the villages to the west, Matala's setting between bay, cliffs and ocean more than makes up for it.

Buses operating the main Heraklion-Ierapetra route connect with local buses. Change at Timbaki if heading back to Heraklion, Mires if going east. There are cars and motorbikes for rent in Matala.

AROUND MATALA

Boat trips will take you to the **Paximadhia Islands** and to beaches further away. Matala's other beach is a scrambling half-hour walk over the headland beyond the caves. It's never empty, but in the afternoon it is usually less crowded than the main beach.

Two Minoan sites – **Agia Triada** and **Festos** – are within easy reach, between Matala and the main east-west road about 12 km away. Festos, once a hilltop palace, looks over the wide valley of Messara, a view rather spoiled by the expanses of huge plastic-covered greenhouses which are a visual blight on much of Crete's coastal farmland. Unlike Knossos, it hasn't been reconstructed and is not very impressive. It's usually very crowded with coach-trip visitors.

Agia Triada is less than an hour's walk from Festos. It's a small site and nothing immediately takes the eye, but it isn't nearly as thronged with visitors and it is possible to let your imagination work in relative tranquillity.

At both sites, you'll see signs advertising the folk museum at **Vori**, about five km away. With an excellent and well-presented collection of traditional tools and implements, it gives a real insight into the harsh demands of peasant life on Crete in the past and even now, and you can only respect the tremendous inventiveness with which Cretans

made the most of limited resources and tools to squeeze a
living from their island. It's run by the Cultural Association
of Messara, and while the Minoan sites have no relevance at
all to modern Crete, this collection, representing life in the
last three centuries to the present day, is essential viewing.

There's more to see at **Gortys**, the Hellenistic/Roman/
Byzantine city whose ruins are on the main east-west highway
about 20 km from Festos. Much more recent, it's also much
less crowded and has a shady snack-bar too. Well worth an
outing from Matala or a stop en route east or west on the
main road round the island.

THE DODECANESE
The Eastern Fringe

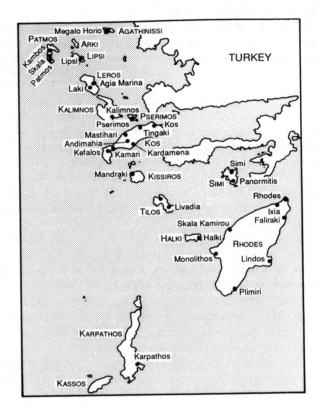

The Dodecanese is a baker's dozen of islands fringing the Turkish coast, only a few miles from most of the group. The military presence on a number of the islands is a symptom of Greece's uneasy relationship with its larger Eastern neighbour.

The name means "Twelve Islands" but it is deceptive.

There are certainly more than twelve, and it's not clear which of the bigger islands in the chain are regarded as the original dozen.

There is plenty of variety in the Dodecanese, from the larger islands of Rhodes and Kos – which experience a huge influx of summer holidaymakers – to tiny outposts like Kastellorizo, Chalki and Tilos. There is even a semi-active volcano bubbling away in its crater on Nissiros.

The group is one of the best places for island hopping. Ferries run from one end of the chain to the other daily in high season calling at all the main islands, and there are direct boats from Piraeus to most of them, as well as connections to other island groups.

Like the Cyclades, the Dodecanese have a distinctive architectural vernacular, typified by tall houses with neo-classical touches and high doors and windows, usually stuccoed and painted in pastel shades. Many have wooden and wrought-iron balconies overhanging precariously from upstairs windows. If you can find a room in a restored or well-kept house they are delightful places to stay: most have back gardens or verandahs overflowing with vines, geraniums, and often banana and palm trees.

The main islands are much more fertile than most of the barren Cyclades, and there is good fishing throughout the group, so food is often better and more varied. In general, the people of the Dodecanese seem to be more relaxed and approachable than their craggy Cretan relatives and you may be invited to join locals for a drink or a coffee. As usual, even a few fumbling words of Greek will work wonders and elicit expressions of admiration for your fluency.

Most – though not all – of the main points of historic interest are medieval rather than ancient, such as the castles of the Knights of St John on Rhodes and Kos.

RHODES

Rhodes, the main island of the Dodecanese, has some of Greece's best beaches, more sunshine than any other island, a fascinating and intact medieval capital and, at Lindos, an

A Turbulent History

The Dodecanese remained under Turkish rule longer than any part of modern Greece except Thessaloniki, Thrace and the far north. In 1912 the Italians grabbed the islands from Turkey and as a reward for choosing the winning side in World War One this piece of petty imperialism was ratified by the Allies. The Italians ruled here until 1943, and left their stamp especially on Rhodes, where they restored much of the old city and left a number of elegant buildings on the waterfront. Their occupying role was taken over by the Germans from 1943/44 and the islands suffered not only from Nazi atrocities – Jewish communities mainly from Rhodes and Kos were deported to death camps – but also in the fighting as Allied forces drove out the occupying troops.

The islands were administered by the Britain under the aegis of the UN until 1949, when they were finally united with Greece, so the oldest inhabitants have known Turkish, Italian, German and British rule before becoming Greek citizens.

archetypically pretty island village. Predictably, these charms have won the hearts of vast numbers of holidaymakers from Britain, Scandinavia and Germany, and the island has a booming holiday industry from April to October. Mass tourism, however, has not been allowed to spoil Rhodes – though it has pushed food, drink and accommodation prices higher than those of any other Greek resort.

RHODES TOWN

The island's capital, built around two great harbours, is really three towns in one – the Old Town, within the medieval walls built by the Knights of St John; the New Town, built in recent years to accommodate and service the holiday visitors; and behind both, the modern residential suburbs.

The Old Town

Happily, the Old Town has been preserved almost intact and in its smaller streets after dark it's possible to forget that there is a holiday boom-town just outside the crenellated walls. Cobbled and arched streets such as Odos Omirou are still more Greek than tourist, with little kafeneions, souvlaki bars and ouzeris which stay firmly shut until the army of daytime sightseers has withdrawn to its hotel barracks for the night. A number of mosques and minarets, some of them still used by the city's handful of Muslims, and plentiful palm trees, give the Old Town a distinctly Levantine flavour.

The main attraction is the **Palace of The Grand Masters**, the heart of the castle-complex built by the Knights. It's everybody's idea of what a medieval fortress should look like, with round towers, fancy battlements and buttresses and huge arched doorways. If it looks remarkably well preserved, that's because it was extensively rebuilt under the Italians after being damaged by an exploding arsenal in 1856. Mussolini intended it to be a grandiose centre for Italian dominion in Greece, and its elaborate mosaics and lavish interior are breathtaking. There are guided tours of the walls and battlements of the Old Town twice weekly – times are posted on the gates of the Grand Palace.

Odos Ippoton, running from the Palace down to Plateia Moussiou (Museum Sq.), has been similarly restored. This street held the lodges of five of the seven Tongues of the Order of St John, whose coats of arms are engraved above each door. The 15th-century Knights' Hospital now houses a small archaeological museum with a collection of finds from Mycenaean to Roman times.

Other points of interest include the **Mosque of Suleiman**, built originally in 1522 to mark Suleiman the Magnificent's conquest of Rhodes and rebuilt early in the 19th century. It is at the opposite end of Odos Panetiou from the Palace of the Grand Masters: opposite it, on Orfeos, is the late-18th-century Turkish library. Another remnant of the Turkish period is the Turkish baths at Platia Arianos, open every day except Sunday.

Sokratous, the Old Town's main shopping and souvenir street, runs downhill towards the harbour from the Suleiman Mosque. At Plateia Simis, just inside the Pili Eleftherias (Freedom Gate) which leads from the old town to the newer harbour-front of Mandraki, you'll see the rather incongruous remains of the 3rd-century BC **Temple of Venus**. The Knights rebuilt Rhodes in their own image so thoroughly that this, and the stadium and Temple of Apollo on Monte Smith, the hill behind Rhodes Town, are all that remains of the once-important ancient city. The Palace of the Grand Masters, some archaeologists believe, is built on the site of an ancient sun-temple. A small pocket of Byzantine-era remains was found recently at a site by the school on Odos Panetiou, and there is the tempting possibility that below these may emerge evidence that the Colossus stood here (see box).

To get a real sense of the scale and complexity of the Old Town's defences, walk around the dry moat between the inner and outer walls (access from the portal behind the taxi rank at Plateia Eleftherias, beside the Syros Taverna or from Salomou Al-Chadeff at the other end) from which you can see the complicated buttresses and bastions, tunnels mined into the foundations by Turkish siege engineers and stone cannonballs fired during the Knights' last stand. These are enormous: it hardly seems possible that any masonry could withstand their impact, but the walls seem to have shrugged them off with hardly a mark.

The New Town

The town of Rhodes is built on a peninsula pointing almost due north. The Old Town's seaward walls enclose the commercial harbour, where inter-island ferries and cruise ships dock, on the east of the point. The New Town, with its esplanade of imposing Italian administrative buildings and arcades, has the yacht and day-cruise harbour of **Mandraki** to the east and beaches on its west and east shores. It's a conglomeration of music-bars, discos and restaurants where you'll find steak, smorgasbord, tandoori or chow mein as easily as Greek dishes, where the FA Cup Final is beamed by satellite to an audience of lobster-pink holidaymakers, and potent and sickly cocktails and draught bitter are the order of the day. The New Town is a cheerfully noisy place in high season, with no pretensions to offering anything but a good time. Many of its bars and restaurants are staffed by British and other European kids spending a working summer in Rhodes. The beaches on either side of the New Town are sandy and clean and by June are jam-packed and fragrant

The Knights of St John

Although the Knights of St John began as an order of "hospitallers" sheltering sick or wounded crusaders and pilgrims to the Holy Land, they gained a reputation for brigandage and piracy. Expelled from Palestine in 1306, they made Rhodes their base, with other strongholds at Kos and on the mainland at what is now Bodrum.

Over two centuries, they built within their miles of walls a city of palaces and lodges for their Grand Master and the "tongues" of the Order, each according to the language of its members. By then they were pirates, preying on anything within their range, and their sails, bearing the indented cross now called Maltese, were as feared as the Jolly Roger centuries later. Their victims were as often Greeks or other Christians as Turks, once again giving the lie to the myth of Crusaders as defenders of Christendom, and it seems likely that their ranks over the centuries were drawn from some of the less savoury elements of European nobility — landless men or younger sons out for gain, none too choosy about the manner of winning it, and not afraid of a scrap. The order was divided into eight Tongues — of Auvergne, Provence, England, France, Italy, Germany, Aragon and Castile — each charged with the defence of a bastion and a section of the wall. Except England and Auvergne, each tongue had a lodge in Rhodes on what is now Odos Ippoton — the Street of the Knights, leading to the grandiose Palace of the Grand Master. The Inn of Auvergne stands on Plateia Simis, close to the walls, that of England on what is now Museum Square. The Masters were elected for life by the membership of the Order. There never were more than about 600 Knights in all: the rest of the Order's fighting strength was made up of lay brothers and men at arms.

The Knights had a good run for their money until 1522, when Suleiman the Magnificent decided their combination of piety and piracy was beyond bearing. A 100,000-strong Turkish army besieged the citadel, backed by an enormous fleet. The Knights held out for six months before negotiating a withdrawal. Fewer than 200 of them survived the siege. In 1530 the Holy Roman Emperor, Charles V, granted them Malta as a base, hoping that they would police the Western Mediterranean against the Corsairs of the Barbary Coast. The Turkish admirals Dragut Reis (a renegade Greek) and Barbarossa pursued them and there was yet another siege — but that's another story. Ernle Bradford's *The Great Siege of Malta* (Pelican) tells it admirably and is a must if you want to find out more about the Knights.

with a blend of a hundred different tanning lotions and potions; and you will pay through the nose for a beach lounger.

LINDOS

The pretty village of Lindos, on the island's east coast some 50 km from the main town, has everything a Greek island village should have: white houses and pebble-mosaic streets in a distinctive style, preserved from ugly development by strict building codes; clean sandy beaches in sheltered bays of glass-clear water; lively nightlife and plenty of places to eat and drink; and all crowned by a clifftop castle of the Knights whose walls enclose an elegant Acropolis of the classical era, when Lindos's perfect natural harbour made it one of the leading cities in this part of Greece. The remains of the ancient theatre, carved into the cliff, can be seen above the village, and the prow of a Lindian galley is carved into the cliff below the stairway leading to the castle. Lindian architecture is distinctive – houses have elaborately-carved arched doorways and courtyards floored with painstakingly laid out mosaics of black and white pebbles. While tourism has prompted much new building, strict planning codes state that traditional elements must be part of any new project or refurbishment, so Lindos has retained its traditional character. You can see some of the most elaborate stonework and pebble floors at the Captain's House bar, at the top of the pebbled stairway leading to the Acropolis and castle.

Nevertheless, Lindos can be a disappointment. Its prettiness is marred by a grudging, greedy, get-rich-quick mentality which is all the more striking in a country where generosity and friendliness are still the norm. Inflated by a seemingly endless flow of visitors, prices are the highest in Greece and service can be impersonal at best, surly at worst.

Drinks, meals and accommodation cost twice as much as in Rhodes Town – you will be charged an arm and a leg for a sun-lounger on a beach which becomes packed with bodies from June to the end of August and the most basic of double rooms, with threadbare blankets and no hot water, can cost as much as a decent hotel in Rhodes Town. Unfortunately for independent travellers, the better accommodation is snapped

Ancient Rhodes and the Colossus

The ancient city-state of Rhodes was a joint venture between the three cities of the island. Lindos, Kamiros and Ialyssos were founded by Dorian settlers around 1100 BC. In 408 BC they combined to build a new capital, which they named after the island itself. Rhodes was famed for its naval skills and was one of the leaders of a league of cities on the Dodecanese islands and on the nearby mainland of Asia Minor.

The Rhodians pursued a flexible foreign policy: they became an ally of Athens after the Persian Wars, but during the Peloponnesian War sided first with Athens, then with Sparta, then with Athens again. In 332 BC they sensibly chose to become allies of Alexander the Great and were among the founders of Alexandria in Egypt, a move which bolstered Rhodes's wealth and power. The Colossus, a giant bronze statue more than 30 metres high, was commissioned by the city from its leading sculptor, Aris, to commemorate Rhodian victory over Alexander's descendant Dimitrios who besieged the city during his struggle with Ptolemy of Egypt. It was toppled by an earthquake in 226 BC and never rebuilt, perhaps because by then Rhodes was past its prime. In 42 BC Cassius (later one of Caesar's assassins) conquered the city and looted thousands of its statues and art treasures. Nobody knows what happened to the wreck of the Colossus, though some sources claim its remains were carried off by Saracen pirates when they conquered the island in 663. By that time, though, Rhodes had changed rulers so often – from Rome to Byzantium, then to Persia – that the bronze wreckage may have simply been taken away piecemeal and melted down for scrap over centuries.

There is a lot of quibbling over just where the statue stood: most guides will claim it straddled what is now the entrance to Mandraki harbour, but some place it at the harbour of Lindos. An exciting new possibility is that archaeologists may unearth hard evidence locating its pedestal on the newly-discovered site inside the walls of the Old Town on Odos Panetiou. This is one of the highest points within the bounds of the ancient city and would have been an obvious choice, some of the experts claim.

up by tour operators throughout the season. Drinks and meals are equally expensive, and quality doesn't usually justify the high prices. Even the Ministry of Culture is in on the act — entry to the Acropolis costs more than at any other historic site in Greece. Bar-owners may harass you if you sit too long over one drink without ordering another, an impoliteness which would be unthinkable anywhere else in Greece.

Despite this, Lindos remains a firm favourite with thousands of visitors, many of whom come again and again. Thousands more visit each day from the other Rhodian resorts, when the village's parking spaces are packed with tour buses. All this means that Lindos is extremely well geared up for tourism. Its streets and beaches are the cleanest in Greece, thanks to a municipality which recognizes that a town that makes its living from tourism has to clean up the mess it leaves behind. The calm bay is ideal for watersports and Lindos is a favourite with water-skiers. Georgios and Colleen Mortzos operate a waterski school throughout the season – there's a day-long shuttle dinghy from the beaches to their offshore raft. Lindos also has several travel and tour agencies arranging everything from onward travel from Rhodes to day-cruises, car and bike rental and excursions. There is a smaller, quieter beach at **Ag Pavlos**, reached by walking around the Acropolis crag from the top of the village.

HARAKI

Very different is Haraki, a fishing-hamlet with a handful of rooms and tavernas about 40 km from Rhodes Town. The village has an excellent sweep of clean, pebbly harbour beach about half a mile long, overlooked by the ruins of yet another knightly castle on a hill to the north. Southward, the beach sweeps away towards Lindos, virtually empty for some ten km until you reach the two or three big hotels at Vlicha Bay, about three km from Lindos.

LARDOS, PEFKAS and GENNADI

South from Lindos, the east coast of Rhodes is an almost continuous stretch of largely undeveloped beach, great for exploring and day-tripping if you have your own transport. There are rooms and pensions at Pefkas, a quieter, cheaper but less postcard-pretty alternative to Lindos, and at the pleasantly green and quiet village of Lardos a kilometre or so inland, and at Gennadi.

INLAND RHODES

Rhodes is hilly, rather than mountainous – its tallest peak, Attaviros, is a mere 1063 metres – and much of the island is green and cultivated. As elsewhere in Greece, water is becoming a problem because of the demands of tourism, growing population, modern plumbing and industry, but Rhodes still has more year-round streams and springs than most of the Aegean's arid islands.

One of the prettiest is at **Petalouda**, the much-hyped "Valley of the Butterflies". This is a misnomer – Greek makes no distinction between moths and butterflies – and the colourful insects which swarm here in June and July are in fact tiger moths. Outside moth season, when no coach parties visit the valley, the mossy little stream with its paths and bridges is cool and quiet. Determined walkers with good shoes can carry on up the valley beyond the end of the stream to the hilltop monastery of **Kalo Petros**.

At **Epta Piges** (Seven Springs) the Italians channelled a number of watercourses into a little reservoir of deep clear water from which to irrigate the lower farmlands. You reach the pool by walking knee-deep through a 160-metre tunnel – take a torch. There is a small restaurant-café by the carpark, overlooking a swift stream. It is a cool, shady place for lunch, though the quiet is interrupted by the hideous shrieking of a flock of semi-wild peacocks.

THE REST OF RHODES

On either side of Rhodes town there are huge holiday-hotel ghettoes. On the west coast, hotels stretch from **Ixia** through **Triada** to **Paradissi** and the island's international airport. On the east side of town, there is another concentration of big hotels at **Faliraki** and **Afandou**. All have excellent beaches but little else.

South of the big resort complex of Faliraki, Rhodes's east coast has excellent beaches, most of them surprisingly uncrowded, and linked by an excellent main road with frequent bus services from town.

THE WEST COAST

South of Paradissi and the airport, is almost untouched by tourism. Between Paradissi and the little harbour of Kamiros Skala this is understandable, as the coast here is a mixture of low cliffs and rocky, unattractive beach. The main attraction is the site of **Ancient Kamiros**, one of the three main ancient cities of Rhodes (weekdays 08.30 – 16.00, Sunday 09.00 – 15.00). The well-preserved ancient site has not been extensively reconstructed, but as the biggest surviving remnant of the days of the Greek city-states on Rhodes it is worth a visit.

Further south, **Kamiros Skala** is a harbour with three tavernas and little else. The passenger ferry Halki sails to the island of the same name daily from here. Twenty km south, the castle at **Monolithos** is perched on a crag which stands apart from surrounding cliffs and looking down to pine-covered slopes on all sides. There are only the walls of the old castle and a small Greek church inside, but the views are splendid. South of Monolithos, there are long and usually windswept pebble beaches backed by rolling hillsides covered with olives and barley fields – it's fertile farming country, very unlike the barren hinterland of most Greek islands.

TRAVELLING

By Air Charter flights from most major British and European airports. Scheduled flights from Athens, Heraklion, Thessaloniki, Karpathos and Kastellorizon.

By Sea Daily nonstop ferries to Piraeus and daily ferries through the Dodecanese (Rhodes/Kos/Kalymnos/Leros/Patmos) to Piraeus. Several weekly ferries to the Cyclades (Santorini) and to the north-east Aegean islands (Samos and Ikaria). There are also international ferries to Marmaris in Turkey and ports in Israel and Egypt. Going to Turkey you must leave your passport with the boat agency overnight for passport control: don't make the mistake of staying overnight in Turkey if you arrived in Greece using a charter flight. This is technically illegal and the return half of your ticket may be confiscated, forcing you to shell out for an expensive one-way scheduled ticket home.

Hydrofoils operate in summer to Tilos, Halki, Simi, Kos and (unreliably) to Kastellorizon. At Kos, you can connect with onward services to Nisiros, Patmos, Samos, Leros and Kalimnos. The main ticket office for hydrofoils is Couros Travel, 34 Karpathou (Tel: 24377). Journey times are roughly half the normal time.

Around the Island The municipal bus service RODA is free within Rhodes Town and cheap elsewhere. The main RODA bus stop is behind the New Market. KTEL buses for longer journeys stop at Plateia Rimini, beside the entrance to the Son et Lumière show. Detailed timetables for travel throughout the island are posted at both stops and are also available from the helpful city tourist office at Plateia Rimini. The main taxi rank is at Plateia Alexandrias, nearby. There are dozens of car and bike rental agencies in the New Town, most of them renting fleets of cheap and cheerful VW-based beach buggies.

WHERE TO STAY

Old Town The cheapest accommodation on Rhodes is in the Old Town, where you can find good, clean though basic rooms in pensions and hotels at low prices. The biggest concentration of cheap pensions and rooms to rent is on **Odos Omirou** and the little alleys either side of it. More expensive options are the **St Nikolis Hotel** at Ippodamou 61 (Tel: 34561/ fax: 32034), a beautifully restored old building with expensive double rooms, well worth it if your budget will run to it. The St Nikolis also has pleasant studio-apartments with fully-equipped kitchens, sleeping two to four, at the same cost as a double room. At Ag. Fanourion 88 the **Hotel Paris** is a mid-priced option.

New Town Most accommodation in the New Town is purpose built for the package holiday market: there are also some smaller pensions and rooms to rent, generally a little more expensive than in the Old Town. **Guest House Stella**, on Odos Dilberaki in the centre of the New Town, has nice double rooms at C-Class prices with en suite toilet, shower and balcony; the older, more basic guesthouse directly opposite has much cheaper doubles with few amenities. In shoulder season you can also find rooms in the larger hotels at surprisingly cheap prices: a double in the large and comfortable **Alexia** costs from around the same as the Stella with en-suite shower and sea-facing balcony.

FOOD AND DRINK
Old Town The Old Town's more expensive restaurants are on the streets closest to the **harbour**, where prices are high for what may well be a mediocre, microwave-warmed meal. There are cheaper and better options further into the streets of the Old Town, especially on and around **Omirou**. On **Plateia Douleios**, in the right-angle between Omirou and Fanouriou, the **Mango Bar** plays rock and blues and serves breakfast, pizzas, beer and cocktails. The **Oasis** restaurant opposite is friendly and good value.

New Town Don't go to the New Town looking for Greek food – but if you suddenly develop a craving for variety, this is the place. Excellent tandoori and other Indian food at the **Shere Khan** on Orfamidou (try the banana cake). Chinese food at **Molly's**. Drinking reflects the New Town's young and international clientele: it's easier to find a B-52 or a tequila slammer than an ouzo, and prices are, by Greek standards, sky high.

The cheapest breakfasts, snacks and fresh juices are in the small cafés and snackbars at the New Market by the bus station, beside the Mandraki harbour: those closest to the harbour cater mainly to tourists, those at the back of the market to local market traders – fresh orange juice, coffee and omelette at the cheapest prices in town. Also within the market, a string of traditional grill-restaurants serve excellent chicken and lamb from the spit and – more intimidatingly – a selection of the spit-roasted offal, mainly liver and intestines, of which the Greeks are particularly fond.

NIGHTLIFE

The New Town throbs with loud music and is full of discos and music bars. Discos tend to charge a hefty entry fee which usually includes your first drink. **La Scala**, the biggest disco-nightclub, is a couple of kilometres out of town behind the big Rodos Palace Hotel. Others include the **Garage** (13 Iroon Politechniou) and **Obsession**, at the Panagou shopping centre.

SHOPPING

Rhodes is one of Greece's main shopping spots thanks to a government decree which gave it duty-free status after becoming part of Greece. As a result the streets of the Old Town are full of liquor stores selling international-brand spirits at tax-free prices. Jewellery and the ubiquitous leather wares are good buys. In the New Town a number of stores sell designer fashion clothing and swimwear at prices pegged to a Scandinavian clientele: they may be cheap by Swedish standards but are no bargain in British terms. Cheaper knock-offs of popular designer names can also be found in the Old and New Town.

Regrettably, Greece does not apparently see fit to enforce the terms of a number of conservation-related treaties which it has signed. Carved ivory and the furs of a number of wild cats are on sale. **Do not buy these**: the goods are likely to be confiscated by UK Customs and you may be prosecuted.

BOAT TRIPS FROM RHODES

A flotilla of day-trip boats leaves Rhodes each day for islands nearby and further afield. Symi is the most popular destination, but the Dodecanese Hydrofoil services make it possible to go as far as Kos (two hours each way), Tilos (80 minutes) and Halki (65 minutes) as well as Symi.

Boats also take day trippers to Lindos and to the east coast beaches between Rhodes and Lindos, including the one where actor Anthony Quinn has a house: he must get sick of it being pointed out to rubbernecking tourists.

All the excursion boats leave from Mandraki harbour, in front of the New Market. A number of smaller boats are also available for charter by the day – good value if you can get a group together and do some hard bargaining. New in Rhodes is scuba diving, until recently looked on askance by Greek authorities in case divers loot archaeological treasures from the seabed: several boats now offer trips for experienced divers and lessons for beginners in the calm clear cove at Kalithea.

NEIGHBOURING ISLANDS

Symi

Tiny Symi is popular with day-trippers from Rhodes. Most boats leave Mandraki harbour at 09.00 – choose from ordinary cruisers such as Symi 1 which take about two hours, fast catamarans (Symi 2 and Rodos) which take less than an hour; or the even faster hydrofoil. Fares start at about £7.50 for the slower boats and are negotiable. Boats to Symi pass within a few hundred yards of the barren and uninhabited Turkish coast.

Symi has two natural harbours. **Pedi**, the smaller of the two, has a medium-sized but unobtrusive holiday hotel, the Pedi Beach, and two or three cafés along a rocky bay. A beach is created each summer by importing sand, and the water is warm and very clear.

Most boats call at Pedi first, then go on to **Yialos**, the island's main port (interchangeably, and confusingly, it is also sometimes called Symi). It takes about an hour to walk from one to the other, passing through the hilltop village of **Ano Symi**: looking down on the red tiled rooftops of the harbour, the white and pastel-yellow houses around the harbour look like dolls' houses. A dozen ruined windmill-towers on the ridge which separates Yialos from Pedi bay are being restored.

Symi's wonderful natural main harbour made it an important Dodecanese trading centre, and the number of dignified harbourside mansions built by its wealthy shipowners in the 19th century reflects this prosperity. Ochre-yellow, white and a particularly vivid lavender-blue are the favoured colours for house decoration: there's a fanciful Italian building at the pierhead which is now the post office and port police HQ. The harbour is ringed by cafés and restaurants which are thronged with day-trippers from midday to mid-afternoon, when the boats leave for the return to Rhodes: after their departure the harbour returns to its slumbers.

Happily, Symiots don't seem to have jacked up their prices to exploit this captive market, and you can eat and drink here better and more cheaply than in most places on Rhodes: the Ouzeri Metapontis, beside the Ionian Bank building on the harbour, has excellent seafood and a friendly owner.

On the harbour front an imitation of the Lindos galley-carving and a plaque mark the spot where Italy formally surrendered the Dodecanese on May 5 1945. Sunnyland Travel, on the harbour front, books accommodation, bike rental and onward travel. The A-Class Hotel Aliki, a luxuriously-renovated mansion on the harbour beyond the port office, is the plushest place to stay.

Tilos
Like some other tiny Greek islands, Tilos has two inland villages named **Megalo Horio** ("big village") and **Mikro Horio** ("little village"). It also has a decent-sized harbour village, **Livadhia**, which thanks to a daily flow of day-trippers from Kos in high season has a couple of tavernas as well as three or four small hotels. Attempts have been made by some British tour operators to put Tilos on the package holiday map but with no great success, and as a result good hotel and pension rooms are often available at negotiable bargain rates. It's about eight km from Livadhia to Megalo Horio, which also has some rooms to rent. There are good beaches at **Eristos** and **Ag Andonios**. Walking and swimming are the sole pastimes on Tilos: Mikro Horio, the tiniest village on the island, is uninhabited.

The island is less than an hour and half from Rhodes on the hydrofoil.

Halki
Further away from Rhodes Town and its masses of tourists and less accessible – boats sail from Kamiros Skala, about 50 km from Rhodes – Halki appeals to solitude-seekers. It doesn't get the masses of day-trippers which Symi attracts, and its pretty harbour – very similar in style to Symi's – is even emptier and calmer. Many of its fine old houses are falling into ruins, though there is talk of renovating some of them as guesthouses. There are rooms to rent and a number of fine and unpopulated beaches within walking distance.

There's a daily (in theory) boat, the Halki, from Kamiros Skala, but departure times vary whimsically from day to day. No timetable is posted and you'll get a number of different predictions of when (and if) tomorrow's boat will leave. Most departures are in the afternoon. The hydrofoil will get you from Rhodes to Halki in under an hour.

Kastellorizon

A peculiarity of politics, Kastellorizon, also called Megisti, is a Greek island in a Turkish harbour. The Turkish resort village of **Kas** is within hailing distance about 500 metres away — there's just enough space to get the dotted line on the map between them. Unhappily, that dotted line is an impassable barrier and you can't go from one to the other. Once a thriving trading port, Kastellorizon fell into the doldrums in the years following the Greek-Turkish war of 1922 and the expulsion of the Greeks of Asia Minor, which is why its only village is now almost a ghost town of elegant houses, very like those of Symi and Halki.

Apart from its glorious isolation it has good snorkelling (though no beaches as such) and one outstanding attraction — the luminous blue sea-cave at **Parasta**, with its rare and endangered monk seals.

Boats from Rhodes take about six hours. There are flights from Rhodes four times weekly. The island has one modern hotel, the Megisti, and some rooms to rent.

KARPATHOS

Midway between Crete and Rhodes, Karpathos is a lonely island. Long sea crossings separate it from Crete and its eastern Dodecanese neighbours. With no nearby coast to shelter it, the island can be windswept at any time of year. Rugged and mountainous, Karpathos has excellent beaches, attractive villages and, despite the recent opening of an international airport which has encouraged the building of two or three medium-sized holiday hotels, it cannot yet be called overdeveloped. Visitors even in peak season are a trickle, not a flood, and the island — third largest in the Dodecanese after Rhodes and Kos — is big enough to absorb them without overcrowding.

Pigadia, the island's main village and ferry harbour, is attractive in an unspectacular way, with a long sandy beach on the bay about 15 minutes' walk away. Despite the appearance of two new hotels, this beach – some two km long – remains uncrowded. **Amopi**, eight km from Pigadia, is smaller and in season more crowded, with two sandy pebble beaches.

Karpathos is an outstanding island for walkers. There is a huge difference between the pastoral landscape of the south, with its lower, cultivated hills and pretty villages – notably **Aperi, Voladha, Othos** and **Piles**, all with sweeping views over the wooded hills and the sea – and the high, bare mountains of the north. Like many of the islands, Karpathos lost many of its people to emigration in the early part of this century, most of them in this case going to the USA but many also leaving to become traders in the Sudan. Many older Karpathians have since retired to their native island, often bringing their cars back with them, which is why you'll see an incongruous amount of Detroit iron on the island's mainly unsurfaced roads, and hear the accents of Brooklyn and Newark, New Jersey in the village kafeneons. Many people have also rebuilt the family home in lavish style, with vivid blue and green plasterwork, archways, domes and always huge masses of bougainvillea. The southern hill villages are green and well-watered.

Northern Karpathos is cut off from the south by its unique geography: the island narrows to a high, steep-sided ridge which falls away to the ocean on either side. In places, this razorback is just wide enough to carry the road built to link the two parts of the island in the late 1970s: from the passenger side of a truck heading over this route you have a clear – and heart-stopping – view over the drop. Faint hearts should get out and walk, or go by boat. The island's highest peak (called, inevitably, Profitis Elias) reaches 1140 metres.

The highlight of northern Karpathos is **Olimbos** (Olympus), a ridge-top village of windmills and traditional houses. Much is made in tourist office literature and guidebooks of this village's "untouched traditional way of life": as a result this traditional way of life has had to make room for a steady flow of rubbernecking visitors and I suspect that tourism, as elsewhere in Greece, is now the main cash earner. Many women in Olimbos – a higher proportion than anywhere else in the islands – do still wear a traditional costume which consists of elaborate embroidery over an indigo-dyed skirt of homespun denim. It's an attractive contrast to the universal black into which custom forces so many women in rural Greek communities, but I can't help suspecting a canny eye to tourism income and the blandishments of tourism officials play as big a part as tradition does in keeping this costume alive.

Perched on this windy height, Olimbos's line of stone windmills must have been the village's biggest asset, for there is always a strong breeze here from either east or west. Eastward, a stream runs through a long, lush valley from Olimbos down to the sea and the little port of **Diafani** with its pebbly bay – about an hour's walk downhill, 90 minutes uphill. On a summer night, frogs croaking in the valley make such an amazing racket that you can hear them up in Olimbos: unfortunately, the same lavish (by island standards) water supply that makes northern Karpathos such a happy home for frogs also breeds swarms of mosquitoes: make sure you have plenty of repellent.

North of Karpathos, separated by a narrow channel from the bigger island, is uninhabited **Saria**, site (confusingly) of the ancient city of Nisyros. There is very little left to see.

To the south, **Kassos** is mostly depopulated, with only a handful of people living in most of its villages, none more than about 40 minutes' walk from the little port at **Emborio**. There is a small beach at **Ammousa** and an even smaller one at Helathros. This is definitely an island for solitude-lovers. Its only other attraction is the stalactite cave at **Sellai**, surrounded by ancient walls.

Buses run infrequently between Pigadia as far north as **Mesohori** and **Spoa**, the jumping-off point for the north: from there it's a full day's gruelling walk over dirt roads to Olimbia, with breathtaking views in all directions. Because there's no public transport, lorries and pick-up trucks tend to be generous with lifts on this road. However, the easiest and pleasantest way to explore the island is by boat. Until the road was built, not long ago, caiques were the only way of getting around Karpathos and the hill village still has its corresponding tiny port below. There are daily caiques from Pigadia and Ammopi to Olimbia and to other secluded beaches and fishing hamlets around the island: you can make a day trip of it or stay overnight. Kassos is served on the Crete/Rhodes route by the same ferries as Karpathos.

TRAVELLING
The island receives charter flights in summer direct from London, and scheduled flights from Athens, Rhodes and Crete, as well as having frequent ferries from Rhodes and Crete.

WHERE TO STAY
There are holiday hotels on the beach close to Pigadia: of these, the small **Romantika**, more like a pension than a hotel, is the pleasantest. Rooms to rent are available at Amopi, Arkasa and Diafani.

FOOD AND DRINK
Karpathos has not so far succumbed to the tide of microwaves which is fast inundating Greece's more developed resorts. The smaller tavernas around **Pigadia's** harbour have good seafood. In recent years a rash of flash cafés has broken out around the harbour: good location but slightly inflated prices. There are good tavernas at **Diafani** and one tiny taverna – the choice is usually between fish or no fish – at **Ag. Nikolaos**, a fishing hamlet with a tiny beach. The hill villages are also well supplied with tavernas – good but usually a limited choice.

KOS

Kos is an island of changing landscapes. The high slopes of the massif of Mount Dikios, dominating the north-east, are rugged and treeless, the lower slopes covered with pine and fig trees. Much of the north and west is a fertile plain of wheat fields and pasture where you will even see the occasional cow – a rare sight in the islands. The central part of the island, around the village of Antimachia and the airport, is a high, windy plateau of thornbush and goat pasture, while the southern tip is mountainous and trackless.

Kos has excellent beaches. These have made it a big package holiday destination for British, Scandinavian and other Northern European holidaymakers, and no beach is without its clutch of holiday hotels.

Kos is the second biggest of the Dodecanese. Like Rhodes, it was a stronghold of the Knights of St John, who left two formidable castles; Turkish and Italian occupiers also left their mark.

KOS TOWN

Looking north and east to the Turkish coast – now studded with holiday apartments – Kos's harbour is dominated by the fortress of the Knights. Less exciting to look at than the elaborate walls of Rhodes, it was a military garrison rather than a town in its own right. The older part of town, built around the harbour with its esplanade of palms and shade trees, is green and shady and its tall palms and surviving minarets – the Yasirli and Defendarli mosques – lend it a Levantine air. On the waterfront east of the castle, the town hall and police headquarters are housed in an Italian building in the wedding cake style. Much of the town was rebuilt by Italian architects after the disastrous earthquake of 1933.

DON'T MISS . . .

Immediately inland from the castle lies the site of **Ancient Kos**, a rather jumbled collection of foundations and toppled columns dating from the fourth and third centuries BC. Many more column drums are haphazardly stored within the walls of the castle. Four distinct sets of foundations mark the sites of the ancient agora, the sanctuaries of Pandimos Aphrodite and of Herakles, and the Christian basilica built in the fourth or fifth century AD on the site of the ancient gallery.

Five minutes' walk away, either side of Odos Grigoriou, are two more ancient sites: a stadium, well preserved and still used for performances, a gymnasium, baths fed by hot springs and – facing the baths – the Nymphaion. When excavated this third-century BC building was thought to be a sanctuary to all the goddesses. More prosaically, it is now known to have been a public urinal.

None of the ancient sites is enclosed and admission to all, and to the castle, is free.

Hippocrates' Tree: Kos's most famous monument is a natural, not a man-made one. That this giant plane tree on the square opposite the castle entrance is indeed the one under which (2,400 years ago) the ancient healer Hippocrates formulated his famous oath and laid the foundations of modern medicine stretches belief a shade. Nevertheless, propped up by scaffolding – and by a Corinthian column borrowed from the ancient site nearby – it is clearly extremely old, and if not the original perhaps one of its saplings: who's quibbling over a few centuries either way? Beside the decrepit tree are the remains of a Turkish fountain.

ALSO WORTH SEEING . . .

The Asklepion – a fourth-century BC combination of temple, sanctuary and hospital – is Kos's most impressive ancient site, some five km from town on a hillside 100 metres above sea level. Divided into three terraces, it sheltered patients, their families and the healer-priests. A Corinthian temple of Apollo – partly restored – and a Doric temple of Asklepios are among the other buildings.

BEACHES

If you stick to the disappointing beaches in and around Kos Town itself you may wonder what all the fuss is about. There's a tatty, pebbly beach east of the harbour and another, bigger and sandier, to the west in front of the new part of town where most of the hotels are. Both have loungers

Hippocrates

The great healer and teacher Hippocrates is a half-mythical figure. Living around 2,400 years ago, he was real enough to leave almost 60 works covering all aspects of medicine. Many of his precepts — such as separating the healthy from the sick to prevent contagion and boiling drinking water to destroy microbes — are central to good medicine today. He stressed the importance of cleanliness and good diet, and he argued that physical health could not be separated from mental and emotional well-being.

Born in 460 BC, Hippocrates studied with the greatest teachers and philosophers of his time, not just in Greece but on long journeys in Africa and Asia. He gained fame for his sound advice to the people of Lemnos when an epidemic struck their island, and became even more widely known in 430 BC when the Athenians credited him with saving them from plague while under siege by Sparta, honouring him with full citizenship and a golden crown. In Athens he became a close friend of the dramatists Sophocles and Euripides.

The famous oath he formulated remains the basic moral code honoured by physicians — though some of its clauses, particularly on abortion, are debatable today. His followers swore by Apollo, Asklepias, Hygeia, Panacea and the whole pantheon to abide by their oath. Students swore to honour their teacher as a parent, to make him a partner in their practice, to share with him at need, to consider his children as their own and to teach them in turn without fee or indenture — not a bad deal for the teacher.

The oath also binds healers to take as their own students only their own sons, the sons of their teacher, and apprentices who have sworn the oath; to use their skills only to help, never to administer a poison or aid an abortion; to leave surgery to surgeons — regarded then as now as a different discipline; not to abuse the bodies of free men and women or of slaves; and to treat whatever they see or hear in the course of their profession as a "holy secret".

and beach umbrellas and you will be harassed by touts if you do not rent one. For less crowded strands and better swimming, head down the west coast towards Tingaki and Mastihari, east in the direction of Bros Therma, or head for the resorts of Kardamaina and Kamari in the south of the island.

TRAVELLING

By Air   Charter flights from main British holiday airports throughout the summer several times weekly. Scheduled flights daily to/from Athens.

By Sea   Ferries daily in either direction on the main Dodecanese/Piraeus route. Ferries also serve the north-east Aegean islands (Kalymnos/Samos/Ikaria/Chios/Mytilini/Limnos) and Kavala weekly.

Ferries sail weekly to Lipsos, Arki, Agathonisi, Astipalia, Fourni, Tilos and Simi.

By Road   Buses are very infrequent: because much of the island – at least around the main town and resorts – is flat, bicycle rental is popular. Motorcycle and Car Rental offices in Kos town and all the resorts. Manos car rental in Kardamena has taken the enterprising step of renting Citroën 2CVs, an ideal car for Greek island roads.

WHERE TO STAY

Finding space anywhere in Kos Town – or for that matter the rest of the island – is a problem unless you are travelling on a package: almost all hotels are dedicated to the package tour market and independent rooms to rent are like hens' teeth. For cheap hotel accommodation try the **Hotel Kalymnos** at Riga Fereou 9, the square beside the harbour (DRX 1,600 single with own toilet and constant hot water) or the **Asclipion** at 154 Marmarou; D-Class hotels include the **Dodekanissos** at Ipsilandou 2 and the **Helena** at Megalexandrou 5. There are plenty of A-, B- and C-Class properties – most of them spread out either side of the harbour and town centre – but most of these are continually block-booked. There are a handful of rooms to rent at **Kardamaina**, mostly full from June to September. A better bet is the **Kamari** beach strip, where there are simple rooms as well as self-catering apartments and studios to let. If all else fails, there is a well-serviced campsite 2.5 km east of Kos town.

FOOD, DRINK AND NIGHTLIFE

Kos is not a gourmet's delight: plenty of internationally bland restaurants catering to a multinational tourist clientele but little variety. Even seafood is often frozen and disappointing. Bars throughout the island tend to be of the cocktail and disco variety, though you will find little kafeneions tucked away in the back streets of Kos Town.

Restaurants line the **harbour front** from one end to the other and continue east along the coast road on the other side of the castle. Sadly, they are much of a muchness, serving mass-produced microwave meals to a mass-produced clientele. **Taverna Platanos**, beside the tree of Hippocrates, at least has a pleasant location; at **Drossia**, on Odos Navklirou, you can sit on the first story balcony and watch the local kamakis sizing up the Scandinavian talent in the bars below.

Navklirou is entered by an ancient gateway drowned in purple bougainvillea. After dark it and the two blocks beside it are a throbbing mass of music bars serving drinks at ridiculously inflated prices to a mixed clientele of holidaymakers and predatory local lads dressed to kill.

THE REST OF THE ISLAND

East Coast

Kardamena, 20 km from the capital on the island's east coast, is Kos's biggest holiday resort thanks to a combination of long south-facing beaches and an international charter airport just five km away. It's a good-time holiday town with little remaining of the tiny fishing hamlet of 20 years ago, but with sand beaches stretching for at least a mile either side of its centre, watersports including parascending, skiing, the ever-popular "doughnut" and windsurfing, and a throbbing tequila-based nightlife centring on a mile-long stretch of bars culminating in George's Club, the town's major boozing emporium, which echoes to the happy shrieking of holidaymakers until two in the morning.

To the north, the slopes of Mt Dikion rise jaggedly out of the Aegean and the volcanic peak of Nisiros beckons on the eastern horizon. Behind Kardamena, which is built on a long stretch of flat coastland, the castle of **Andimachia** on a plateau can easily be taken for a natural formation until a second glance reveals its too angular battlements.

Though its fortified hilltop now encloses only ruins and one small Greek church, this castle built in 1404 must have been even more imposing than the harbour-fort at Kos. There is a knight's crest above the main gate, which is enclosed by a much later Italian-built gun-casement.

Going to Turkey

At least two Greek-owned boats a day, Meander and Hypocrates, connect Kos with the Turkish port of Bodrum, about 90 minutes away, leaving at 09.15 and 16.00. Fares are about £10 one way, £17 return. There are also several Turkish boats, but by a sort of gentleman's agreement the Turks don't actively sell tickets at the Greek end of the service and vice versa. You must leave your passport with the agency overnight. Don't stay in Turkey overnight if you are on a charter flight from Kos: the immigration police will turn you into a pumpkin by confiscating the return half of your ticket. They have a perfect legal right to do this, though it serves no useful purpose.

A further 20 km south, the long grey-sand beach of **Kamari** has become another holiday centre, dominated for half its length by the huge complex of a Club Méditerranée and with more modest new hotels and small apartments built behind the rest of the beach. North around the headland from the Club Med lie two of Kos's last undeveloped beaches, "Paradise Beach" and "Bubble Beach" – both of them a magnet for day-trip boats from both Kardamena and Kamari. Above Kamari, the once-tiny, nondescript farming village of **Kefalos** has become a larger, nondescript farming village on the strength of the new prosperity brought by European Community membership. From here you can hike, bike or drive over dirt roads to a tiny harbour at **Limionas**, five km away on the other side of the island: there's a small sandy beach and one taverna.

West Coast

Kos's westward side is a near-continuous strip of sandy beaches, some of them unpleasantly windswept. The best of these – at Lambi, just west of the main town; Tingaki, 12 km south; Marmari, 15 km south; and Mastichari, 30 km south – are clean and sandy and excellent for watersports. **Marmari** is rated among Europe's best windsurfing beaches and there is a highly-rated windsurfing school at the beach of the Hotel Caravia. The package holiday crowd dominates these as it does the other Kos beaches, and there is virtually no accommodation outside the tour-group hotels.

Interior

Kos's hilly hinterland is surprisingly unpopulated, partly because there has always been fertile farmland on the coastal plain of the west coast and – in more recent years – tourism has drawn many people to work in the town and the beach resorts.

Platani, two km outside Kos, is a pleasant enough little village when not invaded by tour groups stopping to shop and feed en route to or from the site of the Asklipion, two km further uphill from the village. A little further on – surrounded by ill-masked military bunkers – a site has been earmarked for the building of a grandiose International Institute of Hippocrates. The project's aim is to make Kos once again a world centre for the healing sciences. It has been much talked about, progress has been held up by many financial and legal obstacles and its future is still iffy.

Pili, midway between the western slopes of Dikion and the fertile farmlands of the coast, is a pleasant village full of fig-trees, eucalyptus and oleander. Further into the hills, the village of **Asfendiou** is actually several settlements in one. The modern village of **Zia** is a magnet for tour groups experiencing a visit to a "typical Greek village" – honey, herbs and locally-woven rugs in unusual geometric patterns on sale – and Evagelistria, the lowest section of Asfendiou, has a tourist taverna, but hidden away in a fold of the hill are the last villages in Kos untouched by tourism.

Asomatos and old **Zia** are half-ruined and almost deserted except for a handful of ancient women in black. Tumbledown houses are choked by sprawling fig-trees; the village is built just above the line of the last olive-groves, with pine woods and empty rocky slopes above. There are superb sunsets and views to Kalymnos, Pserimos and the Turkish coast. Determined walkers can explore the higher slopes of Dikion from here by dirt roads and donkey track.

NISIROS

Lying about 16 km off the east coast of Kos, the volcano island of Nisiros is a tantalizing silhouette on the horizon seen from Kardamena or Kamari. Seen closer to, its conical volcanic outline and the thick vegetation clinging to the fertile soil of its slopes make Nisiros look almost tropical. Though it has no streams, its slopes are thickly covered with olive groves and clumps of prickly pear.

Though Kos, Turkey and several other islets are clearly in sight from the little main village of **Mandraki**, the waves crashing against the seawall make it feel pleasantly remote from civilization. Indeed, Mandraki could hardly be further from the tan-all-day, party-all-night atmosphere of Kardamena, just an hour's sailing time away. Boatloads of visitors are ferried over from Kos each day and herded up to the volcanic crater, but after they leave in mid-afternoon Mandraki's narrow lanes and tall shuttered houses fall asleep again and the loudest noise is the sound of worry-beads clicking from the kafeneions.

Above the village, the 14th-century monastery of **Panagia Spiliani**, within the crumbling walls of a medieval Venetian castle, is worth climbing the steep flights of steps for. Nisiros's only ancient site is the fifth-century BC fortress at **Palaiokastro**, a stiffish two km hike from Mandraki.

Mandraki is not well endowed with beaches, though you can swim from a clean pebble and boulder beach just around the headland on which the monastery sits. Facing Mandraki, the neighbouring island of **Giali** is gradually being chewed away as its pumice cliffs are quarried for cement, an operation which provides much of Nisiros's income. Giali's sole attraction is an excellent sand beach, with two or three seasonal tavernas – rather marred by the sight of the huge pumice quarry overlooking it.

Better beaches are at **Pali**, the island's second harbour-village, which beats even Mandraki for quiet and seclusion. These too are pebbly, but a two km walk brings you to a long stretch of brown volcanic sand at **Lies**. A big spa-hotel is under way at the beach called Loutra, just outside Pali, where there are hot springs, but as of summer 1991 showed no signs of nearing completion.

Nisiros's other villages are perched on the rim of the volcanic crater itself, looking both out to sea – with wonderful views of the nearby islands and the thickly wooded slopes of Nisiros – and down to the flat land within the crater. **Emborio**, the nearer of the two to Mandraki, is almost deserted and largely dilapidated, though if you follow the whitewashed steps to the highest point of the village you come to a pretty hilltop church in good repair. The tiny old-fashioned general store on Plateia Xatsievangelou doubles as a very basic café – drinks but no food. Set among the hills on the opposite side of the crater, the brilliant white village of **Nikia** is dazzlingly pretty – a welcome contrast to the chemical landscape and stink of the crater far below, it's a composition of pure white and deep shade, sharply defined, with vivid highlights of blue and green paintwork. The church, like many on Dodecanese islands, has an elaborate belltower, in this case surmounted by an anachronistic cross of lightbulbs.

DON'T MISS . . .

The Crater

Around the crater, the hillsides are stained yellow with sulphur and as you get closer to the pit itself the air reeks of it, like the aftermath of a firework party. The crater is a bowl about 250 metres wide and 30 deep. At the bottom, grey mud streaked with brilliant sulphuric yellow is the source of the stench. When the crater is in an active mood the mud bubbles and heaves like the floor of Hell itself. At other times, it's a bit of an anticlimax, but well worth it for the mountain scenery around the crater.

Nearby, a European Community-funded project is attempting to harness the crater's geothermal energy.

TRAVELLING

Mainline ferries call at Mandraki two to three times a week, but the easiest way to get there from Kos is to take one of the many day-trip boats which go from Kos Town, Kamari and Kardamena – you can stay on in Nisiros as long as you like, so long as you keep the plastic card which constitutes the return half of your ticket. The helpful travel agency in Mandraki, Enetikon Tourist Office, rents bikes for trips to the volcano and sells tickets for travel onward to other islands including Tilos.

WHERE TO STAY

There are rooms to rent in **Mandraki**, the cheapest of them at **Pension Drosia** (distinctly spartan). Newer and more comfortable are the **Hotel Porfiris**, **Hotel Romantzo**, both in the village, and the **Hotel Three Brothers** and **Hotel Haritos** by the harbour.

Between Mandraki and Pali the **White Beach Hotel** overlooks a little dark-sand cove. **Pali** has a handful of rooms to rent and a hotel-cum-restaurant, the **Hellenis**, by the harbour.

FOOD AND DRINK

Nisiros comes as a welcome reminder of how good Greek home cooking can be. **Mandraki** has half a dozen good places to eat and most of them serve good, freshly cooked meals at refreshingly affordable prices – generally speaking, standards go up and prices down as you get further away from the harbour where the day-trippers come in. **Mike's Taverna** is one of the best not just in Nisiros but in all the islands, with an affordable, imaginative and varied menu. Mrs Mike, who speaks fluent English as a result of years in Australia, goes out of her way to be helpful to visitors. **To Deilino**, about a hundred metres away, is another good bet for fresh-grilled fish, chicken, octopus and souvlaki and is a great place to watch the sunset over Kos.

KALYMNOS (KALIMNOS)

Kalymnos is an island of deep blue bays and bare grey limestone hills, pockmarked with caves. It's rather bereft of historic or archaeological sites – the main point of interest is a small, crumbling Franco-Byzantine castle above the village of **Chorio**, the old capital of the island.

Like so many island villages, Chorio was built inland to escape the ravages of pirates of one persuasion or another. It is now virtually an inland suburb of Pothia, Kalimnos's bustling little harbour-town and present capital.

Prosperous from a century-old trade in sponges, **Pothia** has taken little notice of tourism until recently, when the dying-off of the sponge fishery has encouraged locals to move into the hotel and restaurant business. The cafés which occupy the whole of its long harbour front are frequented by elderly traders and captains in panama hats or seaman's caps, rather than by tourists, and after the day-trip boats from Kos leave only a handful of foreigners remain.

Pothia is attractive in its busy way, though its single main street carries an inordinate amount of motorcycle traffic and the revving of engines late at night can be hell. It's a good place to see the life of a Dodecanese commercial town which doesn't depend totally on tourism, and much of its traditional architecture of tall stuccoed houses with overhanging balconies and outside staircases can still be seen, especially in the streets inland from the harbour. On the harbour, the municipal building is a fine example of the over-the-top school of Art-Deco-Alhambra architecture favoured by the Italians during their occupation of the Dodecanese, with its dome, arches, round windows and imitation-Moorish detail.

DON'T MISS . . .

Pothia's museum – clearly signposted from the harbour – is an imposing turn of the century mansion which belonged to Nikolaos Vouvalis, father of the Kalymniot sponge industry. Vouvalis had a head office in London and branches in the Saronic islands, Tunisia, Tripoli, Cuba, Nassau and Tarpon Springs, Florida. Judging by the elaborate dining room with its Royal Doulton porcelain and the stiff parlour with its gilt-framed mirrors, oil portraits, plush furniture and wolfskin rugs, there was plenty of money in the sponge trade. It's an incongruous imitation of the fashions of Edwardian England and late-19th-century France, and must have been even more incongruous back in Turkish-ruled, pre-World War One Kalimnos.

BEACHES AND VILLAGES

There's a small and rather scruffy beach about a kilometre out of Mandraki on the south road, signposted to Thermai; unless you are desperate and pushed for time, though, the small resort of **Mirthies**, eight kilometres away, is a better bet. Almost landlocked, the deep bay on which Mirthies and the next-door village of **Masouri** (the two merge) is protected from the sea by the mountainous offshore islet of Telendos. The village has a small, clean beach of pebbles and the water is calm and extremely clear. Two small caiques shuttle back and forth all day to **Telendos**, where there's a rather bigger and less crowded beach and a couple of tavernas – the trip takes about 20 minutes.

Mirthies/Masouri accommodate such package tourism as Kalymnos gets – a surprising amount given its minuscule beaches – but there are quieter pebbly beaches further north, notably at **Emborios**. From its beach, this tiny fishing hamlet seems to be entirely landlocked and the swimming is even better than at Mirthies. There are a couple of tavernas and in summer some basic rooms to rent.

On the other side of Kalymnos, the village of **Vathi** and its tiny harbour Rina are a surprise to the eye after a winding six-km ride along featureless hill-slopes. Turning the final bend, you look down on a deep, wide valley solid from side to side with the greenery of orange groves, made all the more vivid by the lunar landscape of the bare hills on either side. Rina shelters half a dozen fishing boats and the occasional yacht in its steep-walled fjord – the open sea can't be seen from the harbour. It has no beach, and the only place to swim is from the steps at the end of the pier, which lead into deep, clean water. Here, as elsewhere on Kalymnos, the cliffs both shelter the inlet and the village and reflect the sun's heat like natural radiators even after sunset. Kalymnos's little beaches and coves are notably more sheltered than is the norm in the often windy Aegean. A small caique, the Fleyerina, runs daily trips to secluded beaches nearby.

You can walk through the fertile valley and eventually over to Mirthies on the other side of the island: from the head of the valley, though, it's a steep, hot, thirsty and not particularly interesting hike of at least three hours down to Mirthies.

TRAVELLING

By Sea Ferries daily each way to Piraeus/Rhodes and points between. There are frequent day-trip boats from Kos Town and Mastihari. A twice a week connection heads west to Astipalea and Amorgos where you can change for onward travel into the Cyclades.

Around the Island Buses run from Pothia as far as Arninonda on the west coast and Vathi on the east. Motorbike rental available in Pothia and Mirthies. Shared "taxi-buses" are a Kalimnos institution – they're ordinary Mercedes saloons which run on a fixed fare from point to point, leaving when full. At Pothia, they stand by the harbour opposite the Hotel Thermai.

WHERE TO STAY

In **Pothia** the **Hotel Patmos** (not actually a hotel but a pension) has mid-priced accommodation. The **Hotel Thermai**, on the waterfront, is roughly the same price. Both have en-suite shower and loo and hot water. More expensive is the **Hotel Olympic**, another waterfront property of the shoebox persuasion. The scruffy but cheap **Hotel Alma** and **Hotel Crystal** have both apparently succumbed to market forces and closed. Far and away the best value however is the newly-built **Hotel Panorama**, on the zig-zag main street above and to the west of the harbour. It's run by a very helpful and hospitable Greek-Bahamian couple (Tel: 23138). Attractive rooms with en-suite facilities, balcony and breakfast can be had for much the same price as at the rival Patmos and Thermai.

At **Mirthies** most of the accommodation is aimed at tour operator clients but there are also well-appointed rooms and apartments to let. **Studio Australia** is at the Melitzaha Beach end of town. **Ariadne Studios** is at Masouri. Cheaper rooms to rent are available at **Pension Rinio** and more up-market accommodation at the **Hotel Ilios**, with pretty balconies overlooking the bay. **Popi Studios** is set back from the road and covered with bougainvillea.

At **Vathia/Rina** there is a small hotel, the **Hotel Galini**, and rooms to rent at **Pension Manolis** above the harbour.

EXCURSIONS

Day-trip boats run from Pothia to Kos several times a day, and once or twice a week to the main natural attraction on Kalimnos, the sea-cave at Kefala. Boats also run from Pothia and Mirthies to Emborio and other beaches, Telendos and Nera, another offshore islet.

FOOD AND DRINK

Pothia has plenty of cafés and restaurants, ranging from the "smart" modern cafés at the west end of the waterfront where the younger, motorbike-riding set hang out, to the dozen or so older ouzeris and kafeneions frequented by whiskery retired captains and beached divers. Cheaper places to eat are at the east end of the waterfront, beyond the grandiose municipal buildings. Close to the ferry pier, **Zorbas** is one of the best places to eat, with excellent fresh seafood at reasonable prices. The nearby **Do Re Mi** café-bar has live traditional music — not, for once, over-amplified — most evenings.

Mirthies has plenty of beach-side restaurants and bars. There are a couple of modest restaurants at **Rina**, also good for seafood.

LEROS

Unprepossessing at first glance, Leros is an island of low hills and dusty fields separated by bays and inlets even deeper and more sheltered than those of Kalymnos. Its natural harbours made it a prize for both Allied and Axis fleets in World War Two and the island was extensively knocked about as they fought over it. Its main port, Lakki, is still a major haven for Greek freighters.

Leros hasn't become a big hit with foreign visitors and its attractions are rather low-key. Good sheltered beaches and the deep blue water of its bays help to make up for a rather dull landscape. On closer examination, the hills of Leros are far more fertile than they appear at a distance, supporting more cultivation – mainly olives – than either neighbouring Kalymnos or Patmos, and there are some pleasant walks.

Leros has two fair-sized towns. **Lakki**, where the inter-island ferries dock, faces west. Here, the Italian architects responsible for the elaborate public buildings of the Dodecanese had a field day. Every building on the waterfront is a confection of stucco curves, speedlines and portholes, more appropriate to Miami Beach than the bleak hills of Leros. **Platanos** sprawls over a headland on the east coast, with rather grubby harbours either side at Agia Marina and Pandeli. The hill above Platanos is crowned by a Byzantine castle which is being restored: because of the near-paranoid security which surrounds anything even vaguely military in Greece, photography is banned. This may seem odd – why should a medieval ruin be a state secret? – but the fort is still used as an observation post.

Leros has good beaches at Vromolithos about half an hour's walk from Pandeli or Lakki, and Alinda and Gournas about 40 minutes' walk away. Xirokambos, on the southern tip, and Partheni, near the airport at the north end of the island, are both marred by an extensive military presence, with all the rusty barbed wire and cement that goes with it.

TRAVELLING
By Air Scheduled flights from Athens.

By Sea Daily ferries to/from Rhodes and Piraeus, frequent ferries to Samos. Small boats daily to/from Kalymnos and Telendos.

WHERE TO STAY
Few rooms to rent but plenty of older hotels and newer pensions in both **Lakki** and **Platanos**. Much of the better accommodation is occupied by package tour operators in June-August.

FOOD AND DRINK
Platanos/Agia Marina is a better bet than Lakki, which has few tavernas or kafeneions and is somnolent except when the ferry comes in. Platanos, three km away from Lakki, has a surprisingly good choice of places to eat and because the core clientele is Greek, rather than foreign, food is generally better and prices lower than you may expect.

PATMOS

Crowned by an ancient monastery and by the most beautiful village in the Dodecanese, Patmos is an island of great beauty, both natural and manmade. Its rocky hills are a patchwork of terrace-farms divided by dry-stone walls topped with thorns. Fig-trees and prickly pear cluster around houses and villages, and eucalyptus trees, a late introduction, shade roads and streets. A deeply indented coastline gives it plenty of secluded little beaches, and in two places the island is cut almost in two by the sea.

Although it is one of the best-known islands in the chain, monastic conservatism and the lack of a charter airport have kept the excesses of tourism to a minimum, and Patmos's turquoise bays and its many beaches are neither crowded nor overshadowed by hotels, bars and discos.

The island's main village and harbour, **Skala**, is at the end of a deep, east-facing bay, a perfect natural anchorage which makes Patmos a popular port of call for yachts. Above the port, the monastery of St John Theologos, author of the book of Revelations, frowns sternly down. More like a fortress than any western religious building, it is a reminder of a turbulent past when the islands of the Aegean were fair game for Saracens, Corsairs and other seagoing looters. Though it is largely a tourist centre, Skala's tourism is pleasant and low-key. The village is attractively green and flower-filled and its few medium-sized hotels are relatively unobtrusive among the more traditional whitewashed buildings.

Chora, the village which surrounds the walls of the monastery, is one of the most beautiful in Greece, well worth the steep one-hour walk from Skala. It is a mixture of tall mansions and simple village houses which climb steeply to the monastery itself. The colours are austere, an almost monochrome mix of white walls and grey stone windows, door arches and flagstones. It is almost impossible to keep any sense of direction in these narrow, corridor-like streets, stairs and passages, but in any case the best way to see Chora is to wander aimlessly. Like so many traditional Greek villages, it is much bigger than it appears at first sight. To find your way out of the maze, just keep heading downhill.

DON'T MISS . . .

The Monastery of St John
Built in the 11th century, the Monastery was self-ruling under the Byzantine emperors and subsequently managed to keep most of its autonomy under the Venetian Dukes of Naxos and even under the Turks, who – smarter than most Western empire-builders – perceived that religious persecution would only stiffen resistance from their subject peoples. Its founder, the saintly hermit Christodoulos, was given the rule of Patmos by the Byzantine Emperor Alexius 1 Comnenus, whose golden seal can still be seen in the monastery. Other treasures include Byzantine icons, richly-decorated vestments and relics going back to the ninth century, manuscripts and parchments, but perhaps the loveliest aspects of the monastery are the glowing frescoes in the chapel of the Virgin and in the monastery church. Monastery opening hours vary from day to day: the monastery is open every day from 08.00 to 12.00 and at different times in the afternoon and evening. In any case, the best time to make the visit is first thing in the morning. You will not be admitted wearing shorts, a short skirt or short sleeves. However, to preserve decency and accommodate ill-prepared visitors, the monks maintain a collection of "appropriate" garments to lend, and a number of visitors can usually be seen wandering around in an odd assortment of ill-fitting garb.

BEACHES AND VILLAGES
A well as the spiritual treasures of the monastery and the more worldly delights of Skala's bars and cafés, Patmos has some of the best beaches in the Dodecanese. None is large, but all

are uncrowded and clean. In keeping with Patmos's status as a "Holy Isle" (by church and government decree) you will see signs on all beaches inveighing against topless sunbathing and nudity. On all except the town beach at Skala, these seem to be honoured more in the breach than in the observance at least concerning toplessness.

As town beaches go **Skala's** is attractive, though inevitably it is the most crowded on the island. About half an hour's walk away, heading north, **Meloi** has a pleasant but sometimes crowded sand and pebble bay lined with tamarisk trees, with a couple of tavernas. A further half an hour away, **Agriolivado** has a similar beach with more restaurants and cafés, plus windsurfers for hire. **Kampos,** the next bay north, is disappointing, but **Lambi,** much hyped for its coloured pebbles, fulfils its promise. The stones of the beach at first sight appear colourless and dull, but when wet they glow with muted yellows and reds reminiscent of Greek religious frescoes. **Lefkes,** at the foot of a fertile valley, is disappointingly choked with mounds of dry seaweed, not worth the detour.

South of Skala, **Grikos** is the island's most-developed beach village, with several medium-sized hotels and a number of tavernas along a pebbly beach which hardly seems to justify the level of development. On the other side of the island, about an hour's walk away along a hillside footpath looking down to the clear water of Stavros Bay, **Psili Ammos** is the finest of the Patmos beaches. It is an idyllic crescent of real golden sand, shady tamarisk trees and a pleasant taverna on the beach.

TRAVELLING

By Sea Patmos is a hub for the main Dodecanese ferries and routes onward into the Cyclades and the North-East Aegean. Daily (plus) services to Rhodes and points south and to Piraeus, frequent services to Samos and Mykonos. Fast catamarans to Rhodes in summer. Smaller ferries ply between Patmos and the smaller islands of Arki, Lipsi, and Agathonisi en route to Samos (Pythagorion). A long-haul cruise-ferry, the Orient Express, calls fortnightly on its Venice/Istanbul route. There are infrequent ferries to Astipalia and Amorgos in the Cyclades. Patmos is a junction for a number of sometimes competing services: it's worth checking with the Port Authority police to make sure of all the options available.

Around the Island Buses run five times a day between Skala and Hora, from 13.45 to 20.00, and two a day between Skala and Grikou, and one daily between Skala and Kampos. Skala buses stop by the ferry pier opposite the Port Authority building. There are a number of car and motorcycle hire agencies in Skala, and small boats go every morning (10.00) to Psili Ammos, Lambi and Agriolivado beaches, returning every afternoon at 16.00.

WHERE TO STAY

Virtually all accommodation on Patmos is in Skala. The old-fashioned **Hotel Astoria** on the Skala waterfront is one of the cheaper and older hotels. With a café-bar downstairs, it's also one of the noisier ones. Newer mid-priced hotels in Skala are the **Hotel Chris, Hotel Patmion** and **Hotel Skala**, next to each other a hundred metres or so from the main block of cafés and restaurants. The **Hotel Byzance**, the newest hotel in town, is good value.

Finding **rooms** in Patmos is never a problem – fending off the horde of determined ladies who meet the boat to promote their establishments can be. **Pension Sophia**, about 300 yards from the harbour on the main road from Skala to Chora, is one of the nicest: Sophia speaks no English (which doesn't stop her holding long conversations with guests) and is generous with plentiful hot water (not common anywhere), coffee and orange juice, as well as help in finding out boat times. If Skala is booked solid (as can happen in high season) there are a couple of places renting not very good rooms at Meloi and rather better pensions and apartments at Grikos.

FOOD AND DRINK

Skala is one of the more user-friendly island ports – if it's not a pension or souvenir shop it's probably a café or restaurant. Most of them are on the harbour front. The **Old Harbour**, a few hundred metres away in the direction of Meloi, is the poshest and most expensive – worth splashing out on for a last-night banquet.

Focus of the café-bar scene is the **Arion** café, the favourite of a string of café-restaurants in the block either side of the old Hotel Astoria. It's a dignified old high-ceilinged bar with a marble floor and the highest prices in town. For a cheaper and less pretentious place to drink, try the little **Kafezacharoplasteon Houston** on the square beside the post office. The best value grilled chicken and souvlaki is at **Taverna Avgerinos**, in a tiny side street just a minute's walk uphill from the square (open evenings only). Follow the signs to the OTE.

There are two restaurants on the tiny square in the heart of **Hora**, **Vangelis** and **Olympia**. Even pleasanter is the **Patmian House** restaurant, set in one of the narrow streets lower down – follow the signs from the car park beside the Dimarkion building.

EXCURSIONS

Between Patmos and the North-East Aegean islands of Samos and Ikaria stretches an archipelago of tiny inhabited islands, uninhabited skerries and rocks. Of these only Lipsi, Arki and

Agathonisi, and Fourni are inhabited year round: ideal for determined solitude seekers with plenty of books and partners they are still talking to. You want quiet? This is it.

Daily excursion boats connect Lipsi with Patmos in season and there is a thrice-weekly connection to Leros. Once a week the Anna Express goes to Marathi, Arki and Agathonisi, a trio of even smaller and more remote islands.

Lipsi

Lipsi's delightful village has a mostly-new harbour front, backed by a warren of older buildings leading up to its main church. It is clearly a devout community – looking inland from the village you can see at least seven little white churches on the surrounding hillsides, each with its blue dome. One of these (the furthest uphill and to your right as you face inland) used to have a ten-inch naval shell-case pressed into service as a makeshift bell. It sits rusting by the church, a neat example of sword-into-ploughshare.

It's a surprisingly well-farmed little island, with neat terraces making the most of each patch of cultivable land. A large harbour has a small fleet of fishing boats and its shallow, glass-clear water is full of tiny and colourful fish, a handy cross-section of Aegean marine life. There are a couple of excellent fish restaurants by the harbour, and accommodation in the Calypso Hotel (on the waterfront) and a number of pleasant, village rooms.

Lipsi has a pleasant sandy town beach, five minutes' walk from its harbour, which gets busy in the afternoon when local kids head there after school. There's a better, less busy pebble beach 20 minutes' walk further on. Continue for another hour's stiff walking and you come to Lipsi's real gem, a brilliant cove of white sand and shallow, warm turquoise water with one small taverna. If you're only visiting Lipsi for the day, take the "bus" – an open pickup truck with makeshift bench seats – which meets the boat from Patmos: it's well worth the exorbitant return fare.

Arki and Agathonisi

Arki, east of Lipsi, is at the centre of the rocky archipelago, and from its harbour or hilltops it seems on a clear day to be afloat not at sea but in a great lake, bounded on all sides by the hills of Patmos, Ikaria, Samos, the Turkish coast and the other islets nearby. Arki's harbour and only village is tucked away at the end of a long, narrow fjord, hidden from sight of the open sea. Larger ferries like the Nisos Kalymnos can't get in and passengers are taken off by fishing boats. There are a few rooms to rent, but in general Arki makes Lipsi look like a full-scale holiday resort.

It does, however, have superbly clear water and is surrounded by even tinier islands, some of them within swimming distance. One, **Marathi**, has a good beach and a summer taverna.

Agathonisi, east of Arki, is a long, low, barren island, with a village inland. About 200 people live here and it is called **Megalo Chorio** (big village) to distinguish it from the even tinier Micro Horio.

THE NORTH-EAST AEGEAN
The Green Islands

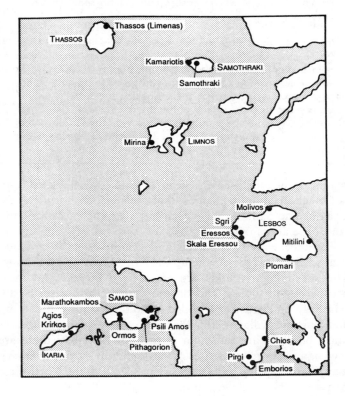

Draw an imaginary line on the map from the southern tip of Evia south-east through Samos to the Turkish coast. South of it, the Aegean is cluttered and spiky with the major and minor isles of the Cyclades and the Dodecanese. North of it, the ocean is emptier and the distance from island to island much greater. Unlike those of the southern archipelagos, though, the

Troubled Waters

Samos and Lesbos were among the great naval powers of ancient Greece, and Samothraki was a most important religious centre to the ancients. The other islands were of less importance in ancient times. More recently — between the Fourth Crusade and Turkish conquest in the early 16th century — they fell into the hands of the Giustiniani, Genoese merchant princes whose castles can still be seen on Chios, Lesbos and Lemnos. During the years of Turkish rule, Chios and Lesbos in particular had sizeable Turkish settlements, traces of which can still be seen. Revolts throughout the North-East Aegean during the War of Independence ended in tragedy or disappointment. On Chios, some 30,000 Greeks were massacred, a 45,000 more carried off to slavery. Samos and Ikaria carried through their rebellion successfully, only to be handed back to Turkey at the end of the war. Like Crete, the North-East Aegean islands had to wait for Turkish defeat in the Balkan Wars of 1911 and 1912 before coming under Greek rule.

islands of the North-East Aegean have no convenient title and not much in common. Samos, Ikaria, Chios, Lesbos, Lemnos, Thassos and Samothraki — each has a character, history and landscape all its own.

Together with two barren and remote islets, Psara and Agios Efstratios, they make up the North-East Aegean group. The seven main islands are among the biggest and most prosperous in Greece and on most of them tourism is still relatively unobtrusive. Wooded mountains and secluded hill and harbour villages, together with some of the Aegean's finest beaches, are the main attractions on most: there are few significant ancient sites, though hilltop castles overlook many harbours and anchorages. The history of the North-East Aegean islands is diverse too.

SAMOS

Fertile and abundant, Samos is an island dominated like no other by shades of green — the vivid splashes of vineyards and planes, the dark spires of cypresses and the dusty silver green of olive groves, set off much of the summer by bright yellow dashes of broom. Samos's peaks, cliffs and crags rise not from barren slopes but from gardens, tiny fields and evergreen woods. Almost 60 km from end to end, Samos is one of Greece's larger islands and a prosperous one from the vineyards and olive groves which cover its hillsides. Its size and fertility have softened the impact of package tourism, though several of its villages have been transformed into holiday resorts over the last ten years.

Samos's beauties are natural rather than man-made: it does not have the gem-like white villages of Patmos or the Cycladic islands. It does, however, have pretty harbours, idyllic white-pebble coves of clear turquoise water, and a backdrop of forest and terrace-covered mountains.

NORTH COAST

Two of Samos's major port towns and its biggest holiday centre lie on the north coast, connected by a good main road.

Samos, the island's capital and main port is a grimy commercial town of about 5,000 people and little appeal: with the rest of the island to explore you won't want to stay here. Its old quarter, **Vathi**, on the hillside above the port, retains some character and is worth wandering through if you have time to kill while waiting for a boat.

Ten km east of Samos, the fishing harbour of **Kokkari** has become the island's most popular holiday centre. It's easy to see why: Kokkari is on a sweep of harbour-bay between two rocky points, looking north to the Turkish coast not far off. There are good pebble beaches to either side of the harbour and in the little cove beyond to the west, and superb white-pebble coves at **Limonakia**, about two km west, and **Tsamadou**, one km further on.

Behind Kokkari, olive groves and the dark green spires of cypresses cover the slopes of Stournara and Karvouni: behind them are the even taller peaks of Ambelos and Profitis Elias. There are some wonderful walks through woods of plane trees and mountain streams which – a rarity in Greece – do not dry up in summer and are bright with dragonflies. Several Samian valleys – like the more famous "Valley of the Butterflies" on Rhodes – are frequented by clouds of crimson-winged moths in summer. Unsurprisingly, Kokkari's beaches, accommodation and café-tables are packed from May to September. If you don't mind plenty of company it is still the finest village in Samos.

Six km west, there's a rather exposed and not very appealing beach at the tiny village of **Avlakia**. A little further, the village of **Ag. Konstantinos** is spread out among vineyards leading down to a boulder beach. Behind its beach-front, Ag. Konstantinos is one big garden, with explosions of pink oleander, crimson bougainvillea and purple morning glory from doorsteps and balconies. Ag. Konstantinos lacks the beaches which make Kokkari so popular and is a pleasant, uncrowded alternative. Like Kokkari, it has impressive mountain scenery inland and is a good base for (fairly untaxing) walks on the slopes of Mt Ambelos. The hill villages of Ambelos, Stavrinithes, Valeontates, Manolates and Vourliotes are all worth a visit, with tiny cafés in plane-tree-shaded plateias.

Villagers are well-used to invasion by rented jeep and bike, but if you arrive on foot by way of the maze of farm paths through the woods you may be accorded a certain respect. More determined walkers can push on from Vourliotes to the now-abandoned monastery at **Vrondanis**: turn left where the tarred road ends for the rocky footpath which leads down to Kokkari.

There is little to see on the north coast between Ag. Konstantinos and **Karlovasi**, the north coast's other major town. A sprawling collection of suburbs of little charm or character, it is admittedly less gritty than the town of Samos. The central square, for buses to the rest of the island and other facilities, is about two km from the ferry harbour. If you have time to kill, there's a good, uncrowded pebbly beach at **Potami**, about half an hour's walk away. The beach – similar to those at Kokkari and Limonakia, but without the huge numbers of sunbathers – has a couple of tavernas and the ruined shell of the 11th-century Byzantine chapel of the Holy Saviour. In fine contrast, an incongruous futurist church of Agios Nikolaos stands on the headland at the east of Potami bay.

SOUTH COAST

Pythagorion, Samos's south coast port, is at the east end of the island about 15 km from Samos town and faces the Turkish hills less than two km away. It has become a popular holiday resort in recent years because it is so close to Samos's charter airport, just five km away, and as a place to stay it is considerably more attractive than either Karlovasi or the town of Samos. This is faint praise, and with a number of other pleasant villages to choose from, Pythagorion ranks rather low: it has two rather scruffy town beaches either side of a large harbour popular with yachts, a harbour front lined with lookalike cafés and restaurants, and a main street full of travel and ticket agencies, car and bike rental offices and souvenir shops. There is a small Frankish keep above the harbour – beside Pythagorion's grandiose church – and within its walls the foundations of part of the ancient town.

The little port is named after Samos's most famous citizen of ancient times, the mathematician Pythagoras. He formulated the theorem governing the proportions of the triangle (the square of the hypotenuse is equal to the square of the other two sides). Pythagorion's other claim to fame is the aqueduct-tunnel built in the sixth century BC by the architect Eupalinos. Until recently it was possible to explore the narrow tunnel into the hillside, but the entrance has now been closed.

Samos, confusingly, has two excellent sandy beaches called Psili Ammos (the name just means "beautiful bay"). The easternmost, and most hyped, of these is some eight km east of Pythagorion. It is easily accessible by rented bike or car but is usually disappointingly crowded. The beach is about 400m long and most of the much-vaunted sand is invisible beneath the packed bodies of dozens of sunbathers. There are two or three good fish tavernas above the little sandy cove. Between Psili Ammos proper and Cape Potami there is a vast stretch of uncrowded (but also unsheltered) pebble beach with a single taverna at its midpoint. Beyond Psili Ammos, the east end of the island is rocky, barren and inaccessible, with a handful of small beaches which hardly justify the effort of getting there.

IREON

The fertile plain west of Pythagorion is a sea of olives and grainfields interrupted only by the island's airport. Inland from here, **Chora** and **Mytilini** are big farming villages largely unaffected by – and uninterested in – the coastal rash of tourism. Mytilini's museum, open erratically, houses the bones of prehistoric beasts found at a large fossil site nearby, among them a giant giraffe named Samotherium and a three-toed pygmy horse.

Ireon, once a tiny fishing hamlet at the west end of this coastal plain, is now a fast-growing holiday resort – not yet as big and bustling as Kokkari but well on the way. It has a fine pebble beach in front of its spread of waterfront tavernas and though building has been explosive over the last ten years it has been done with commendable taste and restraint. One advantage of Samos's almost sub-tropical climate is that bougainvillea and vines quickly cover the worst excesses of tourism development, and at Ireon the emphasis has been on modest hotels, studios and pensions rather than big hotel blocks. Close to the village is the prominent single column which marks the site of the ancient **Temple of Hera** which gives the village its name.

A variety of visitors have carved thir names into the ancient stones; one Reynaud de Cassis in 1738, an Antoine Frisons in 1790, and an Ida Alex of Ohio, in 1926. Until fairly recently this – Samos's only significant ancient site – was unfenced: thanks partly to Ida Alex, it is now enclosed in an ugly chainlink fence topped with barbed wire and as of June 1990 had been closed to the public by the Ministry of Culture.

WEST OF IREON

Beyond Ireon the coast bulges south in a massif of hills covered with olive groves and cypress woods. A winding dirt road, challenging to any form of transport except jeeps or trail bikes, runs from the somnolent hill-village of **Paghondas** round to **Spatharei**, a balcony-village built staircase fashion on the slopes either-side of the road, and on to **Pirgos**, a prosperous if undistinguished farm-village. From Pirgos, the

Pythagoras and Ancient Samos

Neolithic finds at Tigani and Ireon prove that Samos was inhabited 5000 years ago. In Greek times it was settled first by Dorians then — by 900 BC — by Ionians. For two centuries, from around 700 to 500 BC, the island was one of the strongest Ionian states. Its navy was a force to be reckoned with and its sailors and navigators were adventurous explorers. The wealth from this sea trade spurred the arts and sciences and Pythagoras was just one of several generations of scientists and philosophers, among them the astronomer Aristarchus, the first to declare that the earth orbits the sun. Like much of the knowledge of Ancient Greece, Pythagoras's inspiration came from Egypt, where he studied at the court of the Pharaoh Amasis for more than 20 years, and from Babylon, where he was held for a further 12 after the Persian conquest of Egypt. Returning eventually to Samos at the age of 56, he fell out with the tyrant Polycrates who had previously favoured him, travelled through the Greek world, and after settling at the city of Kroton in Italy died there at the age of 80.

Pythagoras's life coincided with Samos's golden age and the rule of the tyrant Polycrates (in the ancient Greek world a tyrant was not necessarily a bad or a harsh ruler, but one who was not elected by the people). There is no doubt that Polycrates was a tough cookie: a number of his rivals, including his brothers Syloson and Pantagnotus, wound up dead or exiled. With an enormously powerful navy of 100 triremes Polycrates taxed passing ships and less powerful neighbouring cities in an early version of the protection racket. A palace guard of 1000 mercenary archers secured him from overthrow and alliances with Naxos, Athens and Egypt kept Samos under his rule free of Persia, which had swallowed Chios, Lesbos and the cities of Asia Minor. In 522 BC the Persian satrap Oroites lured him to a meeting with the promise of treasure. Polycrates's greed was his downfall. The Persians crucified him and after his death Samos came under the sway of the Persians, who put his brother Sysolon on the throne as a puppet. Allied with Sparta and Athens, Samos threw off Persia after Salamis in 479 BC and for a while the strength of the island's fleet rivalled that of Athens. A brief war between the two led to Athens installing a democracy and Samos remained a loyal ally of Athens throughout the classical period.

"capital" of this part of Samos, you can head inland for about 5km to **Mesogia** and **Pandrossos**, two pretty, sleepy old villages high on the flanks of the central Samian massif of Oros Ambelos and Oros Karvouni. Set high above a green, steep-sided valley, these – like the hill-villages of Ambelos's eastern slopes – are a glimpse of Samian village life pre-tourism.

From Spatharei, you can also hike through stream-filled woods and occasional tiny patches of cultivation to the tiny hillside hamlet of **Skoureika** and on through its near-twin **Koumeika** to the long stretch of beach at **Ormos Marathokampou**.

The village of the same name, at the west end of this pebbly bay, is the least-developed of Samos's coastal villages and one of the better places to stay if you want to get away from the crowds. Ormos consists of a couple of streets of older houses built around a small harbour: the architecture is undistinguished but the atmosphere is friendly and relaxed, there is a choice of places to eat and sleep, and the scenery is fine.

For onward travel, Ormos is well placed, about 20 km from Karlovasi. Its biggest assets, though, are the fine beaches at Votsalakia, about half an hour's walk to the west, and Psili Ammos (the western one) about 40 minutes further on. Votsalakia is more than a kilometre of sand and pebble, Psili Ammos almost a kilometre of fine sand, and despite the growing number of hotels and pensions on this beach strip, neither becomes really crowded.

Still further west, **Limionas** is a mostly sandy cove which gets even fewer visitors: it has a good taverna and there are a few rooms to rent. As of late 1991 a small hotel was being built at the east end of this beach. Western Samos is dominated by the treeless massif of Mt Kerkis and its surrounding peaks, a grey limestone fist smashing up out of the treeline. Its highest summit, Vigla, reaches 1435m. Often capped by cloud even in high summer, Kerkis gives the west a microclimate of its own – in spring and autumn it may be raining or cloudy in Ormos when Ireon, only 20 km away, is sunny and dry.

From **Psili Ammos** (west) a very rough road winds steeply round the pine-clad and almost Alpine flanks of Kerkis to the balcony-villages of **Kallithea** and **Drakkai**. Perched high on the mountainside amongst olive groves and orchards, they have dramatic views west to the hilltops of Fourni in the distance. There are a couple of tiny shop-cum-kafeneons in Drakkai.

The summit of **Mt Kerkis** – all the more striking because its bare slopes dominate so much of an island which is elsewhere so green – beckons the determined walker from a number of angles but especially from Ormos Marathokampou and the nearby beach resorts. You can walk to the top of Kerkis from the slopes above Psili Ammos. Take the usual mountain precautions – do not make the walk alone, take plenty of water, wear sensible footwear and tell somebody when you leave and when you expect to be back. It's a full day's hike, even starting early.

TRAVELLING

By Air   Domestic scheduled flights by Olympic Airways from Athens at least twice a day.

By Sea   Ferries daily to Piraeus from Samos town and Karlovasi; four to five times a week to Ikaria, Mykonos, Paros and Naxos; five times a week from Pythagorion to Patmos; three to four times a week to Hios and weekly to Lesbos, Limnos, Kavala or Alexandroupolis in Thrace from Samos Town. The main ticket offices in Samos town are Horiatopoulos for the main Samaina/Ikaria lines service to Piraeus; Regina Travel for the Golden Vergina to Piraeus via Ikaria, Mykonos and Paros; and Pythagoras Tours for the Minoan Lines international service which goes to Kusadasi in Turkey and via Paros, Piraeus, and Kefalonia to Ancona in Italy and for the Agios Rafael to Chios and the North/east Aegean and Thrace. All are on the harbour front within 50 m of the ferry quay. At Karlovasi, the ticket offices are all on the harbour front.

Around the Island   Buses five times a day between Samos and Karlovasi, stopping at Kokkari and Ag Konstantinos; four times a day between Samos and Pythagorion; twice daily between Karlovasi and Ormos Marathokampou. Elsewhere, the bus service is patchy and the idea of running boat trips around the island has not caught on – except at Pythagorion, where there are boats to Psili Ammos. Hence the popularity of renting cars, jeeps and motorbikes. There are numerous competing rental outfits in Samos town, Pythagorion, Kokkari, Karlovasi, Ormos, Ireon and on the Votalakia beach strip. Most of Samos's roads are well surfaced but very steeply curved: drive cautiously. The road from Pirgos to Paghondas via Spatharei is very poorly surfaced, as is the road between Psili Ammos (west) and Drakkoi. Some maps wrongly show a rough road between Drakkoi and Karlovasi: there isn't one.

WHERE TO STAY

Samos Town   There are a few rooms to rent in Samos town but most accommodation is in relatively expensive B- and C-Class hotels. Few will want to spend the night in Samos: if transport connections force you to stay, try the **Hotel Pythagoras** or opposite it the **Hotel Acropolis**, about five minutes' walk east on the main seafront road from the ferry pier and Port Authority building. Between these hotels and the pier is the **Hotel Eleana**, a medium-priced hotel in a gracious old Samian mansion with palm trees in the garden. There are several more adequate but cheerless hotels along the harbour front, between the pier and the central plateia.

Kokkari   In the village, the cheapest, oldest and most basic pensions are those on the rocky point at the west end of the harbour. On the pebbly west beach, there's a long strip of new pensions and rooms to rent:

Hotel Vicky, Pension Virginia and Manolis are among the closest to the harbour and the heart of things. Pension Caryatides, at the west end of this beach strip, is handy for walking to Limonakia and Tsammadou. Pension Limonakia, overlooking the lovely beach cove here, is excellent but always in demand. This is unfortunately true of Kokkari as a whole: it's such a popular and well-known resort that although the village is now almost entirely given over to accommodating visitors, most of the best rooms are booked solid from June to September and even the scruffier ones ask relatively high prices.

Ag. Konstantinos   Pension Kalypso is good value, close to the sea. The new Hotel Atlantis is a pleasant pension on the main road. The Four Seasons is another attractive pension, among vineyards inland from the main road. There are a number of other cheaper pensions and rooms to rent, including those above Taverna Paradisos, the restaurant with the large, shady plateia among plane woods at the east end of Ag. Konstantinos. More expensive but excellent value is the newly-built Hotel Agios, which is close to the sea, surrounded by vineyards and greenery, and has studio-apartments from £15 and two-bedroom duplexes which sleep four for £20.

Karlovasi   In the centre of Neo Karlovasi, the inland part of the town some two km from the port, the Hotel Morfeos is adequate but dull. More usefully, at the port – on the main street about 100 yards away from the harbour itself – the very old-fashioned but adequate Hotel Aktaion is the cheapest place to stay if awaiting a ferry or arriving late. Immediately opposite is Karlovasi's newest and best hotel, the expensive Sandy Bay, which has a swimming pool.

Ireon   Almost every building in Ireon is a pension, guesthouse or hotel – most of them so new that they have not yet been named – and finding a place to stay should be no problem. Most accommodation here has been built to a very high standard to meet the needs of demanding German package tour operators. Prices, however, are very reasonable: a room with its own hot shower and lavatory in Ireon costs only a fraction more than a basic room with shared facilities in Kokkari. Pension Pingouin, above the café-bar of the same name, is pleasant and friendly, as is the older Hotel Hera.

Ormos Marathokampou, Votsalakia and Psili Ammos.   There are a number of old-fashioned rooms to rent, e.g. the small and friendly Hotel Klimataria above the open-air grill restaurant of the same name, and the excellent, new but unobtrusive Hotel Kerkis Bay with rooms from around DRX 4000 double. On the way to the Kampos/Votsalakia beaches, Studio Oceanis and Pavlis Studios are just above Ormos. There are many new studios all along Votsalakia – Studio Panorama and Studio Pelagia are the closest to Ormos, ten minutes' walk from the beach. Restaurant Chrissopetros, nearby, has rooms to rent. Hotel Apartments Agrilimonas Beach is midway along Votsalakia, as is the

Hotel Votsalakia. At the far end of the beach, there are rooms to rent at **Villa Flora** and **White Rock Studios**, which is also within walking distance of sandy Psili Ammos. **Pension Psili Ammos** is at the beach of the same name.

Pythagorion Accommodation at Pythagorion is limited to a number of unexciting holiday hotels, usually booked up by package tour operators. There are few rooms to rent.

FOOD AND DRINK
Food and drink in Samos are among the best in Greece. The island's vineyards supply samaina, a crisp dry white wine, and fokianos, an aromatic rosé, as well as Samos Ouzo and Samos Brandy and a sweet muscat-style dessert wine. Fish is uniformly excellent and there is a bigger choice of vegetable dishes and fruits than on most other islands.

Samos Town Restaurants are almost all on the central square and on the 400 m waterfront and main street between it and the ferry pier. None stands out, but one of Samos's plus points is a plethora of fast food souvlaki and toast places to keep you going if you have just arrived or are waiting for a boat.

Pythagorion The attractive harbour is lined with restaurants. In **Kokkari** the waterfront is lined with restaurants while the tiny plateia immediately behind it is a solid mass of café tables. The smarter the tables the higher the price, but the best value by far is the little old-fashioned psistaria on the main street, opposite Kokkari's grandiose church. **Farmer's Restaurant**, about a hundred metres west, has its own local wine from the cask and some traditional Samian dishes. There are snack-bar restaurants on the beach at both Limonakia and Tsammadou.

Ag. Konstantinos **Taverna Paradisos** is one of the pleasantest locations on the island, with a big plateia under tall planes. On the waterfront, **Taverna Mantra** is a little grill and spit-roast establishment.

Karlovasi has several surprisingly smart places to eat and drink while you wait for your ferry. The **Medousa**, the **Taverna Archipelagos**, and the **Pub Ostria** are side by side on the harbour with shady tables outside: there are a couple of good, cheaper tavernas next door.

Ireon the **Delfin**, **To Kima**, the **Tavern at the Beach** and the fish-restaurant **Aegeon** all overlook the pebble beach. **Hotel Hera** is one of the friendliest places to eat: the **Pingouin** is an attractive new café-bar with tables inside and out.

Koutsi High in the hills on the road which winds between Pirgos and Platanos, the taverna **Koutsi** is in a shady valley among plane trees – a good stop for lunch if you are touring the island.

EXCURSIONS FROM SAMOS

The Turkish coast is the most obvious excursion destination, with the pretty little holiday resort and port of Kusadasi about an hour away and the superbly-preserved Hellenistic city of Ephesus within day-trip distance. If you are not travelling on a charter flight and can stay overnight there are other ancient Greek cities, Miletus and Didime, within easy striking distance of Kusadasi. Most boats for Turkey leave from Pythagorion.

Less exotically, there are also day-trip boats from Samos and Pythagorion to **Patmos**, the tiny island of Samiopoula just off the coast of Samos, and the slightly larger island of **Fourni**. Boats also go to Fourni and Samiopoula from Ireon and Ormos.

IKARIA

A long, thin island lying east-west, its rugged and mountainous interior supporting only a handful of villages, Ikaria is one of the least-visited of the North-East Aegean isles. Its capital, the tiny port of **Agios Kirikos**, is on the inhospitable south coast. Towering cliffs dominate almost all of this coastline, which has no beaches and is inhabited only at Agios Kirikos, the nearby cove of **Thermai** and the tiny and inaccessible hamlet of **Manganitis** some distance to the west. The north coast, too, is rocky and inaccessible, with steep rocky hills dropping straight into the Aegean for much of its length. There are excellent sandy beaches at Armenistis, a little fishing hamlet perched on a headland some 12 km from Evdilos, the island's north-coast port.

Evdilos itself is a very quiet, pleasantly faded little harbour which – after a long period of decline – has begun to wake up with the building of a new harbour and a growing flow of visitors on the ferry from Athens. There is a small black-sand beach just east of the harbour. Beyond Armenistis the tiny pebble-cove of **Nas** has water as clear as vodka, wonderful snorkelling, and is a favourite with nude swimmers and sunbathers. Above the creek which runs into the bay, the foundations of an ancient village are receiving the attention of archaeologists who recently discovered the marble head of a statue.

Despite its rugged coasts, the hilly interior of Ikaria is in places very green, with clear streams flowing year round.

From the spread-out farming village of **Christos-Rahes**, some eight km above Armenistis, there are long walks across the island over a high plateau of streams, woods and goat-pastures. Above this plateau are peaks carved into weird shapes by wind and rain, like the remains of an ancient Mayan temple. Looking south from the triangulation point which crowns the highest of these is like looking over the edge of the world. Ikaria was one of the islands used by right-wing governments both before and after the Civil War and during the Colonels' junta as a place of exile for dissidents, among them the composer Mikis Theodorakis. This policy backfired a bit: the articulate leftists, many of them from Greece's major cities, were allowed some association with native Ikarians and succeeded in converting many of them to their views. As a result, the island is one of the Greek Communist Party's strongholds. Some 80 per cent of the local vote goes to KKE. This remarkable political unanimity leads to a welcome absence of the competing graffiti for rival parties which defaces flat surfaces all over much of Greece.

TRAVELLING
To Ikaria The island is on the main ferry routes between Athens and Samos. The most frequent boats are the Samaina, Icaros and Golden Vergina, which between them call at least daily. Most boats go to Agios Kyrikos but some – less frequently – call at Evdilos, a more convenient port for the north coast beaches.

Around the Island A daily bus goes from Ag. Kyrikos to Evdilos and Armenistis. Taxis (expensive) meet ferries to collect those bound for the north. Jeep and bike rental is available at Ag. Kyrikos and Armenistis, though not as yet on a big scale.

WHERE TO STAY
Armenistis Armena Inn, on the hill above the road into the village, is cheap and excellent value, with comfortable double rooms with en-suite shower (always hot) and balconies with a fine view of the bay. The **Kavos Bay Hotel**, the first of a crop of new hotels which are relentlessly going up, looks out to sea at the north tip of Armenistis. The **Ikaros Pension**, right in the centre of the village, is friendly and has cheap rooms but

---

Radiation is Good for You!

The island's thermal springs, welling up from deep faults, are said to have medicinal qualities and attract a fair number of older Greek visitors to take the waters of the spa at Thermai, a couple of kilometres from Ag. Kirikos. A fairly recent reversal of the view that radiation is necessarily good for you has closed one of the Ikarian springs, which was found to be dispensing alarmingly high doses of hard radioactivity — ironic in an island which, as a number of signs proclaim, is resolutely anti-nuclear.

---

is spartan and shows its age. In July and August, when Armenistis gets numbers of young beach people and backpackers, accommodation can be tight. There is a small pension and some rooms at Nas.

FOOD AND DRINK
A handful of basic tavernas and bars on the quay at Armenistis and the usual sprinkling of waterfront eateries at Ag. Kirikos are the only eating-places. Evdilos, though a ferry-port, is notably lacking in places to eat.

CHIOS

Like Samos, Chios is big, fertile and prosperous. Unlike its southern neighbour, however, it is little touched by international tourism, though it does receive a substantial number of visitors from Athens in summer, many of them with family links to the island. Chios's beaches are unimpressive — one reason for the relative dearth of tourists — but its wonderful medieval villages are a good enough reason for a visit.

While islands further south fell into the hands of Venice or the Knights of Rhodes in the interregnum between Byzantium and the Ottomans, Chios and its neighbours — Lesbos and Samos — became fiefs of the Genoese Giustiniani. Subsequently, under Turkish rule, Chios became a valued source of a pungent natural sweetmeat, the gum of the mastic bush, which grows more prolifically here than anywhere else. The original chewing gum, mastic commanded high prices throughout the Ottoman Empire and a number of Chios's inland villages grew rich on producing it. Chiots were and are among Greece's leading ship owners and a considerable amount of the earnings of Greece's huge merchant marine ends up here.

CHIOS TOWN

Arrival in the busy capital and port of Chios (Chora to natives) is an anticlimax if you are hoping for a picturesque island harbour. It's a big, mostly modern town of office-blocks, warehouses and workshops. Among its redeeming features is a Genoese castle and below it what remains of the old town, a relic of the Turkish occupation.

SOUTHERN CHIOS

Seven km south of Chios town, there's a good sandy beach at **Karfas**. In fact, this is the best beach on the island and is a magnet for people from the town at weekends and for Greek holidaymakers from July to mid-September.

The landscape and villages of the interior are much more interesting than Chios town, though many of them are half-depopulated. The most immediately appealing is **Pyrgi**, whose tall housefronts decorated with elaborate geometric patterns of black and white plasterwork are unlike anything else in Greece. Below the hillside village is its port, **Emborio**, which has a tiny black-pebble beach.

Pyrgi was one of four "mastichochoria" – mastic villages – of southern Chios which grew wealthy on the crop and fell into the doldrums when mastic lost its value. All four are now "agricultural co-operatives" in the hands of village women – part of an initiative by the PASOK-created sex equality commission aimed at rejuvenating rural communities and giving women more say in their affairs. The others are **Olympi**, another hillside port with a good sand and pebble beach about eight km away at Kato Fana, its port; **Armolia**; and **Mesta**, a beautifully restored medieval village where many of the once-dilapidated houses have been restored as guesthouses by the EOT traditional settlements programme.

The south's other big deal is **Nea Moni**, 15 km west from Chios town. This 11th-century monastery, founded by

Constantine IX Monomachos, is probably the finest religious building in the Aegean, its beautiful mosaics an illustration of the golden age of Byzantine sacred art. It's well worth the pilgrimage.

NORTHERN CHIOS

Northern Chios can be a disappointment after the lovely villages of the south. Its woods have been devastated by fire, and many of its villages have never recovered from the Turkish massacres of 1822, when during the War of Independence the occupiers slaughtered tens of thousands of Chiots and carried many of the rest off into slavery. Much of the north is dominated by the 1300-metre Mt Pilineo, which can be climbed from the farming villages of Amadhes and Viki. Marmaro, Chios's second-biggest town, is a mostly modern fishing port with little interest in tourism or for the visitor. **Nagos**, five km west, has a much better beach than the scruffy patch of pebbles at Marmaro, though its 300 metres of sand and pebbles do get crowded from July on.

There is a long, mixed sand and pebble beach running several kilometres south from just beyond the village of Limnia, below the smaller hillside village of Hori.

TRAVELLING
To Chios Scheduled domestic flights several times daily from Athens, once or twice weekly from Mykonos, Samos and Lesbos. Ferries daily in high season to Piraeus, four times a week to Samos, weekly onward via Samos as far as Patmos and Kalymnos. There are three to four weekly connections to Lesbos and at least one sailing a week (the Agios Rafael) goes on north to Limnos, Thassos and either Kavala or Alexandroupolis. There is at least one international ferry a week to Cesme in Turkey.

Around the Island Blue short-haul buses and green long-distance buses leave from Platia Vournaki. Daytime services to Karfas run every half hour. The depopulated north has very sparse services, and as in Kalymnos shared taxis are a standard way of getting about. Cars and bike hire are available only in Chios (there isn't yet enough tourism to generate the rash of rental outfits which line most Greek harbours).

WHERE TO STAY
Finding somewhere to stay in high season can be tricky: though Chios has relatively few visitors, it has even fewer rooms, and you will be competing not only with long-term summer visitors from mainland

Greece and abroad, but also with the handful of tour operators, mainly from Scandinavia, who have begun to block-book some of the better accommodation.

Chios town has a number of hotels from A- to D-Class and some pensions and rooms to rent, all of which are on view from the harbour but none of which have any outstanding appeal.

There are rooms at **Karfas** and **Emborio** and, on the south-west coast, the fishing hamlet of **Pasa Limani**.

Limnia has a handful of rooms and a growing number of nice bungalow-apartments, though from mid-June onward you will be lucky to find anything vacant. Sadly – or perhaps happily – there is nowhere to stay on the postcard-pretty Agia Markela beach, a five-km walk north from Limnia which is the least crowded on the island because of its inaccessibility and lack of facilities.

Far and away the most atmospheric places to stay are **Pirgi** and **Mesta**. In Mesta, the guesthouses operated under the National Tourism Organization's traditional settlements programme start at around £20 and are well worth it: bookable through the NTOG in London, in Athens, or direct (tel: 0271 7319 or 0251 276 908). In Armolia, Mesta, Olympi and Pirgi you may find a room with a Greek family by asking the Women's Agrotourist Co-operatives in the village (bookable through NTOG).

Psara and Inousses

Two small islands within easy reach of Chios provide an odd contrast. Both Psara and Inousses are peaceful almost to a fault. Psara is a rather ghostly place, its population wiped out during the War of Independence. Once there were 30,000 inhabitants: today 500. Surprisingly, this tiny island was — briefly, during the independence struggle – the site of an early Greek parliament before the seat of government moved first to Nafplion and then to Athens. Accommodation is limited, but the former parliament building is now an attractive guesthouse run by the National Tourist Organization. EOT also operates a restaurant in restored buildings on the harbour and there are a couple of other tavernas. Three boats a week go to Psara from Chios. There are no onward connections from Psara.

Inousses comes as a surprise: where you might expect a modest fishing village there are lavish houses and ostentatious yachts in the harbour. The owners are the island's ship owners, among the wealthiest in Greece, and Inousses – the biggest of a surrounding archipelago of nine tiny islets – is very much their preserve. There are a couple of modest hotels, but little else of note, and unless you have a boat of your own the secluded coves on the uninhabited islets are inaccessible.

FOOD AND DRINK

Chios waterfront is lined with tavernas and kafeneions, whose clientele is mostly local: as a result food and drink are better and cheaper than in more tourist oriented islands. **Hotzas**, at Odos Stefanou Tzouri 74, in the old part of town is justly the best known, for genuinely traditional Greek eating and atmosphere – ouzo with meze, wine from the cask, and a bigger than usual menu. At **Karfas** there is a string of beachside tavernas – busy with lunching families from Chios town at weekends, other wise excellent value. Elsewhere, choices are limited: there are several tavernas at **Pirgi** and in **Mesta**, but most beaches have only seasonal snack-bar places.

LESBOS (MYTILINI)

Lesbos, also known as Mytilini, is Greece's third largest island, some 70 km by 50 km. Like Chios and Samos it lies within sight of the Turkish coast, and it shares some of their history, including rule by Genoese princes in the 13th and 14th centuries. Ancient Lesbos was for much of its history an ally of Athens, a centre of trade, naval power and the arts, and the home of the poet Sappho, perhaps history's first feminist. Lesbos's landscapes are a mix of bare hillsides, olive groves and pinewoods and it has some fine sweeping beaches.

Mytilini town is a commercial port whose main point of interest is the castle of the Giustiniani which stands between its two bays and is now a military lookout point. The town's back-streets are grubby rather than atmospheric, and the island's east coast – Mytilini is near its southern tip – has no beaches worth the name.

THE NORTH COAST

Happily, Lesbos has far more attractive places to base yourself and certainly justifies a longer stay than most islands. Top billing goes to **Molyvos**, also called **Mithimna**, one of the most attractive fishing-cum-tourism villages of the north-east islands. Molyvos, a clutter of tiled houses spilling down narrow alleys and flights of steps to a small harbour and pebble beach, is by no means untouched – it is the island's only full-scale holiday destination – but development has been low key and held in check by the NTOG's listing of the village as a traditional settlement to be preserved. More popular with Athenian holidaymakers than foreign tourists, Molyvos retains a strongly Greek flavour. The Genoese castle on the hill immediately above is floodlit at night and is occasionally used for performances during the erratically timed annual summer arts festival.

Midway along Lesbos's north coast, Molyvos is an ideal base for exploring the island. The village's own pebble beach is not one of Lesbos's best – though it is pleasantly shady – but there are better beaches nearby at the village of **Petra**, about half an hour's walk away. Less pretty to look at than Molyvos, Petra has a long sweep of sandy beach fronting farmland, orchards and olive groves. Even better is the beach at **Anaxos**, three kilometres further south and west, where there is a sandy and sheltered bay with a handful of hilly offshore islets.

Further west – and not easily accessible without your own transport – there is an excellent long sand beach, as yet completely undeveloped for tourism, in the bay overlooked by the Genoese mountain stronghold of Antissa. To the west of the bay, the tiny fishing hamlet of Gavadhas offers food and drink.

East of Molyvos, there is a mediocre pebbly beach at **Efthalou**. The old-fashioned thermal baths behind the beach, however, are the main attraction for most Greek visitors. **Skala Sikamineas**, on the very northern tip of Lesbos, is much more attractive. The village surrounds a lagoon-like harbour. In the middle of the harbour, there are cafés and restaurants around a tiny white church at the end of a narrow pier.

THE WEST COAST

Lesbos's best beach, however, is at **Skala Eressou**, below the hillside village of Eressos. It's a long sweep of sand which is, not surprisingly, a magnet for visitors who include a sprinkling of Dutch and British package holidaymakers, Athenians, and a large number of gay women making the pilgrimage to Sappho's birthplace at ancient Eressos, which stood on this beach. Despite this cosmopolitan summer migration, Skala Eressou rarely feels overcrowded.

Even less so is **Sigri**, a little harbour with a smelly Turkish fort (from the evidence, it's frequently used as a public toilet) and a very good white sand beach. Between Sigri and Eressos – a stiff if pleasant enough hike through hilly country with a great view of the sun setting over the sea – is a petrified forest of tree trunks fossilized by volcanic action.

THE SOUTH COAST

Two shallow bays dominate Lesbos's south coast. The most easterly of these, Gera Bay, is only a stone's throw wide at its mouth, separating the villages of Skala and Perama and widening as it runs inland. Further east, the Gulf of Kalloni takes a huge bite out of the centre of the island. Between the two, Plomari is a tumbledown farming town whose mellow old crumbling buildings are rapidly being replaced by raw cement-block houses. **Agios Isidhoros**, three km away, has excellent beaches which are however only barely visible in

summer beneath a tide of Scandinavian bodies. The south
coast's best beach is at Vatera, eight km from the undistinguished inland village of Polihnitos. The shores of the Gulf of
Kalloni are less appealing: the water is so shallow that you
have to wade a great way out before you can swim, and most
of its shores are choked with seagrass.

INLAND LESBOS

Lesbos's size and variety make it ideal for walkers and
explorers. By Greek standards, it is an island of rolling
hills rather than mountains and even its highest mountains
– Olimbos, between Gera and Kalloni bays, and Lepetimnos,
east of Molivos – are less than 1000 m high. The rough road
between Molivos and Skala Sikaminea makes a pleasant day's
walk. Three hill villages – Argellos, Lepetimnos and Sikaminea
– offer refreshment on the way. In the western hills, the
monastery of Perivolis and the Genoese castle at Antissa are
easy walks from the hill village of the same name, on the main
east-west road.

TRAVELLING

To Lesbos   Domestic flights from Athens, Chios, Samos and Rhodes.
Some charter flights from the UK in summer. Ferries from Piraeus direct,
from Chios and from Limnos, Thassos and Kavala.

Around the Island: KTEL buses run frequently between Mytilini and
the central town of Kalloni, but much less frequently – two to three daily
– to points beyond Kalloni. Car and bike rental available in Mytilini,
Molivos and Skala Eressou.

WHERE TO STAY

In **Mitilini** the A-Class **Pension Villa 1900** is the pick of the bunch. The
Rex and the **Sappho** are C-Class hotels and there is a fine seedy old
E-Class hotel, **the Megali Brittania**, on the harbour.

   Molivos has – except in high season – a plentiful supply of rooms to
rent. Among the pensions, **Molivos 1** is an A-Class (not to be confused
with **Molivos 2**, a B-Class hotel) and the **Sea Horse** and **Triaena** are
pleasant B-Class pensions.

   Petra has two C-Class hotels, the **Petra** and the **Ilion**, and a growing
number of rooms to rent. You can also stay with local families through
the **Women's Agrotourist Cooperative** – book through the NTOG or
ask at their office on the plateia.

   At **Skala Eressou** there are a number of places renting rooms, though
standards aren't as high as in Molyvos – this is still a place where many
people sleep out for much of the summer.

FOOD AND DRINK

Mitilini is a bit of a desert, with a harbour-front handful of mediocre restaurants and fast food places – you won't starve, but that's all that can be said for them. **Molivos** is the reverse, with good food, a good choice of places to eat and a pleasant atmosphere in all of them. For fish and seafood, head for the half-dozen tavernas crammed onto the tiny harbour: for a superb view of the night sky, head for the two or three balcony-restaurants on the highest streets of the village, below the castle.

Skala Eressou consists mainly of modest, beachside tavernas along its little tamarisk shaded promenade. **Sigri** has a basic, chicken-to-souvlaki taverna and a couple of kafeneions. **Gavadhas**, the north coast's tiniest hamlet, is a one-taverna place: fortunately, this quayside establishement with its half-dozen tables is excellent, serving delicious spit-roasted meat and fresh charcoal-grilled fish.

At **Skala Sikaminea**, taverna tables cluster around the pierhead-church at the centre of the harbour: it's one of the pleasantest places on Lesbos to eat, perched beside the still, sheltered lagoon at sunset.

LEMNOS

Lemnos is the joker in the North-East Aegean pack, low-lying and barren looking while most of its neighbours are hilly and wooded. A strong military presence, the most obtrusive anywhere in the islands, is evident. Lemnos's relative remoteness is also a deterrent, and as a result, and a compensation, tourism here is very low key. The island's capital, Myrina, is a pleasant surprise. A clifftop castle, built first by the Genoese, then embellished by the Turks, looks over a pretty fishing harbour. The town – despite flocks of Greek soldiers killing time – is much less busy than the bustling commercial ports of Samos, Lesbos and Chios. In fact it's a pleasant backwater, with a harbour-front of old-style restaurants and cafés and many traditional houses in its upper streets, below the castle. Beside the clutch of cafés at the inner end of the harbour, a former mosque is used as a storeroom. Nearby, a washing and drinking fountain adorned with Arabic script testifies to the Turkish era. Facing west, Myrina also gets spectacular sunsets. The sandy beach just outside town gets crowded in season, and some determination is needed to get to Lemnos's other beaches, scattered around the island.

AROUND LEMNOS

The island's main geographical feature is Moudros Bay, the huge inlet which almost cuts the island in two and which – as a major strategic anchorage – is the reason for all the uniforms. Its shoreline, however, is disappointingly rocky and the small town of Moudros itself is of no great interest. Plati, about two km south of Kastro, is the island's best beach though it can be windswept. On the east coast, Poliochni is worth visiting for its 4000-year-old archaeological site, with the remains of a Neolithic walled city. Poliochni is also the jumping off point for one of the North-East Aegean's strangest pocket wildernesses, the sand dunes of the peninsula south of the village: you can walk or bike through the dunes to the monastery of Agios Sozon at the southernmost point of the island.

TRAVELLING
To Lemnos Domestic flights daily from both Athens and Thessaloniki, twice weekly to Lesbos; ferries to/from Piraeus, Rafina, Kavala and Lesbos.

Around the Island four buses a day between Myrina and Moudros. Car rental available in Myrina.

WHERE TO STAY
Myrina is the best base for Lemnos, with accommodation in rooms and a pleasant old-fashioned hotel, the **Aktaion**, which is right on the harbour below the castle. More expensive are the C-Class **Lemnos** and the C-Class **Sevdalis**, both rather soulless.

FOOD AND DRINK
Several good old-fashioned restaurants along the harbour at Myrina, of which **Psarotaverna O Glaros**, overlooking the inner fishing harbour, is the best: superb fish. There are some fast food places around the main square, a couple of minutes' walk inland from the harbour. An interesting old café on the main street, past the square, is furnished with round, green felt casino tables presumably salvaged from some scrapped cruise liner. Inland, it's a bit of a desert, but there are two good tavernas at the hillside village of Atsiki, about eight km from Kastro.

SAMOTHRAKI

It's easy to see why Samothraki became one of ancient Greece's great ritual centres. Its towering silhouette is visible far off, and its highest peak – Fengari, "the moon-mountain" – zooms up to 1,600 metres. Its flanks fall sheer into the sea in many places and Samothraki has no natural anchorages, adding to its air of mystery. Only 3,000 people live on Samothraki, far fewer than on its southern neighbours. The tiny port of Kamaraiotissa, the scarcely bigger mountainside village of Hora above it, and the small spa-resort of Therma on the island's north coast are where most visitors end up staying. Inland, though, there are a number of pretty villages on the slopes of Fengari, whose heights emerge above plane and pine woods. It is an excellent island for walking, though the beaches – very crowded in July/August – are nothing to write home about. Most are pebbly and windy and the best – Pahia Ammos on the south coast is accessible only by caique from Kamaraiotissa.

TRAVELLING
To Samothraki Ferries daily from Alexandroupolis, once weekly from Kavala.

Around the Island Eight buses a day between the port and Hora and Therma. Take the Therma bus to Paleopoli for the Sanctuary site. There are a couple of moped hire shops in Kamaraiotissa.

WHERE TO STAY
Rooms to rent at Hora and around the harbour. Otherwise there is a surprisingly large B-Class hotel, the **Aeolos**, at Kamariotissa and a C-Class, the **Niki Beach**. In season, both are likely to be full, and are rather unexciting.

THASSOS

The Aegean's most northerly island has rolling hills and sandy beaches. Much of Thassos is forested, with pine woods on the flanks of its highest peak, Ipsarion, and chestnuts on the lower slopes. Thassos's excellent sandy beaches are no secret and to anyone arriving from one of the quieter North-East Aegean islands the frequent strips of development in the shape of discos, bars and beach restaurants may come as a surprise, as may the large numbers of summer holidaymakers, Greek as well as foreign. Within spitting distance of the mainland, Thassos is connected by hourly ferries in summer so it's

The Sanctuary

The magnet which draws most visitors to Samothraki is the Sanctuary of the Great Gods. The centre of a mystery-cult which revolved first around a Great Mother, then – with the arrival of colonists from Samos in the seventh century BC – around the fertility-goddess Demeter, it was the region's most important religious site. Highlights of the site are the Anaktoron (initiation hall), Arsinoeion (rotunda) and the Hieron, five of whose pillars have been restored. Though the site is an ancient one, many of the buildings were altered and rebuilt many times over centuries, especially by the Romans. Like so many of the treasures of ancient Greece, such as the marble friezes from the Parthenon or the Venus de Milo, Samothraki's most famous archaeological find was carried off last century. The Winged Victory (Nike) of Samothraki was once mounted on the Nike Fountain, whose remains are on a hillock above the ancient Theatre. Unearthed by the French archaeologist Champoiseau, it is now in the Louvre. There is a copy in the Palaiopolis Museum, next to the archaeological site, and a visit to the museum either before or after visiting the Sanctuary is a must.

Opening hours for site and museum are 09.30 to 15.00 weekdays.

hardly surprising that its accessible shores should have a big following. The island capital – Thassos, naturally, but also called Limenas – is bland, with a crowded town beach and a sprawl of holiday hotels at Makriammos nearby. The best swimming and sunbathing are on the south coast. Potos and Pefkari, neighbouring sandy beaches, are the pick of the bunch, with Pefkari the liveliest and most developed resort on the island. There are good beaches at Astris and Aliki, but neither has much in the way of facilities. Inland, Thassos is a good ramblers' island. To walk up Ipsarion, head for the hill village of Potamia, from which there is a trail marked with the ubiquitous orange dots to the 1200-metre summit – great views over to the mainland.

Another walk worth doing is to Kastro – justly named, this tiny village was built, like many of those in Thassos's hinterland, as a medieval refuge from pirates. When things became more secure in the last century Kastro was abandoned, though a few summer visitors are now restoring its huddled houses.

TRAVELLING
Ferries daily from Kavala, less frequently from Keramoti, Kimi and Agios Konstandinos.

WHERE TO STAY
Most hotels are in Limenas itself, where there are a dozen or so B- and C-Class hotels. In addition there are rooms to rent and some smaller pensions and more modest hotels at Pefkari.

THE SPORADES AND EVIA

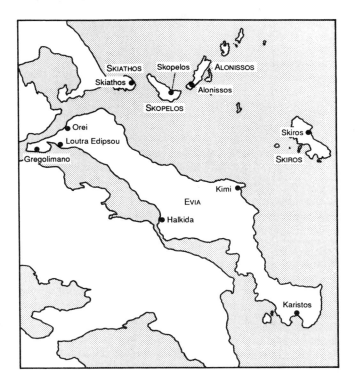

Hilly and cloaked in pine woods, the four islands of the scattered Sporades are slightly cooler in summer than those of the southern Aegean. The main towns of Skiathos, Skiros and Skopelos are among the most attractive in the Aegean. Each island has a distinct character, and all four have excellent beaches.

SKIATHOS

Closest of the inhabited islands to the mainland, and the smallest, Skiathos is by far the busiest. It attracts many British holidaymakers each summer and is beginning to become overdeveloped. It is also a popular resort for numbers of well-off Athenians, as the luxury yachts in its harbour testify. Indeed, with its smart harbourside cafés and bars the port has a touch of the Riviera.

The main town – as usual, bearing the same name as the island – looks rather Italian with its red-pantiled houses and many campanile bell-towers. It surrounds a perfect natural harbour, looking south towards an archipelago of tiny uninhabited islands, each with a tiny beach and clump of pines.

The harbour front is lined with tour agencies, car rental offices and fast food cafés for much of its length. A small island connected to the harbour-front by a causeway holds the remains of a Venetian-Turkish fort and a day-and-night cocktail and snack bar. Ferries and hydrofoils dock at the pier beside the island, smarter yachts and day cruise boats in the fishing harbour on the opposite side: smarter bars and restaurants are to be found along this part of the esplanade.

Much of the island is covered with pine woods, but its greatest glory is its beaches – scores of them. More accessible beaches are rather crowded in high season, but there are many less easily reached coves, especially on the north coast, which are well worth the effort of getting to them.

The island's biggest beach resort is **Koukounaries**, 12 km from Skiathos town (frequent buses), with almost a kilometre of sand backed by pine trees and lined for most of the summer by beach umbrellas and loungers. There are several big hotels and a number of smaller places to stay, all catering to package holidaymakers rather than the independent traveller.

Less easy to get to is **Mandraki**, about 40 minutes' walk over a rough dirt road from Koukounaries. The easiest way to get to this popular stretch of sandy beach is by boat, and in summer scores if not hundreds of visitors arrive each day. There is a multitude of beach bars and tavernas. On the north-west coast, **Aselino** beach is a long bay of fine sand backed by tall bamboos and though it can be reached by bus is far less crowded than Koukounaries. There are no hotels, though the beach is dominated by a large beach bar and café. There is fine snorkeling among the rocks just offshore.

Not far from Aselino by boat but inaccessible by land, **Lalaria** beach is still less frequented for much of the time, though there is a boat-borne influx most days in summer. Nearby stands the former main settlement of the island, the ruined fortress-village of **Kastro**. Built in the 16th century as the only safe haven from the corsairs of the Aegean, this cliff-top settlement was gradually abandoned after independence from Turkey in the 1830s, and Skiathos town, built around the best anchorage on the island from about 1830 on, became the island's capital. There are daily boat trips to Kastro from Skiathos in summer. It's rather a sad place, with little to see except for the ruins of two monasteries and a derelict church whose frescoes are gradually being eroded by the weather. At the end of a winding dirt road, looking north and west towards the hills of Pilion, the modest little monastery of **Ikonistra** is worth a trip. A small café, run by the monks, serves drinks and simple meals, and is a pleasantly cool escape from the heat of the beach.

TRAVELLING

By Air   Frequent summer charters from the UK, Olympic Airways from Athens. The airport is just outside Samos Town.

By Sea   Frequent hydrofoil and ferry connections to the other Sporades and Volos; less frequent ferries to Thessaloniki, Santorini and Crete.

Around the Island   A 12-km stretch of tarred road connects Skiathos town with Koukounaries. There are frequent buses. The Skiathos waterfront is lined with car and bike rental agencies. The easiest way to get to Kastro and the quieter beaches, however, is by boat. A small flotilla leaves Skiathos each morning en route to Mandraki, Lalaria and other beaches on the north and north-west coast, and there are daily boat trips to Kastro. Greek Connection, in Skiathos town, rents speedboats for around £30 a day.

WHERE TO STAY

Skiathos is very much a package tour island (and an up-market one at that) and accommodation for independent travellers is both thin on the ground and quite expensive in high season, though easier to come by outside the July-to-September peak. In Skiathos Town the **Meltemi** pension and the central **Hotel Australia** are good value, as is the **San Remo** hotel at the north end of the esplanade.

The easiest way to find accommodation on arrival, however, is to use one of the numerous travel and accommodation agencies which line the harbour front and act as clearing-houses for unbooked rooms at all prices. There are also villas and larger apartments to rent through several agencies in Skiathos: try the Greek Connection agency on the waterfront, towards the San Remo hotel, which has two-bedroom apartments from around £50 a night.

Immediately in front of the ferry pier, the **Skiathos Villas and Apartments Owners' Association** maintains a kiosk with names and phone numbers of rooms to let and a pay phone for reservations.

FOOD AND DRINK

All the places mentioned are in Skiathos Town: **Taverna Stamatis** is a good fish restaurant overlooking the yacht harbour on the waterfront. Next door, and a good deal cheaper, **Avra** serves souvlaki and gyros, and on the same little parade **Taverna Steki** is a good psistaria-grill. **Jimmy's Bar**, at the end of the fishing harbour, is a nice place for evening cocktails.

Bourtzi, the café-restaurant on the little island which separates Skiathos's two harbour, is open day and night for drinks and snacks and you can swim from the little bathing-quay below it: an ideal place to kill time if you are waiting for a ferry to dock at the pier nearby.

SKIROS

The biggest of the Sporades, Skiros is some two to three hours' sailing from the rest of the group, not far from the coast of Evia. Its main point of interest is the idyllic town of Chorio, a jumble of flat-roofed white houses beneath a dark crag crowned by a monastery and a Venetian castle. Skiros gets its share of visitors in summer, but there are no big hotels on the island nor direct charter flights.

In **Chorio**, the lower parts of the town – especially on the narrow and car-free main street – cater to a mainly Greek summer clientele and are full of restaurants, bars and rooms to rent, some of them in attractive old houses. However, the flashy cocktail bars beloved of Athenians at play have not yet driven out all the traditional restaurants and a couple of the village's older men still cling to traditional costume. Their fantastically pleated, indigo-dyed baggy pants, loose collarless shirts, pillbox caps and uniquely-Skirian sandals look far more comfortable than the bum-hugging denim favoured by today's young Greeks. The tube-like sandals, soled with recycled bits of car tyre, are still commonly worn and you can buy a well-made pair from one of the village cobblers for about £20.

Off the main drag, Chorio is much as it has always been. Village parlours open straight onto the street, offering glimpses of walls hung with hammered copper utensils, elaborately-decorated plates, and ornately-carved furniture draped with patterned rugs. You can wander in Chorio's vertical maze of streets and alleys for some time before emerging triumphantly at the gates of the castle and monastery. On the way, about 50 metres from the gates, pause at the tiny church of Agia Triada to look at the fading glow of its frescoes. From the walls of the ruined Venetian castle there are stupendous views of the sunset over the hills west of Chorio. Below the castle, on a small plateia at the north-west end of the village, stands a bronze statue commemorating the English poet Rupert Brooke, who was buried on Skiros after his death on a hospital ship off Lemnos. His grave is on the barren southern tip of the island. Immediately below the statue of Brooke – which is signposted from the main street – is the Faltaits Museum, which has an excellent collection of traditional weaving, carving, pottery and metalwork.

Below Chorio is a long, sandy, and rarely crowded beach backed by the village of **Magazia** and a row of pensions and modest café-bar-restaurants, about ten to 15 minutes' walk from Chorio itself.

The rest of this roughly hourglass-shaped island does not quite live up to the delights of Chorio. The northern half of the island is marred by a disproportionately large airport and accompanying military bases, or covered by pine forests. The south is strikingly different, its high, bare hills scarred by a maze of dirt tracks being laboriously scraped out by giant army bulldozers.

The island's other beaches are on its west coast. At **Atsitsea** there is a tiny pebbly cove surrounded by offshore islets on the island's west coast, with one small café. Set among pine woods, it is a pleasant excursion from Chorio.

Pefkos, rather more accessible, is a long strip of grey-gold sand with a couple of restaurants, about ten kilometres from Chorio and five from the tiny island port, Linaria.

Linaria itself is little more than a ferry harbour, with a handful of rooms to rent and a couple of tavernas. The big event of the day is the arrival of the ferry or hydrofoil from Kymi or Skopelos. There are a few more rooms, and a small beach, within walking distance around the headland north of the harbour – follow the main tarred road which connects Chorio with Linaria.

TRAVELLING

By Air   Domestic flights from Athens, no international flights.

By Sea   Frequent ferries from Kymi, on Evia; ferries and hydrofoils from Skiathos.

Around the Island   Buses and taxis meet ferries at Linaria to take passengers to Chorio. No public transport elsewhere.

WHERE TO STAY

The pleasant, mid-priced (£10–£15 per person) **Hotel Nefeli** is the best hotel in **Chorio**. There are plenty of rooms to rent in the village – the proprietors will find you if you look as if you are room-hunting. In high season, even the simplest rooms can be expensive by the standards of some other islands, at about £12 for two. **Hotel Elena**, next to the post office as you come into town, is a reasonably priced small hotel. There are a number of pensions and guesthouses at **Magazia**, where you will also find the **Xenia**, the best and most expensive hotel on Skiros at around £35 double.

FOOD AND DRINK

Chorio has a better choice of places to eat and much better food than most island villages. On the main street, **Psistaria O Skiros** is a fine example of an old fashioned grill-taverna with chicken, chops and souvlaki from a giant grill behind the counter. The appropriately named **Sisyphos**, at the foot of the steep main street, is another good restaurant for dinner which, unusually for Greece, serves vegetarian dishes.

The **Ouzo Bar** is a popular old-style ouzo, wine and snackery.

Kafestiatorio O Glaros, at the foot of the hill, serves breakfast, lunch and dinner at good value prices.

Semeli, an ouzeri-cum-croissant shop, is a good place to have breakfast or a snack, serving omelette, fresh fruit juice, toasted sandwiches and a huge choice of croissants with sweet and savoury fillings.

SKOPELOS

A long, thin island dominated by ranges of steep, pine-clad hills, Skopelos has not yet succumbed to mass tourism to the same extent as its near neighbour Skiathos – though it is beginning to get a considerable overspill from Skiathos. For much of its length the coastline falls sharply into the Aegean, and many of its beaches are no more than sandy coves, accessible only by boat.

New building on the outskirts of town has not marred the island's capital, whose typically tall houses rise in tiers above a deep, narrow bay. With their steeply-pitched stone slates and jutting balconies of carved wood and wrought iron, the houses of Skopelos are quite different from the flat-roofed cubes of Skiros or the terracotta villas of Skiathos.

The promenade of **Skopelos town** is lined with pleasant restaurants and café terraces under green shade trees where the entire population takes to the streets after sundown to stroll and chat. There is an adequate sand and shingle beach about one kilometre from the harbour, and most of the newer hotels and apartments have been built nearby, south-west of the older town centre. A monastery and a few fragments of a Venetian stronghold sit atop a low crag overlooking the harbour.

The nearest decent beach is at **Stafylos**, a pretty but crowded cove below steep piny slopes; it's lined with beach umbrellas and there are several café-tavernas and small hotels.

Agnondas, about 15 minutes away by bus, is less crowded, a small harbour-cove with a little pier and three tavernas. A further ten minutes' walk from Agnondas, just off the main road around the island, **Limnonari** is an even better beach of coarse white sand surrounded by cicada-filled pines. There's a small seasonal taverna which also has half a dozen rooms to rent. Further up the west coast, there are excellent and uncrowded beaches at **Milia** and **Elios**.

The island's only other village of any size is **Glossa**, crowning a hillside in the north of Skopelos with its harbour of **Loutraki** — a stop for ferries and hydrofoils from Skiathos — below. Glossa is a mainly modern village of no great interest but pretty views across to Skiathos and the hills of the mainland. Loutraki has an undistinguished beach but some pleasant restaurants and places to stay, and small boats connect it with the other coves and beaches of the island.

Skopelos has been a devout island and has more than the usual quota of churches, monasteries and especially convents. The main village alone has more than 120 churches, and there are a dozen convents and monasteries dotted around the island.

TRAVELLING

To Skopelos Frequent boat and hydrofoil services link Skopelos town and Loutraki with Skiathos, Alonissos and Volos. Daily excursion boats also visit Alonissos and the nearby "desert island" Peristera.

Around the Island Several buses daily on the main road which runs between Skopelos town and Glossa via the west coast. Bikes, jeeps and Citroën 2CVs can be rented in Skopelos town. Caiques go daily round the island in season to Armenopetra and other beaches.

WHERE TO STAY

For independent travellers, the choice is between the two ports: there is virtually no accommodation available outside Skopelos town and Loutraki. At **Skopelos, Pension Sotos** at Plateia 25 Martiou is a comfortable pension in a pleasantly modernized old building. The **Lina Guest House** (Tel: 0424 22637) on the waterfront, above the giftshop of the same name, has clean, light double rooms with shower from about £12. A little further along, the **Hotel Andoni** is a nice, rather old-fashioned hotel with balcony rooms overlooking the harbour.

In practice, only the determined resist the wiles of the gaggle of landladies who meet each ferry to peddle their rooms. Skopelos town has plenty of rooms to rent, most of them in pleasant old houses, and the easiest way to find one is to go with the flow.

At **Loutraki**, the **Hotel Avra** on the beach is small, modern and medium-priced. There is a small nameless pension and a few rooms available to rent nearby.

FOOD AND DRINK

Most restaurants in **Skopelos Town** are on the waterfront at Plateia 25 Martiou, a continuous strip of café-restaurant tables which includes **Taverna Spiros, Estiatorio Psistaria Skopelaki**, the **Apokalypsis Jazz/Rock Music Bar** and the **Ecstasy Cafe**. Two of the best places to eat in Skopelos town are the unrelated restaurants, each called **Platanos** and each under a huge plane tree at either end of town. The one by the harbour is a good breakfast spot with fresh juice, honey and yoghurt, while at the opposite end of Skopelos town the other Platanos serves excellent souvlaki, tyropitta, gyros and salad. In front of the Hotel Adonis, the **Restaurant Maxim** is a good outdoor grill-restaurant.

At **Loutraki, Restaurant Rania** and **Taverna Psistaria Faros** are perched prettily on the hillside above the little harbour and serve good fish and grills.

ALONISSOS

The least visited of the major Sporades, Alonissos is hilly and more barren than its neighbours, with few inhabitants and only two villages – the modern harbour of **Patitiri**, built after the 1965 earthquake made much of the old village of Chora unsafe. Patitiri has location on its side but its functional modern buildings cannot match up to the good looks of the other Sporadic island capitals.

Chora, perched 300 metres above, is much prettier and

some of its derelict houses have been rebuilt as second homes by Athenians and foreigners, a trend which may lead to a renaissance of the village – albeit entirely as a holiday community – over the next few years.

Much of the coast is cliffy and the island's handful of good beaches are easiest to reach by boat – it's a long hot trek overland to get to even the nearest to Patitiri. **Kalamakia**, on the east coast, is a long stretch of sandy beach, so far little developed, as is **Kokkinokastro** ("red castle") about half an hour away by boat. The castle in question is the site of ancient Ikos, and a few stumps of ancient city walls can be seen close to the beach. There are excellent beaches too on the little, uninhabited island of **Peristeri** and on other offshore islets. Caiques ply to these from Patitiri.

One, **Gioura**, has a cave locally claimed as the home of one of the one-eyed Cyclops – worth a visit for its coloured limestone spires and spikes. A Byzantine shipwreck, just off the coast at Agios Petros, is one reason the waters off Alonissos have been declared a marine conservation area.

TRAVELLING
By Sea Plenty of ferries, excursion boats and hydrofoils every day from Skiathos and Skopelos.

Around the Island The caiques which run from Patitiri to the main beaches are the only really sensible way of getting around the island, though walkers will find plenty of tracks to explore around the island's hillsides and patches of farmland, with tiny coves suitable for swimming at the end of many of them.

WHERE TO STAY
Rooms to rent in **Patitiri**, where a clutch of landladies meet most boats, and a growing handful of rooms at **Chora** (much the pleasanter option if space is available). The B-Class **Alkyon Guest House** is the best value accommodation at Patitiri, with 30 beds. There are also two big C-Class tourist hotels, the **Galaxy** and the **Marpounda**, where you may find bargain rates in the off-peak months.

FOOD AND DRINK
Estiatorio Akrogiali, by the beach of the same name just by **Patitiri**, has good seafood and grills. In summer, a couple of "music pubs" open up to satisfy the peak-season visitor's perceived lust for loud music and drinks at three times the normal price.

There are seasonal tavernas at all the beaches on the caique routes: check with boatmen at Patitiri to make sure they are open if you're visiting towards the beginning or end of the summer.

EVIA

This 170 km-long island – Greece's second largest after Crete – hardly qualifies as an island at all. Separated by a narrow gulf from the mainland north of Athens, it is connected at one point by a swing bridge and it feels more like an extension of the mainland coast than an island proper. Technically one of the North-East Aegean group, its nearest offshore neighbours are the Sporades; Skiros is less than two hours away.

Evia is an island of fertile, wooded hills. Its beaches are popular with Greek holidaymakers because of its proximity to Athens, only a few hours' drive away, and there are a number of quite developed resorts, especially in the south-west of the island.

Elsewhere, however, there are pleasant and undeveloped fishing villages and isolated beaches. With its woods of pine and chestnut trees, Evia's hilly hinterland also has some fine walking country.

Halkida, capital of the island, is connected to the mainland by a swing bridge. It's an uninspiring industrial and ship-building town whose main point of interest is the mysterious current which swirls beneath the bridge over the Evripos narrows and which changes direction every few hours for no known reason. The town also has a medieval fortress, one of many to be seen throughout the island. Evia was an important part of Venice's Aegean empire until its fall to the Turks in 1470.

Halkida is roughly midway up Evia's west coast and is the island's main road nexus as well as the principal gateway from the mainland.

North of Halkida much of the island is mountainous, with a large holiday resort and spa on the west coast at Loutra Edipsou. Between Loutra Edipsou and Halkida, **Limni** is an attractive harbour town of Italian-looking tiled houses, popular with Greek summer visitors. It's a quiet, mellow little place for much of the year, with pleasant sand and pebble coves to the north and south. About five km south of Limni, the dirt road comes to a final halt at the little monastery of Galatki, below which is a pretty and often deserted white pebble beach with clear, calm water.

The main road linking Halkida with Cape Artemissio, Evia's northernmost point, is a spectacular drive. **Pefki**, midway along the north coast and facing across to the southern tip of the Pilion peninsula, is quiet and undeveloped. At **Orei**, a prosperous fishing port, a rather grim Frankish fortress squats in the middle of the town.

The biggest concentration of big resort-style hotels is on the heavily developed beaches between Loutra Edipsou and Gregolimano, all popular summer resorts for Greek holidaymakers. **Gregolimano's** long sand beach is heavily commercialized and lined with umbrellas and sun loungers. **Gialtra**, considerably quieter, has a grey sand and shingle beach but little character.

South of Halkida, the island is more heavily populated and its coasts more crowded. Industry and commerce dominates much of the coast road south in the direction of the busy commercial towns of Eretria and Amarinthos, some 60 km from Halkida, and there's no real reason to stop on this drab stretch of coastline. Things start to look up, however, after Lepoura, where the main road splits, one branch heading north to the pretty town of Kimi, the other south to Karistos, Evia's southernmost town.

Kimi, a hilltop town of tall and elegant old mansions, has a huge balcony-plateia shaded by plane trees and packed with café tables. On a clear day, looking east over the tiled roofs of the town, you can see the outline of Skiros, the closest of the Sporades, on the horizon. For all its prettiness, Kimi sees few foreigners and would be an excellent place to relax for a few days if you want to soak up the life of an ordinary Greek town going about its everyday business.

Below Kimi, the dull and dusty little port of Paralia Kimi is worth visiting only as the jumping-off point for the Sporades and other North-East Aegean islands: it consists of a main street of cafés and rooms to rent running the length of a disproportionately long harbour which once served the island's gypsum mines but now sees only passenger ferries.

Heading south from Lepoura the road runs down the spine of Evia through Almiropotamos, an undistinguised village with a lovely stretch of beach below at **Panagia**. Nea Stira, on the coast further south, is a dull sprawl of cement-block "bed factories" with unimpressive sand beaches either side of town. Marmari, a little further south, is similarly disappointing, and it's better to head on to **Karistos**. Far from undeveloped, Karistos has far more character than the purpose-built resorts to the north and is an attractive old-fashioned harbour town whose ordinary life has not yet entirely given way to tourism. The old Venetian fortress named Castello Rosso (red castle) because of the colour of the local stone – it is now known as Kokkino Kastro – can be seen a couple of kilometres inland at the orchard village of **Mili**, which is also the starting point for walking up the 1349-metre Mt Ochi.

It's a three-hour walk from Mili to the Hellenic Alpine Club refuge at the peak, where there are superb views over Karistos towards the mainland; you can either return from here or continue over the massif, a further 3½ hours to the hamlets of Leonosei and Kallianos, among citrus and pomegranate groves, to the sea. If you choose the latter you will have to camp or hitchhike back to Karistos.

TRAVELLING

For independent travellers, one option is to arrive from the mainland via Rafina to Karistos, travel overland up to Kimi and onward to Skiros for island hopping through the Sporades to Volos.

By Sea   There are ferries from the east coast port of Rafin (25 km from Athens) to Marmari and Karistos; from Agia Marina to Nea Stira; and from Arkitsa to Loutra.

Kimi has daily ferries to Skiros and less frequent boats to Lemnos in the N-E Aegean.

By Road   Halkida is the hub of a bus network which connects all points on the main road north and south several times daily. Via the bridge at Halki, there are buses from Athens, Thessaloniki and the major mainland towns. Cars and bikes can be rented in Halkida from several agencies.

WHERE TO STAY

There are vast numbers of pensions as well as the large hotels in the **Loutra Edipsou** strip, most of which will be packed with Greek visitors in July and August. Try the B-Class **Lykourgos**, C-Class **Angela** or C-Class **Anna**, all modest modern little pensions.

In **Halkida** – if you must stay there – the cheapest option is the Hotel Kentrikon, a C-Class at Agelli Gobiou, close to the bus station and bridge to the mainland. Next door, prominently signposted, is the expensive B-Class **John's Hotel**.

At **Paralia Kimi** the C-Class **Hotel Beis**, with double rooms from around £13, is better value than the generally drab and overpriced handful of rooms to rent privately.

At **Karistos**, where independent travellers are a rarity, cheap pensions and rooms to rent are thin on the ground. Try the smallish C-Class **Hotel Als**.

At **Limni**, the best bets are the tiny C-Class **Avra** and **Plaza**.

FOOD AND DRINK

Halkida, like most commercial Greek towns, has better eating than you'd expect. There are a number of fast food souvlaki and grill places around the bridge to the mainland, handy for grabbing a quick snack as you pass through, and a row of more sophisticated places to eat and drink on the promenade along the waterfront north from the bridge.

Kimi proper has few restaurants as such, but **Paralia Kimi** has a row of good little grill-restaurants for those awaiting a boat. At **Karistos** and at other Evia ports and resorts, the presence of largely Greek and therefore discerning clientele means the food is generally better than in resorts populated with foreigners. **Peroulakis**, beside the harbour, is the best of a gaggle of little restaurants close to the sea at Karistos.

INDEX